WHO VOTES NOW?
. . . .

WHO VOTES NOW?

DEMOGRAPHICS, ISSUES, INEQUALITY, AND TURNOUT IN THE UNITED STATES

Jan E. Leighley
AMERICAN UNIVERSITY

Jonathan Nagler
NEW YORK UNIVERSITY

PRINCETON UNIVERSITY PRESS
PRINCETON AND OXFORD

Copyright © 2014 by Princeton University Press
Published by Princeton University Press, 41 William Street,
Princeton, New Jersey 08540
In the United Kingdom: Princeton University Press,
6 Oxford Street, Woodstock, Oxfordshire OX20 1TW

press.princeton.edu

Jacket Illustration: Ballot / Ballot EPS Ballot / Ballot AI Ballot / Ballot JPG Ballot.
© YCO. Courtesy of Shutterstock.

Library of Congress Cataloging-in-Publication Data
Leighley, Jan E., 1960–
Who votes now? : demographics, issues, inequality and turnout in the United States /
Jan E. Leighley, American University; Jonathan Nagler, New York University.
    pages cm
Includes bibliographical references and index.
ISBN-13: 978-0-691-15934-8 (cloth : alk. paper)
ISBN-10: 0-691-15934-3 (cloth : alk. paper)
ISBN-13: 978-0-691-15935-5 (pbk. : alk. paper)
ISBN-10: 0-691-15935-1 (pbk. : alk. paper) 1. Voter turnout–United States–Statistics.
2. Political participation–United States–Statistics. 3. Elections–United States–Statistics.
I. Nagler, Jonathan. II. Title.
JK1967.L45 2013
324.973–dc23
                          2013016995

British Library Cataloging-in-Publication Data is available

This book has been composed in Sabon

Printed on acid-free paper ∞

Typeset by S R Nova Pvt Ltd, Bangalore, India

Printed in the United States of America

10 9 8 7 6 5 4 3 2 1

Jonathan dedicates this book to his parents, for
encouraging reading and civic participation.

. . . .

Jan dedicates this book to her daughter, Anna Johnson.
Yes, I do . . . more than you know.

Contents ....

List of Figures ....

List of Tables.............................

Preface................................

Who votes? And does it matter?

These are not new questions in the study of American politics, but they continue to be important ones, and they motivate what we do in this book.

As the title suggests, we owe an enormous intellectual debt to Ray Wolfinger and Steve Rosenstone, who wrote what is now a classic text on voter turnout in the United States, *Who Votes?*[1] We have written before on the demographics of turnout, and continue to believe that the demographics of turnout are inherently important to questions of democracy and representation.

Intellectually, *Who Votes?* has had staying power. In addition to a rich description of patterns of turnout across demographic subgroups, Wolfinger and Rosenstone (1980) provided insightful analyses that reflected on common beliefs about every demographic characteristic they investigated. In addition, they emphasized the importance of election rules (especially the closing date for registering to vote) as deterrents to voter turnout. Their last chapter concluded on a somewhat surprising note when they suggested that who votes is not that important—that voters and nonvoters have similar preferences, and that if everyone voted, there would be few changes to political outcomes.[2]

Much of what Wolfinger and Rosenstone demonstrated stimulated other scholars to take a closer look. In short, their comprehensive description of patterns of turnout across a wide range of demographic subgroups became a theoretical and empirical springboard for subsequent research. Much of this subsequent research expanded on the

---

1. Published in 1980, their analysis relied on data from the 1972 Current Population Survey—the first scholars who embarked on such a huge data analysis effort. Given computing resources of the day, Wolfinger and Rosenstone could only use a subset of cases from the CPS.

2. Wolfinger and Rosenstone recognized that future political cleavages could change such that the demographic differences they described between voters and nonvoters *could* have meaningful policy implications.

theoretical interpretations of Wolfinger and Rosenstone, while some drilled down to focus in greater detail on the demographic characteristics of interest and changes in their distribution over time.[3] Others, most notably Rosenstone and Hansen (1993), reframed the study of voter turnout to emphasize the importance of campaign context and political elites (e.g., candidate and party mobilization efforts, issues and party competitiveness) as key determinants of voter turnout.[4]

Aside from demographics, *Who Votes?* also initiated sustained attention to whether the legal rules governing elections influence how many vote, as well as who votes. Wolfinger and Rosenstone's (1980) extensive data collection on state election laws and their implementation has been updated in various ways by those focusing on whether election laws influence turnout.[5] Whatever their focus, this wide range of studies shares a common point of departure: Wolfinger and Rosenstone's key observation that demographics are central to understanding voter turnout.

But Wolfinger and Rosenstone's classic work was limited to one presidential election–an election that is now forty years past. And dramatic changes in the demographics of the U.S. population over this long period, along with fundamental changes in political campaigns (e.g., changes in the use and availability of new media, and increased campaign spending) and election laws (e.g., the increase in the availability and use of absentee voting, early voting, and election day registration) suggested to us that there was more work to do.

Others, of course, have considered this intersection of demographics and political engagement—most notably Verba, Schlozman, and Brady's (1995) exhaustive and authoritative study of the demographics of participation other than voting, and, more recently, their study of "political voice" (Schlozman, Verba, & Brady 2012). Both of these studies frame the enduring and central importance of demographics to political behavior in light of normative concerns regarding inequality: if the unequal distribution of economic and social resources has political consequences, it surely must be evidenced in who casts ballots, who engages in political activities, and who expresses political voice.

We, too, frame our investigation of voter turnout in presidential elections in the United States between 1972 and 2008—a period of increasing economic inequality—in light of these normative concerns

---

3. See, for example, Abrajano & Alvarez (2010); Barreto (2005); Cassel (2002); Kam, Zechmeister, & Wilking (2008); Leighley & Nagler (2007); Pacheco & Plutzer (2007); Ramakrishnan (2005); Teixeira (1987); and Tenn (2007).
4. See, more recently, Bergan et al. (2005); Goldstein & Ridout (2002); Holbrook & McClurg (2005); and Parry et al. (2008).
5. See, for example, Brians & Grofman (2001); Hanmer (2009); Knack (2001), Knack & White (2001); and Springer (forthcoming).

about economic and political inequality. We also wanted to examine whether over this same period changes in electoral laws and the nature of the choices offered by the parties had led to changes in turnout. We hope our arguments and evidence regarding demographic patterns of turnout over time, and whether election laws or political candidates can enhance the representativeness of voters, speak not only to scholars but also to citizens, candidates, and journalists. We would not have written this book if we did not think that who votes matters.

Acknowledgments . . . .

Our work on the study of voter turnout began over two decades ago. The effort could not have been sustained without support (intellectual, financial, and otherwise) from many quarters.

First, Ray Wolfinger kindly met with us in 1990 at the annual meeting of the American Political Science Association in San Francisco, when we were first starting our work on studying turnout. His willingness to take time to meet with two junior faculty he did not know, based only on our shared interest in voter turnout, was incredibly generous.

Second, our academic homes during the writing of the book—including New York University, the University of Arizona, American University and, for one pleasant semester for one of us, the European University Institute—provided both financial and scholarly support in many ways. Of course, the most valuable support we received was from our colleagues, for both specific comments as well as general advice on related papers and the book manuscript in its many incarnations. A half semester spent at NYU–Abu Dhabi by Jonathan turned out to be especially productive.

In addition, each of these universities provided outstanding research assistants, without whom the book would be impossible. To name a few: at NYU, Melanie Goodrich provided valuable assistance with coding of CPS data; Adam Bonica wrote very flexible code that let us redo analyses as quickly as we updated data; Nick Beauchamp performed several useful updates to the code base; Andrew Therriault was our source for expertise on Annenberg data; and Lindsey Cormack and Dominik Duell both provided valuable assistance with National Election Studies (NES) data. At the University of Arizona, Jessica McGary provided timely assistance with our initial graphs, and at American University, Amun Nadeem, Michele Frazier, Carrie Morton, and Chelsea Berry provided excellent assistance with background research and supplementary data collection and copyediting.

Third, we gratefully recognize the Pew Charitable Trusts through the Pew Center on the States for providing grant support to us, along with our collaborators Dan Tokaji and Nate Cemenska at the Ohio State University School of Law, for collecting data on state registration and election laws. We rely heavily on this data in chapter 4. We especially appreciate the support of Zach Markovits at Pew, who guided our project to successful completion. The work of Pew's Center on the States continues to be important to a better understanding of democracy in the United States. and we were fortunate to be a part of that work. We also thank Steve Carbo and Demos for providing feedback and constant reminders of the importance of our work, and for giving one of us a chance to present research to policy makers. Over the course of our research on turnout one of us has testified in federal court on the effectiveness of election day registration, and one of us has testified before Congress on the effectiveness of election day registration. We appreciate the opportunities we have had to demonstrate the relevance of our research to important policy matters.

Our travels away from home included invitations to numerous departments and conferences to present our work; we undoubtedly returned from these visits understanding more about turnout and how to write this book than when we began. These colloquia included talks at American University, Columbia University, Harvard, the Massachusetts Institute of Technology, New York University, Hebrew University, the Institut d' Analisi Economica in Barcelona, the European University Institute, the University of Maryland, Princeton University, Temple University, the University of California–Davis, and the D.C. Area Workshop on American Politics.

We also thank Chris Wlezien and Peter Enns, who invited us to Cornell University's conference, "Homogeneity and Heterogeneity" in Public Opinion; Margaret Levi, Jack Knight, and Jim Johnson, who invited us to the "Designing Democratic Government" conference sponsored by the Russell Sage Foundation; and Mike Alvarez and Bernie Grofman, who invited us to a conference on post–Bush versus Gore electoral reform.

Most of the chapters in this book were initially presented at annual meetings and conferences such as those of the American Political Science Association, the Midwest Political Science Association, the Conference on Empirical Legal Studies, and the Southern Political Science Association. Over the years many of the chapters were revised and presented again, imposing on an ever larger number of discussants and fellow panelists. We regret that we cannot recall all of the discussants to whom we are indebted, nor all of the panel participants.

Most recently, we appreciate the comments of Michael Hanmer, Mike Martinez, Betsy Sinclair, Theda Skocpol, and Lynn Vavreck at these meetings. Mike Alvarez deserves special thanks for the many useful insights he has offered in discussions of voter turnout and elections. Jen Lawless, Danny Hayes, and Matt Wright also provided excellent feedback in extended discussions of the project. We thank Orit Kedar for her persistence in offering good advice, even when it was not being followed. Jonathan thanks many coauthors on other projects for their patience while time was taken away to work on this book. And Jan thanks Bill Mishler, coeditor of the *Journal of Politics*, for his patience as Jan's attention was focused on completing this manuscript while journal submissions continued unabated. He is one of many friends and family members who have taken a backseat over many weekends and holidays, especially, as we pushed to complete the book.

As with anyone who works on turnout in the United States, we owe a huge debt to Michael McDonald for the work he does maintaining state-level data. We appreciate his responsiveness to our many questions regarding turnout data as well as many discussions about the research questions we share in common.

In addition, several of our colleagues generously took the time to read various chapters of a draft of the manuscript and provide valuable feedback, including Marisa Abrajano, Lindsey Cormack, Bob Huckfeldt, Jennifer Oser, Costas Panagopoulos, Elizabeth Rigby, and Tetsuya Matsubayashi. And going well beyond what we could reasonably expect in effort and helpfulness, Jamie Druckman and Pat Egan gave us exceptionally useful feedback on a draft of the entire manuscript. We also appreciate Chuck Myers's suggestions, which helped us sharpen the presentation of our arguments, and the patient and helpful production staff at Princeton University Press—especially production editor Karen Fortgang and copy editor Brian Bendlin—who were critical in the last stage of revisions, which, of course, took longer than we had all hoped. And despite all the excellent advice of our colleagues, they bear no responsibility for any remaining errors—that responsibility is ours.

WHO VOTES NOW?

One

$\cdots\cdots\cdots\cdots\cdots\cdots\cdots\cdots\cdots\cdots\cdots\cdots\cdots\cdots\cdots\cdots\cdots\cdots\cdots\cdots\cdots\cdots\cdots\cdots$

Introduction

After every presidential election, commentators lament the low voter turnout rate in the United States, suggesting that there is something wrong with a democracy in which only about 60 percent of its citizens vote. Yet there is little public consternation over the fact that those who do show up at the polls are disproportionately wealthy: while nearly 80 percent of high-income citizens vote, barely 50 percent of low-income citizens do.[1] Given the dramatic increase in economic inequality in the United States over the past thirty years, the silence on this point is all the more striking: apparently the important question for pundits and journalists is not *who votes* but *how many* vote.

Contrast this silence with the strident debates regarding voter identification laws passed after the 2008 presidential election. Low voter turnout aside, many state legislatures passed laws requiring individuals to provide positive identification when voting on election day. While supporters of these laws argued they were intended to protect the integrity of elections, opponents countered that the laws were partisan efforts to depress the turnout of liberal-leaning citizens who also happen to be least likely to already have identification documents—that is, the poor, and racial and ethnic minorities. The common assumption in this debate, whatever the legislative intent, is: *who votes* matters.

The intensity of this debate even up to a month prior to election day in 2012 was likely fueled by pollsters' predictions that the presidential race seemed to be too close to call. In September, media reports and political junkies were claiming that the election would be all about

---

1. We refer to the higher turnout rate of the wealthy compared to the poor as *income bias*.

turnout: Would the Obama campaign deliver the same record-high turnout that it did in 2008? And would the Republican base turn out to support a candidate who had an inconsistent record on many issues important to the base? If, as the pundits suggested, turnout was pivotal to the election outcome, both campaigns were ready: they both raised and spent more money than any previous presidential campaign, and spent a substantial amount of those dollars to mobilize supporters.[2] While we now know that overall turnout in 2012 was lower than in 2008, what we do not know is whether who was mobilized to vote led to Obama's victory or, more specifically, whether the presence of these new voters would influence the policies he would later produce.

If nonvoters preferred the same policies as voters, we might not care very much about who votes: however many or few citizens cast ballots on election day, the same preferences would be expressed. Yet we show in later chapters that this is not the case. Voters and nonvoters do not prefer the same policies. Our conclusions thus challenge the conventional wisdom regarding voter turnout and policy preferences in the United States. In a now classic study of voter turnout in the United States, Wolfinger and Rosenstone (1980) claimed that who votes does *not* matter, arguing that because the political preferences of voters and nonvoters are similar, there are few representational inequalities introduced by the failure of all eligible voters to participate in the electoral process. Similarly, most simulations of the effects of turnout in presidential and senatorial elections suggest that the same candidate would win even if all eligible citizens voted.[3]

But these studies focus exclusively on the differences in *partisan* and *candidate* preference between voters and nonvoters, and consider these two differences as the only relevant consequence of changes in turnout. They do not consider whether any *policy* consequences would result should all eligible voters cast ballots. We argue that in determining whether who votes matters it is important to compare preferences of voters and nonvoters *over issues*, not just preferences *across candidates or parties*. A growing body of political science evidence supports this common sense conclusion: that policy makers cater more to the wishes of voters than nonvoters.[4] If we accept that elected officials pay attention to what voters want, then comparing the preferences of voters and nonvoters over issues, not just candidates or parties, matters. The question is straightforward: do nonvoters support the same policies that voters support?

2. "The 2012 Money Race: Compare the candidates"; http://elections.nytimes.com/2012/campaign-finance; accessed December 3, 2012.
3. See Citrin, Schickler, & Sides (2003); Highton & Wolfinger (2001); Martinez & Gill (2005); and Sides, Schickler, & Citrin (2008).
4. See Griffin (2005) and Martin (2003) for evidence on this point.

A simple example illustrates why preferences on policy issues, not just candidates, or parties, matter. We might observe that both 55 percent of nonvoters and 55 percent of voters prefer the Democratic candidate to the Republican candidate. But if voters' preferences for the Democrat are based on the promise of liberal social policies, and non-voters' preferences for the Democrat are based on the promise of liberal economic policies, then the nonvoters are going to suffer for staying home. Once elected, the Democrat is likely to respond to the social policy wishes of the voters, and be more likely to ignore the economic preferences of the nonvoting supporters who would like redistributive economic policies. As a result, who votes matters for the most basic outcome of politics: who gets what.

In this book we examine voter turnout in every U.S. presidential election from 1972 through 2008.[5] We address four questions regarding the changing political context of turnout. First, how have the demographics of turnout in presidential elections changed or remained the same since 1972? Second, what have been the consequences of the broad set of election reforms designed to make registration or voting easier that have been adopted over the past several decades? Third, what is the impact of the policy choices that candidates offer voters on who votes? And fourth, is Wolfinger and Rosenstone's conclusion that voters are representative of nonvoters on policy issues accurate, and therefore, who votes does not really matter?

Our findings on these four questions advance our understanding of turnout and its consequences for representation in fundamental ways. Our empirical evidence on the demographics of turnout shows that over a period of increasing economic inequality, the income bias of voters has remained the same. The rich continue to vote at substantially higher rates than the poor. While this difference is very large, it has not increased substantially.

A second finding of note is that, contrary to the claims of many reformers that making voting easier would dramatically change who votes and how many vote, some electoral reforms modestly increase turnout but by no means produce changes in turnout anywhere near large enough to close the gap in turnout rates between the United States and many of the other industrialized democracies. Reforms intended to make voting easier have led to increases in turnout, and in competitive elections this 2 or 3 percentage-point increase *could* change the outcome of any given election.

Third, we find that politics matters: when candidates offer distinct choices, eligible voters are more likely to turnout. Though we are

5. Our choice of 1972 as the first election we study is largely practical, based on the availability of data.

interested in the demographics of turnout, and believe that it is important to study demographic representation, we also believe that turnout is inherently political. On this point the intellectual debt is owed to Key (1966), who rightly observed that voters are not fools: they cannot vote as a reflection of their self-interest if they are not offered relevant choices. For Key as well as many scholars of party politics, elections are choices about policies, or candidates, or parties; they are not determined solely by demographics. We demonstrate how the policy choices offered by candidates influence whether individuals choose to cast ballots. If citizens see no differences in what candidates are offering, then, there really is very little reason to show up at the polls. We underscore the politics of turnout in this regard, for we believe that candidates offering distinct choices to citizens constitutes another mechanism by which voter turnout might be increased, and could also lower the income bias of voters.

Finally, and contrary to the conclusions of Wolfinger and Rosenstone, our empirical evidence demonstrates that voters are *not* representative of nonvoters on economic issues. Voters and nonvoters had different policy views in 1972 and have had different policy views in every election since then. This difference is substantial, and results in consistent overrepresentation of conservative views among voters compared to nonvoters. That these differences are reflected primarily in citizens' views on economic issues is a distinctive feature of this finding. That these policy differences have been ignored over several decades of increasing economic inequality make our finding all the more important. Our evidence on these differences is clear, and we hope that it is sufficiently persuasive to change the conventional wisdom among scholars and journalists alike.

We believe that the study of who votes is made all the more important by the dramatic increase in economic inequality that has occurred in the United States since 1972. We are today a country in which fewer people have a greater proportion of the wealth than in 1972. For this reason alone, documenting that voters are significantly wealthier than nonvoters and voters are *not* representative of nonvoters on redistributive issues is critical information for evaluating the nature of electoral democracy in the United States. To paraphrase Vice President Joe Biden, this is a big deal.

1.1 Economic Inequality, Income Bias, and Turnout

The potential importance of economic issues suggested by our example above seemed to be realized in the 2012 presidential campaign, with much of the campaign rhetoric, advertising, and debates focused on government programs whose impact varies across economic groups, programs intended to increase job creation, and access to health care. Prior to the 2012 election economists and sociologists had identified a dramatic increase in income inequality as a distinguishing feature of American life over the past several decades (Danziger & Gottschalk 1995; Farley 1996; Gottschalk & Danziger 2005). Between 1972 and 2008, for example, the share of household income going to the bottom fifth of the distribution decreased from 4.1 percent in 1972 to 3.4 percent of income by 2008. During that same time the share of income going to the wealthiest fifth of the population *increased* from 43.9 percent of income to 50 percent of income, and the share of income going to the top 5 percent of households *increased* from 17.0 percent to 21.5 percent.[6]

Estimates of differential income changes over time are even greater when considering persons in the top 1 percent of the income distribution. Between 1979 and 2007 this group's after-tax household income increased by 275 percent, while the after-tax household income of others in the top quintile (those in the 81st through 99th percentile of the distribution) increased by 65 percent. The corresponding figure for the bottom quintile is a mere 18 percent (Congressional Budget Office 2011).[7] Whatever measures are used, the bottom line is clear: Americans live in a more unequal economic society today than they did in 1972.[8]

Popular and journalistic attention to the politics of inequality increased after the 2008 housing collapse and subsequent recession, fueled by the Occupy Wall Street movement as well as economic issues abroad. So, too, in the last decade has scholarly attention to issues of inequality and the potential conflicts among equality, representation, and wealth increased (American Political Science Association 2004; Beramendi & Anderson 2008; Hacker 2006; McCarty, Poole, & Rosenthal 2008; Page & Jacobs 2009). The conclusions drawn in most of these studies are rather pessimistic with regard to the maintenance of *political* equality in the face of increasing *economic* inequality. With empirical evidence documenting that elected officials respond more to the preferences of the wealthy than to the preferences of the poor, democratic equality is doubtful.[9]

---

6. U.S. Census Bureau, Current Population Survey, Annual Social and Economic Supplements. Table H3, accessed November 7, 2011, from http://www.census.gov/hhes/www/income/data/historical/inequality/index.html.
7. See Jones and Weinberg (2000) for a comparison of different measures of income inequality for the period 1967–2001.
8. See also Piketty & Saez (2006, 2003).
9. See Bartels (2008); and Gilens (2012).

But this tension between economic and political inequality is not new. In fact, political inequality in voter turnout is not new at all. Since 1972 the wealthy have always voted more than the poor, and hence have always been overrepresented at the polls (in both presidential and congressional elections). But now the income and wealth gap between the wealthy and poor is much greater than it was in 1972.

What existing research does not address is whether the difference in turnout between the wealthy and poor has increased over the past thirty years. In fact, our earlier research on this point suggested that this income bias had been relatively stable from 1972 through 1984. But what has happened since then? Are the wealthy overrepresented even *more* today than they were in the 1970s, the 1980s, or 1990s?[10] We show that there has been remarkable stability in income bias in turnout despite the remarkable changes in income inequality since 1972.

1.2 Policy Choices and Turnout

The overrepresentation of the wealthy in voting or other forms of political participation is often understood to reflect that wealthy individuals also tend to have other resources (e.g., education, political interest, or stronger social and political networks) that make it easier for them to vote, or more likely to be targets of candidate and campaign mobilization efforts. But we argue that to understand income bias in turnout we must explicitly address the important role of the issue positions offered by candidates to citizens in each election. This theoretical argument is grounded in the very basic observation that elections are about choices— not just choices about parties or candidates but also choices about policies. To the extent that candidate issue positions appeal differentially to the wealthy and the poor, we would expect to see differences in how these individuals assess the value of voting.

We begin with the notion of the turnout decision as a cost-benefit calculation: citizens will vote when the costs of voting are perceived to be less than the benefits of doing so (Downs 1957). We argue that when citizens are offered distinctive choices on public policies, they are more likely to vote because these policy choices are a component of the benefits offered those who vote. Our account of turnout includes not just the choices made by voters but the choices made by candidates as to what

---

10. Schlozman, Verba, and Brady's (2012) finding that there is substantial education and income inequality in access to and use of new, electronic forms of participation makes revisiting this question for the most common form of participation in democratic politics in the United States today—voting—all the more important.

issue positions to take. We know that turnout is not constant over time—it rises and falls from one election to the next. Recognizing the critical role of candidates and the policy positions they take can help to explain this variation in turnout across elections. An important focus of our analysis thus includes the choices offered to the voters by the candidates.

We develop and test this model of turnout in light of our interest in the income bias of voters. We want to know whether, over this period of increasing inequality, the poor and wealthy believe that they have a choice to make, and whether those choices matter for individuals' decisions to vote. Given the large degree of income bias in the voting population, we also want to know whether the policy choices offered matter more for the wealthy than for the poor.

Citizens often describe why they did not vote, or do not plan to vote, as reactions to the candidates: "I don't like either of them"; "they don't represent me"; "they are not talking about what's important to me." While these self-reports as explanations of behavior may not be especially enlightening, they do suggest that citizens are aware of candidates and how they compare, at least on some dimensions. And they suggest that some citizens might see candidates as offering distinctive choices—at least some candidates, in some elections—regardless of citizens' levels of education, cognitive abilities, or interest. But if candidates do not offer distinctive policy choices, or if the choices they offer are more relevant to the rich than they are to the poor, then they effectively eliminate the ability of citizens (or poor citizens) to express their policy preferences through voting. The choices offered citizens thus become a key factor helping to explain why some citizens vote and others do not—and whether voters are representative of nonvoters.

1.3 Economic Inequality and Voting Inequality

To consider the importance of policy choices to turnout in the context of increasing inequality, we draw on Meltzer and Richard's (1981) argument that as the mean income of a society diverges from the income of the median voter (as it does with increasing inequality), then voters below the median have more incentive to favor redistributive government policies. The logic is straightforward: if a larger share of income is concentrated in fewer hands, then the majority of the electorate has more to gain by using the tools of government (such as the tax code) to redistribute that money to themselves. If the top income quintile has 50 percent of the income, then the other 80 percent of the electorate has substantial incentive to tax the rich. If the top income quintile only has 25 percent of the income, the incentive to support redistribution is less.

The logic of this median voter model of candidate choice implies that the importance of redistributive issues for voters' candidate choices is greater in times of increasing economic inequality. This implication was at least casually supported by political events and campaign rhetoric in the 2012 presidential election.

Two limitations of the Meltzer and Richard model, however, are that: (1) it assumes that all individuals will choose to vote; and (2) it assumes that the median voter will choose the tax rate directly rather than facing a choice of policy options offered by competing parties or candidates. Our key insight is that in deciding to vote or not, the impact of increased economic inequality on turnout will be conditioned by the nature of the political choices offered by the political parties. Individuals may not be given the option by either party to substantially redistribute income from those above the median income level to those below it. They can *only* respond to the choices offered by the candidates based on their assessment of the difference in benefits (or costs) reflected in the candidates' stated policy preferences.

We hypothesize that in calculating the benefits of the choices offered, individuals compare the policy positions of each candidate to their own position: the greater the difference between the attractiveness of the two candidates' policy positions, the more likely individuals are to vote. In addition, Zipp (1985) has hypothesized that the policy positions of candidates could influence turnout through a different mechanism. He suggests that the more alienated voters are by candidates' positions, the less likely they might be to vote. Consistent with this, we hypothesize that individuals compare their own policy preferences to the positions of both candidates: the greater the difference between individuals' preferred policy positions and the position offered by the closest candidate, the less likely they are to vote.

In the context of economic inequality, with the salience of redistributive issues heightened, what happens to turnout depends on what the poor and wealthy perceive as the policy preferences of the candidates. We propose two very different (hypothetical) scenarios, one of which leads to a decrease in income bias in the face of increased economic inequality, the other an increase in income bias in the face of increased economic inequality.

In the first hypothetical scenario, income bias is predicted to decrease when the poor believe that one candidate offers significantly more in the way of redistributive policies than the other candidate. Because they see a redistributive policy choice, the poor are thus less indifferent between candidates' or parties' policy positions than they would be if the candidates offered the same positions. Believing that they have a relevant choice to make regarding redistributive policies, the poor become *more* likely to vote as rising inequality increases the salience of redistribution. These relevant choices are also more clear to the wealthy, so with rising inequality the wealthy also become *more* likely to vote.

The aggregate effect of both groups voting at higher rates might be a constant rate of differential turnout between the poor and wealthy. But if the poor initially are voting at *much* lower rates than the rich, then the aggregate turnout effect on the poor will be larger than the effect on the rich because there are more nonvoting poor to be mobilized by increasing inequality than there are nonvoting rich to be mobilized.[11] Thus, in this first scenario, income bias in turnout is *decreased* by a rise in economic inequality.

In the second hypothetical scenario, income bias is predicted to increase when the poor believe that neither candidate offers a relevant choice on redistributive issues, and are thus more *alienated* than the wealthy from both parties and candidates. As income inequality increases and the salience of redistributive issues rises for the poor, this alienation leads to lower levels of turnout relative to the rich as the poor believe that the political system is not responding to or representing their interests. At the same time, with a rise in inequality and neither candidate threatening to redistribute income, the wealthy would be placing greater emphasis on a *lack* of redistribution, and therefore would be less alienated and *more* likely to vote. Thus, in this scenario we see an *increase* in income bias in turnout.

In both of these scenarios, what is key in determining who votes is not just the income or socioeconomic status of individuals but the behavior of parties and candidates. If one party offers redistribution, then the poor are likely to see a difference between the parties, and both the poor and wealthy will vote more as economic inequality increases. If neither party offers redistribution, then the poor are likely to become more alienated, and their turnout will, all things equal, decrease as economic inequality increases. In these same circumstances—with neither party offering redistribution—the wealthy would likely be less alienated and vote more. All of these observations are fully consistent with formal models of voter turnout that equate the benefits that individuals receive from voting with the utility derived from candidate policy positions.

It is important to realize here that *movement* by the candidates or parties is *not* required for increasing economic inequality to lead to increased turnout of the poor. As increasing economic inequality raises the salience of redistribution, if the poor perceive *any* difference between

---

11. We emphasize that since the voting we are discussing is voting on *candidates*, not *policies*, the poor would only have an increased incentive to vote *if* some candidates were promising to tax the rich.

the two parties on these issues, they would be less indifferent between the two parties, and more likely to vote; with lower initial levels of turnout of the poor, the aggregate consequence is less income bias in turnout. If the poor do not see redistributive choices offered by candidates they will be more alienated and less likely to vote, resulting in greater income bias of voters. The fundamental implication of our argument is that, theoretically, increasing economic inequality could lead to higher *or* lower income bias of voters—with the actual outcome predicated on the policy choices offered by candidates.[12]

1.4 Voter Turnout and Election Laws

Since 1972, most states have passed legislation to reduce the costs of voting by making it easier to do so; many supporters of reforms such as absentee voting, early voting, and election day registration have argued that doing so would increase voter turnout. As a result, voters in many states today may cast no-excuse absentee ballots by mail, may cast in-person votes for a lengthy period before election day, or, for those not already registered, may choose to both register and vote in person on election day.

Most of these reforms have been passed with some expectation that their adoption would lead to a more representative set of voters by increasing the turnout rates of less educated, lower-income individuals. The logic is that if states lower the costs of voting, those least likely to vote—and thus most underrepresented as voters—would be more likely to cast a ballot. Recently some states have adopted more rigorous voter identification requirements that are clearly *not* designed to make it easier to vote. Opposition to these efforts has focused on how requiring positive identification at the polls actually makes it harder for everyone to vote—especially the poor, and racial and ethnic minorities.

Our focus here is on those election law reforms intended to make voting easier, reforms that have often disappointed their supporters. One observation about some of these reforms is that making it easier to vote simply makes it easier to vote for those already inclined to do so, and thus *widens* the turnout gap between rich and poor, or the more educated and less educated.[13] This conflicts with the traditional view, espoused

---

12. Again, our claim differs from the argument of Meltzer and Richard (1981) because they do not at all consider competing parties; in their model the decisive voters simply choose the amount of redistribution by the government.

13. Rigby & Springer (2011) argue that reforms making it easier for the registered to vote will increase income bias as the set of people who are registered are wealthier than the set of people who are not registered.

forcefully by Wolfinger and Rosenstone (1980), that making it easier to vote allows those at the bottom of the socioeconomic status scale (those who have the hardest time clearing the administrative hurdles) to more easily meet the legal demands, and thus be more likely to cast ballots.

As Wolfinger and Rosenstone showed, the date for the cutoff of registration to vote (i.e., the closing date, or the number of days before the election that registration closed) was a key factor in determining turnout in 1972. But what about more recent reforms? Election day registration lowers the cost of registration and voting, making it a one-step rather than two-step process. In-person early voting and No-excuse absentee voting have also been adopted in efforts to make voting easier. In-person early voting allows individuals to cast ballots prior to election day; in these states "election day" has often become "election two weeks." No-excuse absentee voting allows voters to request a mail-in ballot even if they will be in the state on election day and would be able to vote in person at a polling place. This form of voting also lowers the cost of voting as individuals do not have to wait in line at the polling place.

Our focus on these four reforms is motivated by the fact that they are most central to the ten presidential elections that we study, both in the number of states that have adopted them and in the number of individuals who take advantage of them.[14] And because most research on these reforms has been limited by its typical focus on one reform in isolation from others, and by relying on limited periods of time, the effects of these reforms deserve continued attention. We think it important to provide a definitive answer to the claim that these reforms increase turnout, and also consider whether they matter *more* for those individuals least likely to vote.

We provide robust evidence of both the efficacy and the limitations of these reforms. We show that reforms such as election day registration and absentee voting have increased turnout when adopted, but we also show that the effects are more modest than what some reformers may have hoped for.

1.5 Data and Chapter Outline

In the following chapters we present a wealth of empirical evidence based on several data sources. We rely heavily on the U.S. Census Bureau

14. A recent set of reforms we do *not* study are reforms requiring stricter forms of identification, such as photo ID; there is simply not enough data available at this time to evaluate their impact on turnout.

Current Population Survey (CPS) as it provides the largest samples of nationally representative data collected on the American population for the 1972–2008 period that allows us to distinguish between voters and nonvoters. The primary limitation of the CPS is that the data are limited to demographics and do not include any questions relating to the policy positions or political views of respondents. When we turn to questions regarding how party and candidate evaluations of citizens influence their turnout, or how much voters share the policy preferences of nonvoters, then, we must turn to other data, and for that we rely primarily on the well-established American National Election Studies (NES), a biennial survey of representative samples of U.S. citizens. In addition, we use the 2004 National Annenberg Election Study to assess the representativeness of voters' policy positions. The NES provides us with the advantage of using repeated questions over time, while the Annenberg study provides more contemporary, election-specific questions on which to base an assessment of the electorate's and voters' policy views.

Our analyses of the impact of election laws on turnout utilizes new data on election laws. To improve upon previous research we use data collected on state voter registration and election administration laws for each election since 1972.[15] Because we combine data on election laws at the state and year level with data on turnout at the state and year level, we can estimate the impact of those changes in electoral laws on turnout using standard cross-sectional time series techniques. This allows us to draw robust causal inferences as we observe the effect over time of changes in laws within a state, conditional on changes happening in all other states.

In chapter 2 we use data from the CPS to provide an extensive description and discussion of aggregate and demographic group-specific turnout rates since 1972, focusing on education, income, race, ethnicity, age, gender, and marital status. We find that turnout of *eligible* citizens has not declined since 1972, and that the overrepresentation of the wealthy versus the poor among voters has remained stable and large over time. However, we see substantial changes in the relative turnout rates of men and women, blacks and whites, and younger and older adults.

In chapter 3 we introduce the theoretical framework that guides our analyses and discussions of the determinants of voter turnout. We adopt a model of turnout that poses an individual's decision to vote as a reflection of the costs and benefits of engaging in such behavior. Then, for each presidential election year since 1972, we estimate turnout as a function of our demographic characteristics of interest. These estimates

15. This project was generously funded by the Pew Charitable Trusts in 2008 and 2009.

allow us to estimate the impact of one demographic characteristic (such as income) on turnout while holding other demographic characteristics (such as education and race) constant. We refer to these estimates as "conditional" relationships, and graphically represent how the conditional relationships among these characteristics and turnout vary over time and by election year. Our findings in this chapter, too, suggest that the conditional relationships between education and turnout, and income and turnout (i.e., "conditional income bias") have been relatively stable (or modestly reduced) since 1972. We also find important changes in the conditional relationships between age, race, gender and turnout.

In chapters 2 and 3 we consider two distinct aspects of income bias because they address two very different, yet equally important, questions. In chapter 2 we examine whether poor people vote less than rich people and whether these differences change between 1972 and 2008. This is important empirical evidence, for turnout differences between the poor and wealthy likely have important political consequences for the political representation of the poor and policy outcomes. This bivariate relationship is what we mean when we use the term *income bias*, referring to turnout patterns or the representativeness of voters: the poor are a smaller percentage of voters than they are of the electorate, while the wealthy are a larger proportion of voters than they are of the electorate.

In chapter 3 we want to know if poor people vote less than rich people, *once we condition on other characteristics*. We might, of course, observe that rich people vote more than poor people; but that observation does not clarify whether they vote more simply because of life cycle effects (because when people are older they have more income, and we know that they generally vote more) or because of some other reason. We refer to conditional relationships favoring the turnout of the rich regardless of this group's differences in other demographic respects as *conditional income bias*. Similarly, we might want to ascertain whether once we know a person's level of education, does knowing his income tell us more about the probability that he will vote? Or if we observe that Hispanics vote less than Anglos, we might want to know if that is because Hispanics, on average, have less income and education than Anglos, or because they are on average younger than Anglos.[16] Or could there be another explanation? To sort out these possibilities, we would want to know if Hispanics vote less than Anglos *conditional on* levels of income, education, and age. It follows that we also want to know if these conditional relationships have changed from 1972 to 2008.

16. We use the term *Anglos* to refer to non-Hispanic whites.

In chapter 4 we describe the nature and variety of changes in voter registration and election administration laws since 1972. States vary tremendously as to how easy it is to register and to vote, and previous research suggests that these laws affect who votes because they change the cost of voting (Brians & Grofman 2001; Fitzgerald 2005; Highton 1997; Karp & Banducci 2001; Knack & White 2000; Wolfinger & Rosenstone 1980). Yet most of these studies rely on cross-sectional data, and usually consider the influence of one reform at a time. We provide aggregate (state-level) analyses of the effects of changes in these rules on voter turnout. These analyses help us address the question of whether overall voter turnout has increased as a result of these legal changes. We find modest effects of election day registration, of absentee voting, and of moving the closing date for registration closer to the election on overall turnout. The effect of early voting is less clear.

In chapter 5 we consider how the policy positions offered by candidates influence voter turnout. We expect that larger differences in the policy positions of candidates are associated with a higher probability of voting. Using NES data, we examine the impact of individuals' percep-tions of candidates' policy positions—how they compare to each other, and how they compare to the individuals' preferences–on individuals' decisions to vote. We find that individuals are more likely to vote when they perceive a greater policy difference between the candidates. We also find that the poorest Americans have become more indifferent between candidates in recent elections—that is, they see fewer differences between candidates now when compared to wealthier Americans.

In chapter 6 we consider whether voters and nonvoters differ in their policy preferences using both NES and Annenberg data. We find, contrary to conventional wisdom, notable differences in both of these comparisons, especially on redistributive issues. We conclude that the seeming consensus that it would not matter if everyone voted is simply wrong, and has been wrong for a long time. That these differences have been ignored in political discourse as well as scholarly research is all the more striking given the increase in economic inequality experienced in the United States.

Over the next five chapters we document changes in the demographics of turnout in the United States, and the effects of changes in electoral laws on turnout. While we show distinct changes in turnout of certain groups over the time period, we mostly highlight the remarkable stability of the overall level of turnout and the stability of the relative turnout of *most* demographic groups. In 1972, U.S. turnout was relatively low compared to that of other industrial democracies, and exhibited high levels of income bias. In 2008, after decades of various electoral reforms, U.S. turnout remained relatively low compared to that of other industrial democracies, and still exhibited high levels of income bias. We also highlight the consistency with which voters are not representative of the electorate on redistributive issues; they were not representative in 1972 nor were they representative in 2008. In chapter 7 we return to broader questions of representation and inequality in U.S. presidential elections.

Two
. . . .

Demographics of Turnout

Our interest in this chapter is whether changes in demographics and changes in the distribution of income in the American electorate (i.e., those who are eligible to vote) are also reflected in the composition of the voters (i.e., those who actually cast ballots). We focus primarily on how the turnout rates of different demographic groups have changed, or not changed, over time, and the extent to which voters in 2008 are more or less descriptively representative of the electorate than voters were in 1972. Of special interest, given the notable increase in economic inequality and the well-established relationship between socioeconomic status and voter turnout, is whether the voting population overrepresents the wealthy (relative to the poor) more today than it did in 1972.

Demographics remain today, as they were in 1972, major components of analyses regarding the determinants of mass political behavior in the United States. Whether drawing on the intellectual traditions of the Columbia school established by Lazersfeld, Berelson, and Gaudet in *The People's Choice* (1948) or the Michigan model pioneered by Campbell, Converse, Miller, and Stokes in *The American Voter* (1960), scholars have consistently demonstrated the importance of socioeconomic status, race, ethnicity, gender, age, and marital status as predictors of numerous aspects of electoral behavior and public opinion.

But the demographics of the United States have changed dramatically since the time of Wolfinger and Rosenstone's seminal work on voter turnout in the 1972 presidential election. The civilian population has increased from fewer than 208 million people in 1972 to over 303 million people in 2008.[1] The proportion of Anglos (non-Hispanic whites) declined from 83.2 percent of the population in 1970 to 65.6 percent in 2008.[2] And the proportion of African Americans in the population increased from 11.1 percent of the population in 1972 to approximately 13 percent of the population in 2008, while the proportion of Hispanics (of any race) has increased from 5.7 percent in 1970 to 15.4 percent in 2008.[3]

At the same time, the proportion of noncitizens in the voting-age population has increased substantially. In 1972 less than 2 percent of the voting age population were not citizens, but in 2008 8.4 percent of the voting-age population were not citizens.[4] McDonald & Popkin (2001) discuss additional requirements for voting eligibility and argue that in addition to citizenship, increasing numbers of institutionalized individuals as well as the greater number of states disenfranchising convicted felons has led to a larger percentage of voting-ineligible individuals in 2008 compared to 1972. Whereas the number of persons ineligible for these reasons was very small in 1972, it was over 1 percent of the voting age population in 2008.[5]

Changes in the size of various demographic groups since 1972 have also been accompanied by changes in economic status. Median income in 1972, all races combined, was $21,800, compared to $26,800 in 2008.[6] But change in the median income of women, compared to men, has been substantially greater: for women over the age of fifteen, the median income in 1972 was $12,100, compared to $21,00 in 2008. In contrast, the median income of men over the age of fifteen actually decreased from $34,700 in 1972 to $33,600 in 2008.[7]

1. Total population figures from U.S. Census Bureau, 2011, Statistical Abstract, table 2. These numbers exclude armed forces personnel.
2. Proportion of Anglos for 2008 from U.S. Census Bureau, 2012 Statistical Abstract, table 6: Resident Population by Sex, Race, and Hispanic-origin Status: 2000–2009; proportion of Anglos for 1970 calculated from U.S. Census data.
3. Proportion of blacks and Hispanics for 2008 from U.S. Census Bureau, 2012 Statistical Abstract, table 6: Resident Population by Sex, Race, and Hispanic-Origin Status: 2000–2009; proportion of blacks for 1970 calculated from Gibson and Jung (2002, table 1).
4. For data on the proportion of noncitizens among the voting-age population, see McDonald (2011)
5. For data on the proportion of ineligible persons among the voting-age population, see McDonald (2011).
6. All incomes reported in these comparisons between 1972 and 2008 are in constant 2010 dollars, in this and the following two paragraphs. All figures are rounded to the nearest hundred dollars.
7. Median income data in this and the following paragraph on individuals over the age of sixty-five are taken from U.S. Census Bureau, Current Population Survey, Annual Social and Economic Supplements, table P-8AR: Age—People, All Races, by Median Income and Sex: 1947 to 2010.

Men over the age of sixty-five have fared much better. In 1972, the median income of men age sixty-five and over was $17,500 in constant 2010 dollars; in 2008, it had risen to $25,800. The income gains of women over the age of sixty-five were not as great, with their median income increasing from $8,900 in 1972 to $14,700 in 2008. Aside from these gender differences, however, it is clear that, as a group, income of individuals over age sixty-five has risen since 1972.

Among racial and ethnic groups, blacks have experienced the greatest proportional increase in median income, from $15,900 in 1972 to $22,200 in 2008. While whites' median income increased from $23,000 to $29,400 in 2008, Hispanics' median income increased only slightly, from $18,300 in 1974 (1972 data not available) to $21,000 in 2008.[8]

2.1 Measuring Voter Turnout

Our analyses in this and subsequent chapters primarily rely on three national survey sources, all of which include questions that ask individuals (or informants) whether they voted in the most recent election. The Current Population Survey (CPS), conducted by the U.S. Bureau of the Census, is a monthly survey of approximately 50,000 households. Respondents are asked about behavior of other household members, providing information on approximately 90,000 individuals per month.[9] In November of even-numbered years, the CPS includes a short battery of questions on voter participation. In particular, respondents are asked whether or not they voted in that month's election, and whether or not they were registered. It is the especially large sample size that makes the CPS a valuable resource in studying voter turnout (see appendix 2.1). Along with the overall smaller sampling error, the sample includes enough people at different levels of education and income to accurately note differences across time in the participation of subgroups of interest of the population. And finally, the CPS has a substantially smaller

8. The data reported for whites for 1972 are not reported for white non-Hispanics, while the data reported for 2008 are restricted to white Non-Hispanics because the census did not include a Hispanic origin question until after 1972. Given the relatively small proportion of Hispanics in the United States in 1972, we believe that this comparison for median income is fairly accurate. Median income data by race and Hispanic origin are taken from U.S. Census Bureau, Current Population Survey, Annual Social and Economic Supplements, table P-4. Race and Hispanic Origin of People (Both Sexes Combined) by Median and Mean Income: 1947 to 2010.
9. We will refer to the 90,000 as *respondents*, though technically only those directly interviewed are truly survey respondents.

nonresponse rate than both academic surveys and surveys conducted by news organizations. In an era when voters and nonvoters are increasingly difficult to contact, the high quality of the CPS survey makes it an invaluable resource for studying turnout.

However, the CPS is limited to demographic characteristics and cannot be used to study other important determinants of voter turnout such as political preferences, attitudes, or psychological orientations. The CPS thus cannot be used to assess the consequences of who votes with respect to the representation of policy preferences. For these purposes, then, in later chapters we turn to the American National Election Study (NES) and the National Annenberg Election Study (NAES), both of which include a wide range of questions regarding demographics, attitudes, political preferences and voting behavior. The NES, a biennial survey of 1,000–2,000 U.S. citizens, provides the advantage of having time-series data on many of these questions, and provides us with the opportunity to assess electoral changes over time. Alternatively, the NAES includes a wider range of policy preferences, has larger sample sizes on some questions, and (unlike the NES) includes noncitizens in its sampling frame. We thus use the 2004 NAES to provide some additional validation of our findings based on the more standard NES surveys. Detailed question wording from the NES and NAES is provided in appendix 6.1.

One possible limitation of using any of these self-reports of voter turnout is that individuals may fail to accurately report their past behavior. Whether unintentionally or intentionally misreporting, the concern with self-reports is that they might introduce systematic measurement error in our estimates of voter turnout. This is not an issue if different demographic groups have approximately equal rates of misreporting. But if, for example, high-income individuals are more likely to overreport than are low-income individuals, then any inferences we can make with respect to differences across income groups are compromised.

This potential problem has been addressed by numerous scholars using comparisons of self-reported turnout in the NES with validated turnout (i.e., where the NES confirmed or disconfirmed respondents' self-reports by using official county-level voting records). These comparisons are available for the NES for the 1976 though 1988 surveys. Previous research comparing the reported and validated vote in the NES suggests, indeed, that higher-status individuals are more likely to overreport than are lower-status individuals, in part because they are more sensitive to the norm of voting as expected of "good citizens" (Granberg & Holmberg 1991; Hill & Hurley 1984; Silver, Anderson, Abramson 1986). These studies also report that there are significant differences in misreporting rates between blacks and whites, with blacks being more likely to overreport voting. Whether such patterns are the same for the 1990s and early 2000s is not clear.[10]

However, there is some evidence to suggest that the NES-validated vote measures also have systematic shortcomings and should be used cautiously. Traugott (1989) examines the NES validated turnout measures, for example, and reports that in some years the proportion of records where insufficient information was provided to attempt validation was as high as 15 percent (Traugott 1989; Traugott, Traugott, & Presser 1992). Also, recent research suggests that misreporting rates may be less of a problem than previously claimed (Berent, Krosnick, & Lupia 2011).[11] The necessary assumption that we need to make for our inferences documenting changes over time in relative turnout rates of different demographic groups is that differences in misreporting rates across demographic groups are stable over the time period examined.[12]

Our analyses in this chapter and chapter 3 rely on the CPS self-reported turnout measure because we are primarily interested in demographic changes over time–and we have no reason to believe that misreporting rates are not stable over time.[13] Our primary measure of turnout in this chapter is a measure of the turnout of citizens in the voting-age population (CVAP), as is typically done in analyses of registration and turnout rates.[14]

However, with the increase in the noncitizen population over this time period, analyzing only citizens could mask differences between voters and the general voting-age population, a set of nonvoters that includes those who choose not to vote and those who legally cannot vote. Since we are interested in knowing how descriptively representative voters are, this second comparison provides useful information. Thus, we also use the CPS survey data to compute a second measure of turnout, based on the

10. On the validity of the aggregate NES self-report estimates of voter turnout over time, see Burden (2000) and McDonald (2003).

11. While Katz & Katz (2010) suggest a method to correct survey misreports with other survey data, we would need to have validated survey data from each election year and assume the misreporting mechanism is similar across surveys as different as the CPS and the NES.

12. Bernstein, Chadha, & Montjoy (2003) find that misreporting rates across states are stable over the period they analyze: 1980 to 2000.

13. In chapter 6, where we use the NES self-reported vote, we also briefly discuss findings based on the NES validated vote for the years in which it is available, 1976–88. However, given the few years in which it is available, as well as the various problems with the validated vote measures identified by Traugott (1989), we do not believe that this alternative measure is clearly superior to the self-reported vote for our purposes.

14. Because the CPS is a survey of households, the sample is restricted to persons who are not incarcerated at the time of the survey. It thus includes people who are prohibited from voting based on a felony conviction but are not incarcerated.

Table 2.1. Estimates of Voter Turnout in Presidential Elections, 1972–2008.

	CPS CVAP[a]	CPS VAP[b]	NES CVAP[c]	McDonald VAP[d]	McDonald VEP[e]
1972	64.6	63.0	72.8	55.2	56.2
1976	63.6	61.6	71.6	53.5	54.8
1980	63.9	61.3	71.4	52.6	54.2
1984	65.0	62.1	73.6	53.3	55.2
1988	62.4	58.9	69.7	50.3	52.8
1992	65.5	61.3	75.1	54.7	58.1
1996	58.4	54.2	72.9	48.1	51.7
2000	59.5	54.7	72.7	50.0	54.2
2004	63.8	58.3	76.6	55.4	60.1
2008	63.6	58.2	77.6	56.9	61.6

[a] Self-reported turnout of citizens computed by the authors from the Current Population Survey for each year. Individuals coded as *Don't Know, No Response, or Refused* by the Census Bureau are treated as having not voted.

[b] Self-reported turnout of voting-age population computed by the authors using data from the Current Population Survey, 1972-2008.

[c] Self-reported turnout of citizens computed by the authors using data from the American National Election Studies Time Series Cumulative Data File, 1972-2008.

[d] Turnout rate of voting-age population based on vote for highest office as computed by McDonald (2011). Data for 1972 and 1976 are from McDonald and Popkin (2001); data for 1980–2000 are available at http://elections.gmu.edu/voter_turnout.htm.

[e] Turnout rate of voting-eligible population based on vote for highest office as computed by McDonald (2011). Data for 1972 and 1976 are from McDonald and Popkin (2001); data for 1980–2000 are available at http://elections.gmu.edu/voter_turnout.htm.

voting-age population (VAP). In this measure we include noncitizens in the denominator when we compute turnout.[15]

Our estimates of voter turnout between 1972 and 2008 are reported in table 2.1, which includes three measures based on self-reports or informant reports in surveys: the reported CVAP and VAP measures from the CPS, and the self-reported measure from the NES. Table 2.1 also includes two turnout measures based on official reports of the number of ballots cast: *voting-age* and *voting-eligible* turnout, as calculated by McDonald (2011). McDonald uses official totals for ballots cast, and the best available estimates of the voting-age population in the states to estimate the first measure. He then adjusts the denominator for the number of noncitizens in each state, as well as other individuals ineligible to vote to generate the second measure.[16]

15. As with our CVAP measure, our VAP measure does not include *currently* institutionalized felons ineligible to vote in the denominator; it thus somewhat overstates the turnout of the voting-age populations.

16. Other individuals ineligible to vote include disenfranchised felons; see McDonald (2011).

As expected, the estimate of turnout is always larger by approximately three to six percentage points when the measure is restricted to citizens (i.e., the CVAP vs. the VAP). This difference, however, is greater in more recent years as the number of noncitizens in the United States has increased. According to McDonald's estimates, over 8 percent of the voting-age population in the United States in 2008 were not citizens. Thus, including those noncitizens in the denominator will immediately reduce any computed turnout rate quite substantially.

Between 1972 and 2008, the turnout of citizens in the United States was higher in some elections than others, ranging from a low of 58.4 percent in 1996 to a high of 65.5 percent in 1992. However, there is no downward trend in the data, as many have claimed previously (e.g., Miller 1980; Reiter 1979; Rosenstone & Hansen 1993; Teixeira 1992). When we look at turnout of the population including noncitizens, we see that 1972 had the highest level of reported turnout, with turnout generally declining since then. Again, this follows from the arithmetic: with an increase in noncitizens (i.e., people not eligible to vote), the denominator in this calculation is simply increasing faster than the numerator.

Our NES self-report measure also suggests that turnout has either increased or stayed the same since 1972. Given the exclusive focus of the NES on political and social issues (and the resulting sample bias toward more highly educated, politically engaged individuals), the NES self-report estimate is higher than both of the CPS estimates. Since 1996, the NES self-report has provided a substantially higher estimate than the CPS CVAP self-report (a difference of over seventeen percentage points in 1996).[17]

Each of these three survey measures (NES, VAP, and CVAP) are all much higher than the "official" rate based on ballots cast as reported by state officials. However, we note that despite the use of the term, there *is* no "official" turnout rate for the United States. While the various state governments certify how many votes were cast for each election, they simply do not know with certainty the number of citizens eligible to vote. Thus, any measure of turnout is by necessity based on an estimate of the eligible (or voting-age) population, and even the "official" turnout numbers cannot be used as an independent benchmark to demonstrate the inaccuracy of the survey measures.

While none of these measures is without error, what we see is that none of these survey measures reflect a trend of decreasing voter turnout among voting-age citizens over time. This is an important point, as much

---

17. See Traugott (1989) and Berent, Krosnick, & Lupia (2011) for analyses of why NES-reported turnout is so high.

has been made of an alleged decline in U.S. voter turnout since 1972. However, our results are consistent with the analysis of McDonald and Popkin (2001), which showed that when looking at the turnout of voting-age *citizens* there has been no decrease in turnout.

2.2 Measuring Socioeconomic Status

Our major focus on the demographics of turnout is on socioeconomic status, though we also consider race/ethnicity, age, gender, and marital status in some detail (see appendix 2.1 on question wording and response categories for each of these variables). We conceptualize socioeconomic status as reflecting the resources and opportunities available to individuals to interact and engage politically, socially, and economically; individuals with higher status have greater resources to assume the costs of such behaviors, and also have more ways to participate in these spheres.

Wolfinger and Rosenstone's detailed analysis of education, income, and occupation as determinants of voter turnout, however, led them to conclude that there is no generic status variable related to voter turnout (1980, 34–35). That is, while education was strongly and positively related to voter turnout in 1972, the relationship between income and turnout was much weaker, and was unrelated to voter turnout once an individual achieved a threshold of financial security. Occupational status was not associated with voter turnout at all in 1972; instead, occupational differences reflected particular attributes or characteristics of the occupation (e.g., its reliance on the government).

Largely as a result of these empirical findings, the standard analytical approach in most studies of voter turnout over the past several decades has been to rely primarily on education and income (but not occupation) as indicators of socioeconomic status. We follow such a practice here in order to be consistent with this earlier work.

As we have argued earlier (Leighley & Nagler 1992b, 727, 730–32), education, income, and occupation as measures of class are plagued with measurement error, a key reason for some of the conflicting findings reported in previous research on class bias over time. Occupation is especially troublesome with respect to categorizing particular jobs as either white collar or blue collar, as well as with respect to temporal validity (made all the worse in the CPS by a notable coding change in 1970). In addition, the distinctive attributes of particular professions with respect to those dimensions that Wolfinger and Rosenstone (1980) identified as relevant to voter turnout are especially difficult, if not impossible, to measure reliably over time.

We continue to believe that income is the most meaningful available measure of socioeconomic status to use in studies of turnout. Income is the most widely used and recognized demographic criteria by which government distributes benefits and therefore seeks to influence social and economic life. Thus, if poor people do not vote, they could find economic policy being written in ways that disadvantage them. However, if poorly educated people do not vote they would not be likely to find government policy explicitly written to disadvantage them, *as government policy does not generally mention one's level of education.* And this relationship of government policy to income happens both at the spending end (through means-tested benefits programs) and the taxing end through a tax code that sets different rates for people at different income levels. Thus we proceed to primarily focus on *income bias*, rather than *socioeconomic class bias.*

Our measure of individuals' income over time is not the discrete income category into which the individual is categorized but instead reflects where the individual is relative to the entire income distribution in a given year. We do this in part because in each year the CPS arbitrarily defines a set of income categories, and the size and range of these categories varies a great deal over the time period of interest.

We measure income in each year by assigning individuals to one of five income groups (i.e., quintiles), combining the CPS income categories for each year. As the categories do not map perfectly into quintiles (i.e., the first several CPS income categories may yield slightly more or slightly less than 20 percent of the respondents), we randomly assign people in overlapping categories into quintiles so that each quintile represents 20 percent of the distribution.[18] By assigning individuals' self-reports of income to one of these five quintiles in each year between 1972 and 2008, we use a more meaningful measure of income over time, and thus one that allows us to draw more meaningful inferences about the relationship between income and voter turnout.[19] As quintiles are a standard reporting unit for income measures, our individual-level measure is thus comparable to aggregate-level measures of income change.[20]

---

18. In earlier work (Leighley & Nagler 1992b) we did not smooth out the quintiles generated by CPS categories, leading to criticism that they were not comparable over time (Freeman 2004). With the procedure we use here the quintiles are comparable over time.
19. Note that in the multivariable estimates that follow based on cross-sectional data, this coding has no effect. However, it is critical for comparability of estimates across years.
20. Much of the recent change in the income distribution has been *within* the top quintile. However, we do not see much efficacy in examining the turnout rate of the top 1 percent of the income distribution, because even if they all voted, they would still only have 1 percent of the vote.

Conceptually, education reflects the skills and information gained by individuals and, though it is typically achieved at relatively early stages of life, has been documented to determine a host of life chances, including income level and occupation type. This likely reflects another key aspect of education as a measure of status: it is closely linked to family background. Individuals with higher levels of education are more likely to come from families with higher levels of education. Levels of education also likely reflect attitudinal characteristics of individuals who seek to achieve more education or who become more engaged in politics because they have basic information about interests and issues.

As Nie, Junn, and Stehlik-Barry (1996) and Tenn (2005) argue, the meaning of education has changed over time. Someone with a college degree in 1972 was much rarer than someone with a college degree in 2008 (12.0 percent vs. 29.4 percent of people over twenty-five years of age, respectively), and someone who failed to graduate from high school was rarer in 2008 than 1972 (13.4 percent vs. 41.8 percent, respectively).[21] Comparisons of the level of education over time badly conflate selection into education with level of education. Thus for education, too, a measure of relative education is more suitable for testing differences in the effects of education over time. We measure education not by the number of years of formal schooling attained (as is usually done) but instead by assigning each individual to one of three categories representing the education distribution in each year (i.e., bottom third, middle third, top third).[22]

2.3 Measuring Race and Ethnicity

As scholars of racial/ethnic politics are well aware, thorough data on race and ethnicity are rarely available, even in the case of the U.S. Census. Until recently, "ethnicity," in Census Bureau terms, refers to identifying as Hispanic or Latino, while "race" refers to identifying as white, black, or African American, American Indian/Alaska Native, Asian, or Native Hawaiian or other Pacific Islander. Individuals identifying as Hispanic or Latino can also identify as belonging to any racial category.

21. U.S. Census Bureau, Current Population Survey, table A-2: Percent of People 25 Years and Over Who Have Completed High School or College, by Race, Hispanic Origin and Sex: Selected Years 1940 to 2012; accessed October 25, 2011, at http://www.census.gov/hhes/socdemo/education/data/cps/historical/tabA-2.xls.
22. As with income, when CPS education categories do not allow us to precisely determine which third of the income distribution a respondent is in, we use random assignment.

Our analyses focus primarily on three racial/ethnic groups: Anglos (i.e., non-Hispanic whites); African Americans (non-Hispanic blacks); and white Hispanics, because these are the three largest and most commonly politically identified groups during the period of analysis.[23] The large size of each of these groups throughout the period allows us to draw more accurate inferences regarding changes in the relationship between these demographic characteristics and voter turnout. We do not distinguish between Hispanics on the basis of their native origin due to our inability to maintain consistency over time. Thus, our description of Hispanic turnout, and our conditional comparisons of Hispanic turnout and Anglo turnout, are all averages over the full set of Hispanics.[24]

Even focusing on only these three groups is challenging because of changes in question wording over the study period. The Current Population Survey did not include a "Hispanic Origin" (i.e., ethnicity) question until 1976, and so our analysis of ethnicity and voter turnout is restricted to the 1976–2008 time period. In 2000 the response categories of this question were revised to "Hispanic or Latino Origin" and "Not Hispanic or Latino."

The CPS has also revised its question wording regarding race over the period of our analysis. From 1972 to 1988 there is a consistent coding of white, black, and "other." From 1992 through 2000 individuals could identify as one of four races: white; black; American Indian or Alaskan Native; and Asian or Pacific Islander. The category "other" included everyone else. In 2004, a new set of response categories was provided, and for the first time respondents were allowed to select one *or* *more* races when they self-identified, and they could also choose a sixth racial category, "some other race." However, the entire set of new 2004 categories comprised less than 2 percent of choices of respondents over 2004 and 2008. So the effect on our analyses of the additional categories is likely to be small.

---

23. We use the term *Hispanic* to refer to those who identified as either Hispanic or Latino. Because conventional census and scholarly and popular terminology for different racial and ethnic groups has changed over our period of study, we use related terms interchangeably (e.g., *black* and *African American*, or *Hispanic* and *Latino*), but try to use the terminology that most closely matches that used in the data sources upon which we rely. When there are changes over time, and we are referring to the entire period, we typically use the more recent terminology. For coding purposes, those listing multiple races were coded as "other" in 2004 and 2008.

24. See Highton & Burris (2002) on the differences in turnout rates among Hispanics of different national origin.

2.4 Demographics of Turnout, 1972–2008 (CPS)

We begin our analysis of voter turnout in presidential elections by examining differences in turnout rates by education, income, race/ethnicity, age, gender, and marital status. We do this to answer the fundamental question of descriptive representation: does the set of individuals who cast ballots share the same distribution on demographic characteristics as the set of individuals who are eligible to vote? In other words, does the set of voters "look" like the set of eligible voters? If voters are demographically similar to the electorate (i.e., eligible individuals) then we can conclude that in this basic sense, voters are descriptively representative. In chapter 3 we will turn to models that give the conditional relationship between these demographic characteristics and the likelihood of voting over time—that is, we will examine whether voters are representative of the electorate for each demographic characteristic, while conditioning on, or controlling for, other demographic characteristics.

Figures 2.1 through 2.7 graph report turnout rates by education (bottom third, middle third, and top third of the distribution), income (low to high quintiles), race/ethnicity (white, black, Latino, other; as well as white non-Hispanic, black non-Hispanic, white Hispanic, and other), age (18–24, 25–30, 31–45, 46–60, 61–75, and 76–84), gender, and marital status (married vs. nonmarried). In each of these figures the horizontal axis represents each presidential election year, while the vertical axis represents the percentage of individuals in each demographic group who report having voted. Changes over time in the turnout levels of each group can then be assessed by examining the movement (i.e., ups and downs) of each line, while differences in turnout rates across the demographic subgroups can be assessed by the distance between lines. The larger the distance between each line, the greater the turnout differences are based on the demographic characteristic of interest.

Figure 2.1 graphs turnout by thirds of the education distribution, and figure 2.2 graphs turnout by income quintile. The graphs for turnout by education and income levels are similar in that there are distinct differences across each demographic category, and these differences are observed for every election year between 1972 and 2008. In each election, individuals with higher levels of education are more likely to vote than individuals with lower levels of education, and individuals with higher levels of income are more likely to vote than those with lower levels of income.

In addition, while the differences in turnout across education and income levels (i.e., the distance between the lines) appear to be similar over time, the actual turnout rates vary across the period. Between 1972 and 1988, for example, turnout seems to be relatively stable, with a

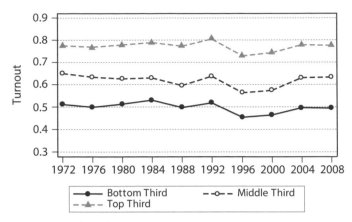

Figure 2.1. Turnout by Education, 1972–2008.
Note: Entries are the self-reported turnout rate of the citizen voting-age population for each demographic group. Computed by the authors using data from the Current Population Survey.

notable increase (across all subgroups) in 1992, followed by a drop in turnout (again, across all subgroups) in 1996, and then increases in most subgroups in each election from 2000 to 2008. Regardless of these changes, the difference in turnout between the highest and lowest education group is about the same in 2008 as it was in 1972 (13.8 percentage points). For income, however, it appears that the difference in turnout between the highest and lowest income groups is slightly smaller in 2008 than it was in 1972 (25.3 percentage points in 2008 vs. 28.8 percentage points in 1972), with the lowest two income groups voting at increasing rates in each election after 1996.

These patterns confirm the enduring significance of education and income for patterns of voter turnout, and suggest that income bias of the voting population has been remarkably stable over time. Note that there are two important observations here: first, that the income bias of voters is large, and has been large in every election since 1972; and, second, changes in income bias over time have been rather small. In addition, that turnout of each group moves together suggests that the turnout of each group responds similarly to election specific factors. We return to this point in chapter 5. More broadly, we note that what we do *not* see is an increase in income bias in turnout that is anything like the increase in income inequality over this period. Thus, if the increasing income inequality over the period we examine has affected politics, it has done so through mechanisms other than through causing any substantial change in the representativeness of the voters.[25]

25. See Bartels (2008) for a similar observation.

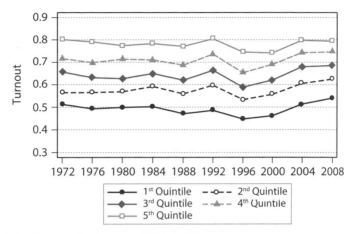

Figure 2.2. Turnout by Income, 1972–2008.
Note: Entries are the self-reported turnout rate of the citizen voting-age population for each demographic group. Computed by the authors using data from the Current Population Survey.

In contrast to the relative stability in patterns of turnout by education and income we saw previously, we see substantial differences in relative turnout by race, ethnicity, age, and gender over time. We provide two separate graphs of turnout by ethnicity to show different combinations of ethnicity with race, and because of constraints in the available data. Figure 2.3 graphs turnout by race and ethnicity separately from 1972 to 2008; the categories for white, black, and other *include* Hispanics, *and* we include turnout of Hispanics as a separate measure in figure 2.3.[26] Figure 2.4 graphs turnout by ethnicity from 1976 to 2008, classifying respondents into four categories: white non-Hispanic, black non-Hispanic, other non-Hispanic, and white Hispanic.[27]

Examining white non-Hispanic turnout over time as we do in Figure 2.4 is especially important because the makeup of those classified as white in 2008 is much different from the makeup of those classified as white in 1972. In 1972, most of the U.S. population could be characterized adequately as black or white, but by 2008 the homogeneity of the white racial category became questionable, as white Hispanics,

26. Note that in this graph respondents can appear in multiple categories: the Hispanic category includes white Hispanics, and the white category includes white Hispanics.
27. There are so few nonwhite Hispanics in the sample that we omitted them here and only analyze white Hispanics. However, as this constitutes almost all Hispanics in the United States, our inferences about turnout of white Hispanics could be used to describe Hispanics generally without offering the caveat that they are white Hispanics.

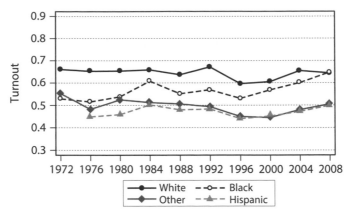

Figure 2.3. Turnout by Race, 1972–2008.
Note: Entries are the self-reported turnout rate of the citizen voting-age population for each demographic group. Computed by the authors using data from the Current Population Survey.

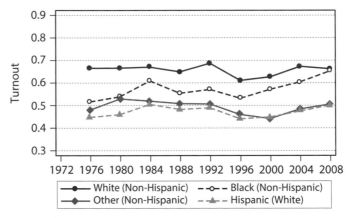

Figure 2.4. Turnout by Ethnicity, 1976–2008.
Note: Entries are the self-reported turnout rate of the citizen voting-age population for each demographic group. Computed by the authors using data from the Current Population Survey.

a much larger group than in 1972, were now politically distinctive from white non-Hispanics. Thus, the black versus white categorization is not adequate for examining racial/ethnic group differences over this time period. Obviously the set of whites in 2008 included a much higher percentage of Hispanics than did the set of whites in 1972, and as Hispanic whites vote at a much lower rate than non-Hispanic whites, we would be failing to measure what is a politically relevant demographic characteristic in combining the groups.

Figure 2.3 illustrates the dramatic change over time in turnout of these groups. Turnout of blacks increases from 53 percent in 1972 to 65 percent in 2008. Thus, where thirty years ago black turnout lagged substantially behind white turnout, in 2008 it was the same as white turnout. Note that black turnout first increased between 1976 and 1980, spiked substantially in 1984, declined through 1996, and then increased again. The high levels of turnout in 1984 and 2008 are consistent with claims of the importance of Jesse Jackson's presidential candidacy in 1984 and Barack Obama's candidacy in 2008 (see Tate [1991, 1993]; and Philpot [2009]). But it is also important to note that the trend toward increasing turnout of blacks relative to whites is observable outside of these elections. We note that this is a direct comparison of turnout rates *without* conditioning on income and education, where we would expect the lower levels of income and education of blacks to lead to lower turnout rates for blacks than whites.

This increase in black turnout has potentially important electoral consequences. Black turnout in 1972 was only 52.9 percent; in 2008 it was 64.7 percent. According to exit polls, Obama won 95 percent of the black vote in 2008. If black turnout in 2008 had been only what it was in 1972, Obama's overall vote share would have dropped by 1.2 percentage points. And, of course, given the geographic distribution of blacks, this would have meant more than 1.2 percentage points in some states and fewer in others. The point, of course, is that in a close state, 1.2 percentage points could easily be pivotal. Obviously the large impact here is because of the overwhelming support blacks give to Democratic candidates. Whereas Obama's share of the black vote was 52 percentage points higher than his share of the white vote, his share of the women's vote was only 7 percentage points higher than his share of the men's vote.

We also see changes in the turnout of Hispanics and Anglos over this time period. Figure 2.4 gives the turnout for white non-Hispanics, other non-Hispanics (Anglos), white Hispanics, and black non-Hispanics.[28] Anglo turnout follows the same pattern as that reported for the education and income groups: it is relatively stable until 1988, with a notable spike in 1992, followed by a drop in 1996 and then increases in 2000 and 2004. White Hispanic turnout, on the other hand, increases between 1976 and 1984, and then again from 1996 to 2008, after declining or remaining constant in 1988 and 1992. The key point here is that whereas black turnout increased considerably from 1972 to 2008, Hispanic turnout has increased much less. The 21.7 percentage-point gap in

28. Because of data availability, this graph starts in 1976 rather than 1972.

turnout between Anglos and white Hispanics that existed in 1976 shrank to a 16.1 percentage-point gap in 2008, with much of this shrinkage happening from 1976 to 1984. In 1984 and 1988 the gap was 16.5 percent and 16.6 percent, respectively. It did not drop below this level again until 2008, when it returned to 16.1 percent. Given the greater organization of Hispanic political groups compared to 1972, as well as the increasing size of the Hispanic community, the size of the gap in 2008 is striking.[29]

Figure 2.5 shows patterns of turnout across age groups between 1972 and 2008 and also documents changes in the demographics of turnout. The most striking change here is in the dramatic increase in voter turnout in the oldest age group (76- to 84-year-olds). In 1972, less than 60 percent of this age group reported voting, but by 2008 that proportion had increased to nearly 75 percent. This increase resulted in the turnout of this oldest group exceeding turnout of 31- to 45-year-olds and 46- to 60-year-olds, at the same time that it approaches the turnout levels of 61- to 75-year-olds (the group with the highest levels of self-reported turnout.) As was the case in 1972, the youngest age group (18- to 24-year-olds) reports the lowest level of voting in every election year (with a notable spike in 2004 and a slight increase in 2008).

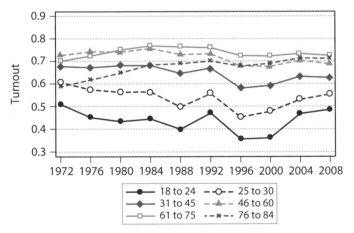

Figure 2.5. Turnout by Age, 1972–2008.
Note: Entries are the self-reported turnout rate of the citizen voting-age population for each demographic group. Computed by the authors using data from the Current Population Survey.

29. To be clear: we are talking about the gap in turnout *of citizens*!

We note that this increase in turnout is especially important because it coincides with demographic changes in the age distribution of the population. While 76- to 84-year-olds made up 4 percent of the citizen voting age population in 1972, they made up 5.4 percent of the citizen voting age population in 2008 (see table 2.2 for details on population proportions for other demographic groups in 1972 and 2008). Combining these changes with their increased turnout rate, their share of the voters increased from 3.6 percent in 1972 to 6.0 percent in 2008.

These results likely reflect that older Americans are healthier and wealthier today than they were in 1972, and are likely to be more active. But they are also consistent with what many observers of real politics have argued: that older Americans have become more politicized.

Changes in turnout patterns of men and women also emerge when we examine self-reported turnout from 1972 to 2008 (fig. 2.6). In 1972, women were less likely to report voting than were men, though since 1984 women have been consistently *more* likely to report voting than men. And the trend has been quite steady. By 2008 the gap in turnout between men and women had grown to over 4 percentage points. Some scholars have attributed increased participation by women to an increasing number of female candidates and national political figures (Atkeson 2003). Women have also entered the labor force in larger numbers over this period.

We note that this change is potentially important to election outcomes. Women vote Democratic at significantly higher rates than do men. Thus, this change in turnout rates in effect makes the set of voters more

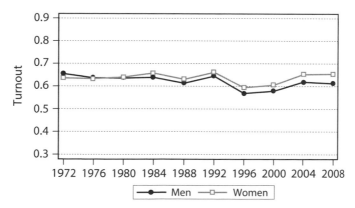

Figure 2.6. Turnout by Gender, 1972–2008.
Note: Entries are the self-reported turnout rate of the citizen voting-age population for each demographic group. Computed by the authors using data from the Current Population Survey.

Democratic than they would otherwise be. For example, in 2008, Barack
Obama received 56 percent of women's votes and only 49 percent of
men's votes. Had women and men voted at the same rate in 2008 that
they did in 1972, Obama's overall vote share would have been 0.16
percentage points lower.

The final demographic characteristic we examine is that of marital
status. As shown in figure 2.7, turnout of both married and single
individuals has varied somewhat over time, but these changes are similar
for the two groups: the turnout of single individuals increases in the
same elections where the turnout of married individuals increases, and
similarly for decreases in turnout. The turnout levels of both groups are
fairly similar in 2008 to what they were in 1972, despite a fair amount
of variation in the later elections. And single individuals continue to vote
at levels substantially below the levels of married individuals.

More generally, then, what we see in these bivariate relationships over
time is the enduring importance of education and income, compared
to the more fluid relationship between turnout and race, ethnicity,
age, or gender. Determining whether earlier findings that education is
more important than income as a determinant of voter turnout are
still correct requires a multivariable analysis of the type we conduct in
chapter 3. Perhaps over this period of increasing economic inequality,
both education and income remain important, but income has become
more important than education. We will return to this question in
chapter 3.

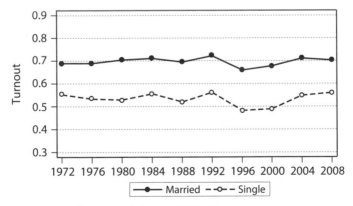

Figure 2.7. Turnout by Marital Status, 1972–2008.
Note: Entries are the self-reported turnout rate of the citizen voting-age
population for each demographic group. Computed by the authors using data
from the Current Population Survey.

2.5 A More or Less Representative Voting Population?

As Wolfinger and Rosenstone noted, "In short, voters are not a micro-cosm of the entire body of citizens but a distorted sample that exaggerates the size of some groups and minimizes that of others" (1980, 108). Based on the differential turnout rates documented in figures 2.1 through 2.7, it would seem that 2008's voting population was indeed, on most dimensions, as distorted as was the 1972 voting population.

While looking at the level of turnout of each group over time is useful for seeing what has been happening, normatively we are concerned with representativeness. The obvious question is, does a group's share of *the votes* match its share of *the population*? To provide a more systematic portrait of changes in electoral representativeness over time, we compare the representativeness of the 1972 and 2008 voting populations using a representativeness ratio similar to that used by Wolfinger and Rosenstone (1980, table 6.1) and Rosenstone and Hansen (2003, table 8.2). This ratio for each demographic group is computed by dividing the group's proportion of voters by its proportion of the voting-age citizen population. If the group is equally represented when comparing their proportion of voters to their proportion of the voting-age citizen population, then the representativeness ratio equals one; if the group is overrepresented as voters compared to the voting-age citizen population, then the ratio is greater than one; and if the group is underrepresented as voters compared to the voting-age citizen population, then the ratio is less than one.

Table 2.2 illustrates the calculations of representativeness for 1972 and 2008. To both make it comparable to Wolfinger and Rosenstone's original table and to illustrate the issues in comparing groups across time, we show representativeness for two measures of education. The first measure is simply level of education. Here we have four categories: less than high school graduate; high school graduate; some college; and college graduate and beyond. The second measure is placed in the education distribution, and here we have whether the respondent is in the bottom, middle, or top third of the education distribution. The table thus shows that the representativeness of the voting population with respect to *level* of education has changed drastically. In 1972, persons with less than a high school education had a representativeness ratio of 0.79, but by 2008 it had dropped to 0.62. However, if we simply look at persons in the bottom third of the education distribution, the representativeness ratio did not change. It was 0.79 in 1972, and 0.78 in 2008. Of course, the other thing that changed was the distribution of education in the population. Whereas 36.6 percent of the citizen voting age population in 1972 had less than a high school degree, in 2008 the corresponding number was only 11.2 percent.

Table 2.2. Representativeness of Voters by Demographic Groups, 1972 and 2008.

	1972			2008		
	% of CVAP[a]	% of Voters[b]	Ratio: Voters/ CVAP[c]	% of CVAP[a]	% of Voters[b]	Ratio: Voters/ CVAP[c]
Less than High School	36.6	29.0	0.79	11.2	6.9	0.62
High School Grad	37.5	38.7	1.03	31.7	27.4	0.86
Some College	14.3	16.8	1.18	29.6	31.6	1.07
College Grad and Above	11.7	15.5	1.33	27.5	34.1	1.24
Education—Bottom Third	32.8	25.9	0.79	31.9	24.7	0.78
Education—Middle Third	33.6	33.8	1.01	34.6	34.5	0.99
Education—Top Third	33.6	40.3	1.20	33.5	40.8	1.22
Income—1st Quintile	20.1	15.9	0.79	19.5	15.5	0.79
Income—2nd Quintile	20.0	17.3	0.87	19.6	18.0	0.92
Income—3rd Quintile	19.8	20.0	1.01	19.8	19.9	1.00
Income—4th Quintile	20.1	22.1	1.10	20.4	22.4	1.10
Income—5th Quintile	20.0	24.7	1.23	20.8	24.3	1.17
Age 18–24	18.3	14.3	0.78	12.8	9.3	0.76
Age 25–30	12.9	12.0	0.93	10.6	9.2	0.87
Age 31–45	24.9	26.6	1.04	26.4	26.0	0.98
Age 46–60	24.6	27.5	1.12	28.7	30.8	1.08
Age 61–75	15.4	16.6	1.08	16.2	18.3	1.13
Age 76–84	4.0	3.6	0.91	5.4	6.0	1.11
Women	53.0	52.3	0.99	52.1	53.7	1.03
Single	30.9	26.4	0.85	46.0	40.5	0.88
Black	10.0	8.2	0.82	12.1	12.3	1.02
Hispanic	—	—	—	9.5	7.4	0.78

[a] Entries in the first and fourth columns are the percentages of citizens in the voting-age population in the referenced demographic group, for 1972 and 2008, respectively. Computed by the authors using data from the 1972 and 2008 Current Population Surveys.

[b] Entries in the second and fifth columns are the percentages of voters in the referenced demographic group, for 1972 and 2008, respectively. Computed by the authors using data from the 1972 and 2008 Current Population Surveys.

[c] Entries in the third and sixth columns are the ratios of the demographic group's share of voters to the demographic group's share of the citizen voting-age population, for 1972 and 2008, respectively. Values less than 1 indicate underrepresentation of the specific demographic group among voters, while values greater than 1 indicate overrepresentation of the specific demographic group among voters. Computed by the authors using data from the 1972 and 2008 Current Population Surveys.

The 2008 voting population is more representative of blacks than was the 1972 voting population, with the representation ratio increasing from 0.82 to 1.02. We also see changes in representativeness across age groups. In 1972 persons between the ages of seventy-six and eighty-four were underrepresented among voters (ratio of 0.91), but, in 2008 this group was *over*represented among voters (ratio of 1.11). In contrast to these notable changes, the representativeness ratio for women increased only slightly, from 0.99 to 1.03. For singles, their representativeness ratio barely changed (0.85 to 0.88).

In addition to representativeness, table 2.2 shows the share of votes held by different groups. Comparing the percent of voters column in 1972 with the percent of voters column in 2008 highlights several politically meaningful changes. Whereas in 1972 76- to 84-year olds had 3.6 percent of the votes, in 2008 they had 6.0 percent of the votes. Single people had 26.4 percent of the votes in 1972, but 40.5 percent of the votes in 2008. And blacks had 8.2 percent of the votes in 1972 and 12.3 percent of the votes in 2008. Given the differences in voting patterns of blacks versus nonblacks, and single people versus married people, these shifts in the share of votes have potentially important implications for election outcomes.[30]

2.6 More or Less Income Bias?

Research on and discussions of income bias in turnout can focus on two very different questions, both of which are important. Being precise about which question is being addressed is critical to knowing the proper way to answer the question.

First, if we are asking whether lower-income people are less well represented among the voters than among the voting age population, then we do not need to condition on other characteristics of the lower-income population. Those other characteristics are irrelevant to the question. We simply need to compare the fraction of the votes cast by lower-income people to their fraction of the eligible voting population. This is what we do in table 2.2.

But, second, if instead we are asking whether a lower-income person is less likely to vote than a similar higher-income person—that is, one who shares the lower-income person's other demographic characteristics (e.g., the same age, education, ethnicity, and gender)—then we would

---

30. See Teixeira (2010) for a fuller analysis of the electoral implications of demographic change.

need to proceed differently. To answer this question we would, of course, need to condition on other characteristics potentially associated with income and turnout. If we observe that, on average, lower-income people vote less than higher-income people, we might want to know if this difference in voting rates can be explained by other observable demographic characteristics of the respondents. In the case of income, we might want to know this based on concerns of representation and fairness. We know that income generally increases as people get older, but we would not want to infer that poor people vote less simply because younger people vote less.

Answering this second type of question also allows us to do two things. First, it indicates what needs to be explained beyond what is in our model. If Hispanics vote less than Anglos on average, but vote at the same rate as Anglos once we condition on education, income, and age, then we would not need to look for other causal explanations of why Hispanic turnout is low relative to Anglo turnout. We would have found that Hispanic turnout is lower than Anglo turnout because Hispanics are less educated, have less income, and are younger. But, if Hispanics vote less than Anglos even *after* conditioning on other demographic characteristics, then we would need to look for other explanations to explain why that is so.

Answering this second question also provides useful information if we are interested in the marginal *effect* of different attributes on turnout, and are trying to draw causal inferences from observed conditional relationships between individual characteristics and turnout. We note that drawing causal inference about the relationship between observable characteristics and turnout in cross-sectional data is problematic. But we are still interested in these conditional relationships.

Our earlier work on income bias has addressed both of these questions and suggested that income bias had not increased between 1972 and 1988. Our earlier analysis (Leighley & Nagler 1992b) focused primarily on two different tests of changes in income bias. First, we examined changes in the turnout of different income quintiles over time. Increasing differences between the turnout of members of the top and bottom income quintiles over time would be evidence of increasing income bias, as would differences between the turnout rates of each income quintile and overall turnout. We found these differences to be surprisingly small from 1972 to 1988.

Second, we tested for changes in the conditional relationship between income and turnout, controlling for other demographic characteristics associated with voter turnout (i.e., race, gender, age, marital status, living in the South), to assess whether income as an explanatory variable became stronger over time. Should income bias in turnout be increasing, then the conditional relationship between income and turnout should increase, or the relationship between other characteristics associated with turnout and income would have to change. Using a probit model of voter turnout, we found that the conditional relationships between turnout and both income and education were relatively stable between 1972 and 1988. These two sets of evidence led to our conclusion that there was little (almost no) change in income bias between 1972 and 1988.[31]

The data we report in table 2.2 suggests that income bias is similar in 1972 and 2008 and thus that it has not changed dramatically since 1988. Specifically, the representativeness ratio for the poorest income group is the same in 2008 as it was in 1972, the ratio for the second poorest quintile increases by .05, and the ratio for the middle quintile changes only from 1.01 to 1.00. The fourth quintile stays the same at 1.1, while the wealthiest quintile's score decreases from 1.23 to 1.17. This decrease in overrepresentation is the largest change among all the income groups.

These findings contradict Freeman's (2004) and Darmofal's (2005) conclusions that income bias has increased. We believe that some of the disagreement in the literature on whether income bias has increased or not (in the form of inconsistent or inconclusive evidence) reflects the particular way in which income bias is measured, the particular statistical approach used to examine income bias, and the particular time periods chosen for study.

For example, we note that one must be cautious in drawing conclusions regarding income bias when examining only the top and bottom income groups. The simplicity of comparing the extremes of income distribution likely overlooks the economic diversity of American society, as well as the possibility that notably different patterns of income gains and losses across income groups may have vastly different political consequences. One might imagine, for instance, a relatively stable rate of income bias over time when comparing the turnout of the wealthiest quintile to the poorest—but quite different political implications would likely result if at the same time middle-income voters are either energized or demobilized by economic and political circumstances.

We also argue that it is all the more important to examine income bias over a series of elections. Early studies noting the income bias of the voting population assumed that as turnout (supposedly) declined in the 1970s it was lower-status individuals withdrawing more quickly

---

31. Using similar measures, Shields & Goidel (1997) both expand on and confirm these conclusions in the case of midterm elections between 1958 and 1994.

than higher-status individuals—though the decline was implicitly viewed as a process occurring over the course of several elections (see, e.g., Burnham [1980, 1987, 1988]; and Reiter [1979]). Assessing income bias across a long series of elections allows us to determine to what extent income bias in the voting population is malleable from election to election, or instead moves in the form of small changes tending in the same direction.

Analyses of changes in income bias over time are fundamentally constrained by the time period considered, as well as assumptions regarding the linearity of changes over time, either in theory or practice. That is, if we seek to test for an increase between two points in time, then which two points are chosen may make a difference for our conclusions. The data presented in table 2.2, for example, may reflect these two particular election years: one in which George McGovern is running as a liberal Democrat and one in which John McCain is running for election in a time of war as a conservative Republican, the latter with a marked increase in aggregate voter turnout. This evidence cannot tell us whether the substantive finding that there is decreasing representation of any one group would differ if instead we compared 1980 to 2008, or 2000 to 2008.

From a practical perspective, this means that when evaluating income bias over time one must consider whether year-to-year changes are as notable as an underlying trend over time. The possibility of election-specific changes in income bias independent of overall turnout is intriguing, as we know that candidates, issues, and party strategies often differ substantially across elections, and that some elections take place in periods of increasing economic inequality while others do not. Hence, changes in income bias might be observed only in particular periods within the broader time frame of the analysis. If year-to-year changes dominate the trend, then it suggests that income bias responds to specific political interests and is thus potentially malleable by elites.

Our analysis of income bias from 1972 to 2008 focuses primarily on differences in turnout across income groups, but we also present differences in turnout across education groups since these data are often presented in analyses of socioeconomic bias more broadly defined. Figures 2.8 and 2.9 plot the representativeness scores for income and education groups for each election from 1972 through 2008.[32]

Again, we see that the representativeness of the voting population with respect to the electorate has basically remained stable since 1972 for both income and education. The middle-income group is fairly represented,

32. The representativeness scores for income and education, as well as representativeness scores and similar representativeness graphs for race, ethnicity, age, gender, and marital status, are included in appendix 2.2.

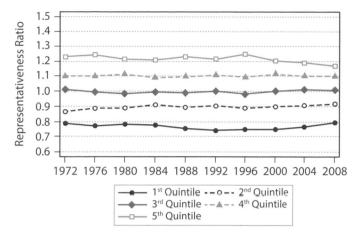

Figure 2.8. Representativeness of Voters Compared to Citizens, by Income, 1972–2008.

Note: Entries are the ratio of the income group's share of voters (based on self-reported vote) to the income group's share of the citizen voting-age population. Values less than 1 indicate underrepresentation of the specific income group among voters, while values greater than 1 indicate overrepresentation of the specific income group among voters. Computed by the authors using data from the Current Population Survey.

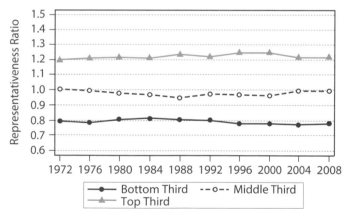

Figure 2.9. Representativeness of Voters Compared to Citizens, by Education, 1972–2008.

Note: Entries are the ratio of the education group's share of voters (based on self-reported vote) to the education group's share of the citizen voting-age population. Values less than 1 indicate underrepresentation of the specific education group among voters, while values greater than 1 indicate overrepresentation of the specific education group among voters. Computed by the authors using data from the Current Population Survey.

with the group's representativeness score very close to 1 for the entire period, while the highest two income groups are overrepresented. While there are slight variations from election to election, the level of representation for these three groups seems to be fairly stable. The lowest two income groups, in contrast, are underrepresented, with representativeness scores generally between 0.7 and 0.9. Though changes are still quite small, it appears that the second income group's representativeness score increases over time, while the lowest income group's representativeness score dipped slightly in the 1980s, but rebounded from 2000 to 2008. The relatively flat lines associated with these representativeness scores indeed suggest that income bias in the voting population, as measured by income, has remained relatively stable over time. We emphasize here that we are not interested in arguing about whether the representativeness of the bottom income quintile has gone from 0.79 to 0.81. Our point is that it is very stable, and that changes in the distribution of income dwarf changes in the distribution of votes.

To put this in perspective we can compare changes in the share of *income* held by the bottom income quintile to changes in the share of the *votes* held by the bottom income quintile. This quintile had their highest share of income (5.5 percent of total income) in 1972, and their lowest share of income (4.0 percent of total income) in 2008. This is a drop in 27 percent of the group's share of income.[33] In contrast, the highest recorded share of votes held by the bottom quintile during the period we examine was 15.9 percent of the total votes (in 1972). The group's lowest share of the votes held was in 1992, when the bottom quintile had 14.0 percent of the total votes. This means that the largest drop in *vote share* for the bottom quintile over this period was 12 percent. Thus comparing the loss in income share to the (temporary) loss in vote share over this period, we see that the loss in income share is almost two and a half times the loss in vote share. And by 2008 the share of votes held by the bottom quintile had rebounded to 15.5 percent, and was thus 2.5 percent below the share held in 1972.

We see similar results for education. Not surprisingly, given the importance of education as a predictor of voter turnout, the two highest education thirds have representativeness scores close to or greater than 1 throughout the entire period, while the lowest education group is underrepresented for the entire period. But there is no substantial shift in the magnitude of under-representation for the lowest group, though we see some election to election variation.

---

33. Note that we are using percent of the original quantity here, not percentage points. Thus, the 27 percent drop in income share for the bottom income quintile is calculated based on the 1.5 *percentage-point* drop from 5.5 to 4.0 as (100*[1.5/5.5]).

2.7 Representation: Of the Eligible or the Available?

Normatively we believe that in a fair world, poor people and rich people should have proportionately equal shares of the votes; each citizen's right to a ballot should carry equal weight, even though her wealth may be decidedly unequal. For example, the people in the bottom fifth of the income distribution should have 20 percent of the votes, and the people in the top fifth of the income distribution should have 20 percent of the votes.

One group's proportion of the population may differ from its proportion of the votes for two very different reasons. First, legally eligible members of income (or other relevant) groups may differ in their average likelihood of voting, and those groups such as the poor (whose members are less likely to vote than the rich) will be underrepresented among the voters—that is, represent a smaller proportion of votes than their presence in the population. Second, some groups may contain a larger proportion of people legally ineligible to vote than other groups. For instance, more among the poor than the rich may be legally ineligible to vote because of prior felony convictions, or more of the poor than the rich may be noncitizens. Most studies and discussions of income bias focus on the first explanation in that ample evidence documents that the legally eligible poor are less likely to vote than the legally eligible wealthy.

However, legal issues of voting eligibility also affect the representativeness of the poor relative to the rich. Although poll taxes and such devices have been effectively eliminated, states nonetheless maintain the ability to determine who is eligible to vote.[34] The key requirement common to state electoral requirements is citizenship. While this does not explicitly disenfranchise the poor, noncitizens residing in the United States are more likely than citizens to be poor.[35] And because the poor are more likely than the wealthy to be ineligible to vote, they are then less likely to be represented among the voters.

One might argue that analyses of income bias that are restricted to the *eligible* population misconceptualize the population that merits representation if elections are to truly reflect the interests of all those governed by elected officials. An important alternative approach to assessing income bias in the voting population is to compare the relative proportion of the poor in the *resident* population, rather than in the *eligible* population, to their proportion among the voters. Changes in income bias can then be measured using this different conceptualization

---

34. For example, many states restrict felons from voting.
35. In 2008, median household income of citizens was approximately $51,000, compared to less than $38,000 for noncitizens (DeNavas-Walt, Proctor, & Smith 2009).

and provide an alternative assessment of the representation of the poor and the wealthy in U.S. politics today. As the proportion of ineligible voters has increased substantially over this period due to an increase in noncitizens among the population, we could see changes in this measure of income bias even if the behavior of *eligible voters* has remained unchanged over time.

Figures 2.10 and 2.11 present this alternative measure of representativeness, where all voting-age individuals, rather than just voting-age citizens, are included in the denominator of the representativeness ratio. For both education and income we see that the representation of the people at the bottom of the socioeconomic scale suffers compared to the measures based on citizens only (presented in figures 2.1 and 2.2). In 2008, the representativeness ratio for *citizens* in the bottom income quintile was 0.79, compared to 0.75 for the voting-age population.[36] And in 2008 the representativeness ratio for *citizens* at the bottom of the education scale was 0.78, while the representativeness ratio for all

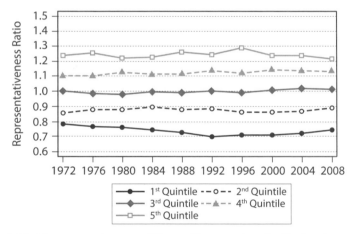

Figure 2.10. Representativeness of Voters Compared to the Voting-Age Population, by Income, 1972–2008.
Note: Entries are the ratio of the income group's share of voters (based on self-reported vote) to the income group's share of the voting-age population. Values less than 1 indicate underrepresentation of the specific income group among voters, while values greater than 1 indicate overrepresentation of the specific income group among voters. Computed by the authors using data from the Current Population Survey.

36. See McCarty, Poole, & Rosenthal (2008) for more on the relationship between citizen and noncitizen income.

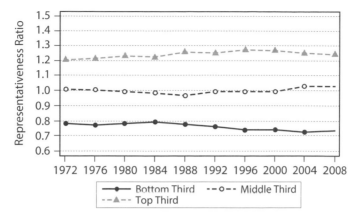

Figure 2.11. Representativeness of Voters Compared to the Voting-Age Population, by Education, 1972–2008.
Note: Entries are the ratio of the education group's share of voters (based on self-reported vote) to the education group's share of the voting-age population. Values less than 1 indicate underrepresentation of the specific education group among voters, while values greater than 1 indicate overrepresentation of the specific education group among voters. Computed by the authors using data from the Current Population Survey.

persons was only 0.74. Thus, our answer to the question of whether income bias of voters *relative to the voting-age population* has increased is different from our answer to the question of whether income bias *relative to the set of eligible voters* has increased. Income bias relative to the voting-age population *has indeed increased.*

2.8 Conclusion

The evidence we have presented in this chapter is based on the most comprehensive and systematic data available on voter turnout in the United States between 1972 and 2008. We have reported several important facts about voter turnout since 1972. First, voter turnout in presidential elections since 1972 has not declined systematically. Instead, it has been slightly higher in some elections, and slightly lower in other elections. Overall turnout levels seem to reflect as much about the political context of each election as they do about citizens' underlying motivation or willingness to participate in the electoral process.

Second, the relationships among income, education, and voter turnout are quite strong: the probability of a highly educated or wealthy

individual casting a ballot is much, much higher than the probability
of a less-educated or poorer individual casting a ballot. As a result,
the income bias of U.S. presidential voters is large, even huge. Third,
these differences in turnout have been remarkably stable over this thirty-
six-year period. During a period marked by truly massive changes in
economic inequality, we do *not* find a significant increase in income bias
in turnout of the electorate. There may have been a small increase, but
nothing substantial, and certainly nothing to suggest a large relationship
between changes in economic inequality and turnout. When we move
beyond the electorate to consider the voting-age population (including
noncitizens), however, there has been an increase in income bias since
1972.

Fourth, there is less stability in turnout patterns by age, gender,
and ethnicity since 1972 compared to those of education and income.
There has been a small shift in the relative turnout of women and men.
Women are now more likely to vote than men, and the gap has been
widening. Because women comprise a group that makes up more than
50 percent of the electorate, and behave substantially differently from
men in their vote choices, this is potentially quite an important political
shift. There has been a substantial change in black turnout relative to
white turnout since 1972. However, the increase in Hispanic turnout
has been much smaller, and turnout of Hispanic citizens still lags far
behind turnout of non-Hispanic whites. Finally, we have documented a
large increase in turnout of older voters relative to turnout of younger
voters.

The centrality of demographics in models of voter turnout underscore
their fundamental importance to the resources and strategies of both
citizens and elites. These basic comparisons provide an initial baseline
for the importance of demographics to voter turnout. In chapter 3
we discuss in greater detail the theoretical importance of each of
these demographic characteristics and how they might relate to each
other. We then test whether the stability of education and income as
primary determinants of voter turnout hold when we condition on other
demographic characteristics of interest.

Appendix 2.1: Current Population Survey: Sample and Variable Details

Data for the Census Bureau's Current Population Survey November
Supplement was taken from data provided by Unicon, a private firm that
sells individual-level census data repackaged so that it is easier to extract
common variables across multiple years. It is simply a repackaging of the

data; coding decisions must still be made by the analyst (in this case, the authors). Thus we provide the Unicon variable name below.

> **Turnout:** This is self-reported turnout. We treat blanks in the data set as missing data; we treat "dont know," "no response," and "refused" as not having voted. This coding lets us match what the Census Bureau reports as the turnout rate in their published summaries of CPS data. [Unicon Variable: *votecast*.]
>
> **Education:** We use respondents' self-report of education to place them in either the bottom, middle, or top third of the education distribution for the year of the election. For people whose reported education category would straddle different thirds of the distribution, we use random assignment to place them. [Unicon Variable: For 1972–90, we use *grdhi* (highest grade completed). For 1992–2008, we use *grdatn* (highest grade attended), then combine this with *grdcom* (grade completed).]
>
> **Income:** We place respondents in the appropriate income quintile based on reported total family income. [Unicon Variable : *faminc*.]
>
> **Age:** Respondent's reported age. Recoded into six categories: 18–24, 25–30, 31–45, 46–60, 61–75, and 76–84. The variable is top-coded at 84 years. (Thus, we do not report on turnout of those over 84 years of age.) [Unicon Variable: *age*.]
>
> **Gender:** self-reported. [Unicon Variable: *sex*.]
>
> **Marital Status:** Self-report. Coded as 1 if married with spouse present; otherwise 0. [Unicon variable: *marstat*.]
>
> **Citizen:** Coded as 1/0, self-reported. [Unicon Variable: *citus* (1978–92), *citstat* (1994–2008), *notreg* (1972–76)]
>
> **Three-category Race Variable:** This variable is coded as black, white, or other. It is based on respondent self-report. For 1972–88 the census coding was white, black, other. In 1996–2002 the categories American Indian or Alaskan Native and Asian Pacific Islander were added. We coded both of these as "other." In 2004 and 2008, respondents could choose from many sets of multiple-race categories. As these codings constituted barely 2 percent of respondents, we also coded these multiple race categories as "other." [Unicon Variable: *race*.]
>
> **Hispanic:** This is a self-report based on a question of origin or descent for 1976–2000. Responses of Mexican American, Chicano, Mexican, Puerto Rican, Cuban, Central or South American, or other Spanish were coded as Hispanic. For 2004 and 2008, this is a respondent's self-report to being Spanish, Hispanic, or Latino. This variable is not available for 1972. [Unicon Variable: *spneth*.]
>
> **Other Ethnicity Codes:** Coding for white Hispanic, White non-Hispanic, black Non-Hispanic, and other were created by combining the three-category race variable and the Hispanic variable.

Appendix 2.2: Additional Data on the Representativeness of Voters, 1972–2008

Table A2.2.1. Representativeness Scores for Demographic Groups, Comparing Voters to Citizens, 1972–2008.

Group	1972	1976	1980	1984	1988	1992	1996	2000	2004	2008
Less than High School	0.79	0.78	0.77	0.76	0.73	0.69	0.67	0.65	0.62	0.62
High School Grad	1.03	0.99	0.98	0.96	0.94	0.92	0.89	0.88	0.88	0.86
Some College	1.18	1.14	1.12	1.11	1.10	1.09	1.08	1.06	1.08	1.07
College Grad and Above	1.33	1.35	1.33	1.31	1.33	1.29	1.32	1.30	1.25	1.24
Education—Bottom Third	0.79	0.78	0.80	0.81	0.80	0.80	0.78	0.78	0.77	0.78
Education—Middle Third	1.00	1.00	0.98	0.97	0.95	0.97	0.97	0.96	0.99	0.99
Education—Top Third	1.20	1.21	1.22	1.21	1.24	1.22	1.25	1.25	1.22	1.22
Income—1st Quintile	0.79	0.77	0.78	0.77	0.76	0.74	0.75	0.75	0.76	0.79
Income—2nd Quintile	0.87	0.89	0.89	0.91	0.90	0.91	0.89	0.90	0.91	0.92
Income—3rd Quintile	1.01	0.99	0.98	1.00	0.99	1.00	0.99	1.00	1.01	1.00
Income—4th Quintile	1.10	1.10	1.11	1.09	1.10	1.11	1.10	1.11	1.10	1.10
Income—5th Quintile	1.23	1.25	1.21	1.21	1.23	1.21	1.25	1.20	1.19	1.17
Age 18–24	0.78	0.71	0.68	0.68	0.64	0.72	0.61	0.61	0.73	0.76
Age 25–30	0.93	0.91	0.88	0.86	0.79	0.84	0.77	0.8	0.83	0.87
Age 31–45	1.04	1.06	1.06	1.04	1.03	1.02	0.99	0.99	0.99	0.98
Age 46–60	1.12	1.16	1.15	1.16	1.16	1.11	1.16	1.14	1.10	1.08
Age 61–75	1.08	1.12	1.17	1.18	1.22	1.16	1.24	1.21	1.15	1.13
Age 76–84	0.91	0.95	1.01	1.05	1.10	1.07	1.16	1.16	1.11	1.11
Women	0.99	1.00	1.00	1.01	1.01	1.01	1.02	1.02	1.02	1.03
Single	0.85	0.83	0.83	0.85	0.83	0.86	0.83	0.82	0.86	0.88
Black	0.82	0.81	0.84	0.93	0.88	0.87	0.91	0.95	0.94	1.02
Hispanic	x	0.69	0.72	0.77	0.77	0.76	0.75	0.75	0.74	0.78
White (Non-Hisp)	x	1.04	1.04	1.02	1.03	1.04	1.04	1.04	1.05	1.04

Note: Entries are the ratios of the group's share of voters (based on self-report) to the group's share of the citizen voting-age population. Values less than one indicate underrepresentation of the group among voters, while values greater than 1 indicate overrepresentation of the group among voters. Computed by authors using data from the Current Population Survey.

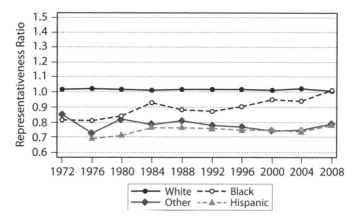

Figure A2.2.1. Representativeness of Voters Compared to Citizens, by Race, 1972–2008.
Note: Entries are the ratios of the racial group's share of voters (based on self-report) to the racial group's share of the citizen voting-age population. Values less than 1 indicate underrepresentation of the specific racial group among voters, while values greater than 1 indicate overrepresentation of the specific racial group among voters. Computed by the authors using data from the Current Population Survey.

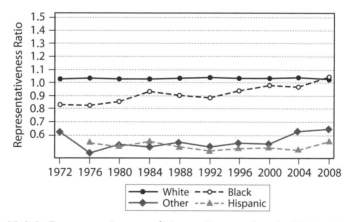

Figure A2.2.2. Representativeness of Voters Compared to the Voting-Age Population, by Race, 1972–2008.
Note: Entries are the ratios of the racial group's share of voters (based on self-report) to the racial group's share of the citizen voting-age population. Values less than 1 indicate underrepresentation of the specific racial group among voters, while values greater than 1 indicate overrepresentation of the specific racial group among voters. Computed by the authors using data from the Current Population Survey.

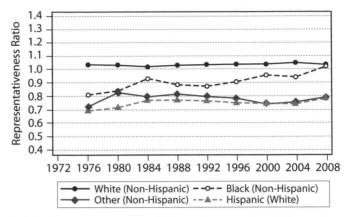

Figure A2.2.3. Representativeness of Voters Compared to Citizens, by Ethnicity, 1976–2008.
Note: Entries are the ratios of the ethnic group's share of voters (based on self-report) to the ethnic group's share of the citizen voting-age population. Values less than 1 indicate underrepresentation of the specific ethnic group among voters, while values greater than 1 indicate overrepresentation of the specific ethnic group among voters. Computed by the authors using data from the Current Population Survey.

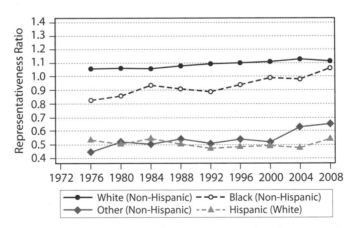

Figure A2.2.4. Representativeness of Voters Compared to the Voting-Age Population, by Ethnicity, 1976–2008.
Note: Entries are the ratios of the ethnic group's share of voters (based on self-report) to the ethnic group's share of the voting-age population. Values less than 1 indicate underrepresentation of the specific ethnic group among voters, while values greater than 1 indicate overrepresentation of the specific ethnic group among voters. Computed by the authors using data from the Current Population Survey.

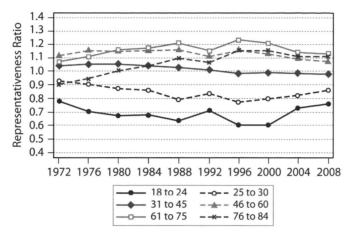

Figure A2.2.5. Representativeness of Voters Compared to Citizens, by Age, 1972–2008.

Note: Entries are the ratios of the age group's share of voters (based on self-report) to the age group's share of the citizen voting-age population. Values less than 1 indicate underrepresentation of the specific age group among voters, while values greater than 1 indicate overrepresentation of the specific age group among voters. Computed by the authors using data from the Current Population Survey.

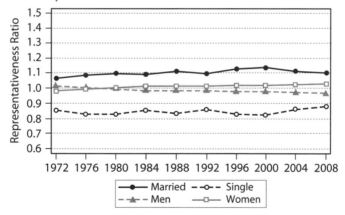

Figure A2.2.6. Representativeness of Voters Compared to Citizens, by Marital Status and by Gender, 1972–2008.

Note: Entries are the ratios of the marital status/gender group's share of voters (based on self-report) to the marital status/gender group's share of the citizen voting-age population. Values less than 1 indicate underrepresentation of the specific marital status/gender group among voters, while values greater than 1 indicate overrepresentation of the specific marital status/gender group among voters. Computed by the authors using data from the Current Population Survey.

Three

....

Theoretical Framework and Models

Since 1972, "who votes" in presidential elections has both changed and remained the same in important ways. As was shown in chapter 2, individuals with higher levels of education and income are much more likely to vote than those with lower levels; Anglos and blacks are more likely to vote than Hispanics; married individuals are more likely to vote than single individuals, and older individuals are more likely to vote than younger individuals. Our findings on income showed that income bias did not change between 1972 and 2008 despite large increases in economic inequality: among citizens the wealthy were overrepresented among voters, and the poor underrepresented, at about the same levels as they were in 1972. In other words, the wealthy had proportionally more votes than the poor in 1972, in 2008, and in every presidential election in between.

If we simply wanted to know if the rich had proportionately more votes than the poor, and if this has changed since 1972, then we could stop here. However, one might argue that *who* the wealthy and poor are in other respects has changed since 1972, and that ignoring these differences limits our understanding of income bias. It is one thing to say a rich person is more likely to vote than a poor person; it is a different thing to say that, all other things being equal (e.g., education, age, gender, ethnicity), a rich person is more likely to vote than a poor person. The latter approach assesses whether among otherwise identical individuals those with more income are more likely to vote than those with less income and therefore to be overrepresented in the electorate. Assessing income bias after conditioning on other demographic characteristics thus underscores the differences in the representation of the rich compared to the poor while accounting for other factors—such as education, age, and gender—associated with turnout. We refer to this type of income bias as _conditional income bias_, which we measure by estimating a multivariable model of voter turnout using income as well as the other demographic variables we examined in chapter 2 as predictors of turnout.

Another advantage of this approach is that it provides additional information on the nature of the relationship between each demographic characteristic we measure and turnout over time. The bivariate relationships we described in chapter 2 may reflect in part the fact that social resources tend to be correlated. For example, individuals with higher levels of education also tend to have higher levels of income, and older individuals tend to be wealthier than younger individuals. Our analyses of the conditional relationships between demographic characteristics and turnout allow us to determine whether the bivariate relationships observed in chapter 2 remain when conditioning on other demographic characteristics.

This analysis provides valuable insights. If the conditional estimates of the effects of demographics such as race, ethnicity, and gender do not parallel the bivariate results (e.g., that older people are more likely to vote than younger people; that Hispanics are less likely to vote than whites; or that women are more likely to vote than men) then we can conclude that the changing bivariate turnout rates for these groups result from either the changing demographic (i.e., compositional) characteristics included in our model or other politically relevant factors. If the conditional estimates confirm the bivariate turnout patterns observed in chapter 2, then changes in turnout of these groups since 1972 must be explained by something other than the demographics we study (e.g., factors such as party contact, candidate targeting, or issue mobilization).

A few examples illustrate the importance of these analyses. We saw in chapter 2 a change in the relationship between age and turnout over time, with older individuals becoming increasingly more likely than younger individuals to vote. We would like to know if that is because the observable characteristics (income, education, etc.) of different age groups changed, or because there is something else about these different age groups that is changing and affecting turnout. Another example is provided by our finding that black turnout increased markedly between 1972 and 2008. We suspect this increase reflects in part that blacks now have higher levels of education and income than they did in 1972, but it might also reflect changes in other factors that influence turnout (e.g., political empowerment). While evidence on the latter possibility is beyond the scope of this book, we can provide some evidence on whether other demographic characteristics associated with race might help to account for the changes in African American turnout we observed in

important ⟶

chapter 2. We also found in chapter 2 that Hispanic turnout increased much less than did black turnout. Is that because Hispanic levels of income and education did not go up as much as black levels of income and education, or is it because of something else? The same questions are raised by our finding that women now vote more than men. Is that because the relative levels of income and education have changed since 1972, or is it because something else changed?

If we do observe differences in turnout between groups in this chapter after conditioning on demographic characteristics, then we or other scholars would want to examine this by either considering other demographic characteristics not included in our model (e.g., labor force participation, attitudinal explanations, mobilization efforts of elites, or some combination of these factors).[1]

Finally, these multivariable analyses are relevant to discussions of the causes of voter turnout. While we are careful not to interpret our empirical estimates of the relationships between demographic characteristics and turnout as definitively causal in nature, a necessary condition for such relationships to be causal is that they are not spurious correlations observed because the demographic characteristic of interest is correlated with some other variable related to turnout. Thus, establishing a conditional relationship between each demographic characteristic and turnout is a necessary step toward determining causality. And, consistent with our focus on examining change—or the lack thereof—over time, we want to know if the conditional relationships among all of our demographic variables and turnout have changed since 1972.

3.1 Costs, Benefits, and Demographics

It would be impossible to find a study of voter turnout in presidential elections where demographic characteristics are not central to the enterprise. From the initial classic election studies (where voter turnout was at best a marginal consideration), to Wolfinger and Rosenstone's *Who Votes?* (1980), to analyses of recent elections, most discussions of voter turnout put substantial emphasis on the relationships among education, income, age, gender, and turnout.[2]

Most studies, too, utilize a cost/benefits framework to interpret empirical evidence, assuming that voter turnout is a "rational," rather

1. See, for example, Gay (2001); Tate (1993); and Barreto (2005).
2. See, for example, Abramson, Aldrich, & Rohde (2003); Campbell et al. (1960); Lazarsfeld, Berelson, & Gaudet (1948); Rosenstone & Hansen (1993); Verba & Nie (1972); and Verba, Schlozman, & Brady (1995).

than expressive, act. Downs first modeled individuals' decisions to vote as a reflection of the relative costs and benefits of voting: "if the returns to voting outweigh the costs, he votes; if not, he abstains" (1957, 260). Downs argued that when voting is costless, only indifferent individuals will abstain, but that when voting is costly, some indifferent individuals will vote and some with preferences will not vote. The latter cases result when the costs of voting outweigh the benefits, and they are not uncommon because the benefits associated with voting are, as Downs originally described them, "miniscule." Downs argued that four factors influence the individual's returns from voting: her perceptions of the policy differences between the parties, of the closeness of the election, of the value of voting itself, and of how many other citizens she thinks will vote (1957, 274).

Downs's portrayal of voting as a rational act provoked numerous scholars' efforts to explain its obvious empirical contradiction: if this theory yields a prediction of zero turnout, then why do we regularly observe citizens voting? Possible solutions to this puzzle include adding a fixed benefit to the calculus (i.e., the value of democracy continuing, civic duty); the real or perceived likelihood of being pivotal being incorrectly assumed (by theorists) or perceived (by citizens); and incorporating consumption or expressive benefits into the model.[3]

Perhaps most persuasive among these responses is Aldrich's (1993) claim that voting is not an especially good example of a collective action problem; it is instead such a low-cost, low-benefit activity that tiny differences in costs and benefits can result in positive turnout. Aldrich argues that conceptualizing the act of voting in this manner results in a critical role for strategic politicians, whose campaign tactics are likely to influence turnout levels regardless of individuals' rational calculations regarding voting.

We follow Aldrich's conceptualization of voter turnout as a rational activity, and we interpret the meaning of demographic patterns in voter turnout as reflecting individuals' differential abilities to subsume costs and benefit from voting. We also extend this argument in chapter 5 to consider the strategic actions of politicians.

3.2 Model Specification

We analyze the demographic determinants of voter turnout over time in this chapter by estimating a multivariable logit model of turnout that

---

3. Examples of these arguments can be found in Engelen (2006); Ferejohn & Fiorina (1974, 1975); Fiorina (1976); Hinich (1981); Palfrey & Rosenthal (1985); Riker & Ordeshook (1968); and Schuessler (2000). See also Jackman (1993) and Miller (1986) on these points.

includes seven demographic characteristics (education, income, age, race, ethnicity, gender, and marital status) as explanatory variables for each presidential election year from 1972 to 2008. Our interest here is in assessing the relative strength of the relationships between demographic predictors and turnout, both with respect to changes over time and with respect to other demographic characteristics. And, of course, we are especially interested in changes in the conditional relationship between income and the probability of voting over time as additional evidence of patterns in income bias since 1972.

The data are taken from the Current Population Survey (CPS), November supplement, for each year.[4] We would prefer to estimate a model of voter turnout consisting of all the demographic characteristics of interest as well as indicators of elite mobilization and state electoral laws that previous studies have reported to be associated with voter turnout. But that is not possible, for two reasons. First, the Census Bureau did not include a question regarding ethnicity in the 1972 CPS and, second, the Census Bureau does not have individual state identifiers for the 1976 CPS. This means that for 1972 and 1976, we cannot estimate our preferred model as we can from 1980 onward.

To provide as much continuity over time as possible, as well as assess the importance of Hispanic ethnicity as a determinant of turnout, we thus estimate two separate models in this chapter. The first model consists of all demographic variables available for the 1972 through 2008 elections, and thus does not include an indicator for Hispanic ethnicity, nor state-level variables. The second model consists of all demographic variables (including Hispanic ethnicity), and is estimated for 1976 through 2008.[5] Since neither of these models include elite mobilization or state legal characteristics, we refer to both of these models as demographic models and distinguish them by specifying whether variables for Hispanic ethnicity are included or not.[6]

We estimate a logit model for each year. We do this because we are specifically interested in comparing coefficient estimates across years.[7] Using alternative strategies such as pooling across years, or using a multilevel analysis or a shrinkage estimator (where we would assume parameters are drawn from a common distribution across years) would not allow us to make inferences regarding the changes over time that we

---

4. Coding details for each demographic variable are included in appendix 2.1.
5. In the multivariable models which include Hispanic ethnicity we use a more detailed coding. We include dummy variables for white non-Hispanic, white Hispanic, and black non-Hispanic in the model, with other non-Hispanic being the omitted category.
6. We note that given the small proportion of Hispanics in the population in 1972, differences between the two sets of model estimates are quite small.
7. Models were estimated using R, and with standard errors clustered at the state level.

are interested in. By estimating separate models for each year we do not assume a commonality across years and do not impose that assumption on the data-generating process.

In estimating a multivariable model we generally describe the "dependent" variable as being "caused" by the right-hand-side explanatory variables. However, the assumption of causality is not based on the data analysis or the model specified but on a model of the real world presumed by the analyst. The data analysis is merely showing the conditional relationships among the observed data and not establishing causality. To be consistent with conventional usage, we will refer to the *marginal effect* of one of our explanatory (right-hand-side) variables on turnout. However, we are not making the claim that such observational evidence demonstrates causality.

To offer an example, we show below that the marginal effect of income on turnout (as measured by moving from the bottom to top quintile) is approximately 18 percentage points: ceteris paribus, persons in the top income quintile are 18 percentage points more likely to vote than persons in the bottom income quintile. While we refer to this as a *marginal effect*, we do not necessarily believe that this is a strictly causal relationship. We are not asserting that simply giving a person more income would make her more likely to vote. What we are claiming is that, ceteris paribus, persons with more income *do* vote more (approximately 18 percentage points more) than persons with less income.

As explanatory variables we include: measures of which third of the education distribution the respondent is in; measures of which income quintile the respondent is in; a set of dummy variables to measure which age group the respondent is in; and dummy variables for gender, marital status, race, and whether or not the respondent lives in a Southern state.[8] By estimating the effects of demographics on turnout separately for each election year, we allow the marginal effects of each demographic characteristic to vary by election. We can then compare these specific election-year estimates over time to assess whether the strength of their effects on turnout increases, decreases, or remains the same.[9]

---

8. In 1976 the CPS does not identify the specific state a respondent is in for every state, as several states shared values for the state identifier variable. But we can identify respondents in every state except Arkansas, Deleware, Kentucky, Louisiana, Maryland, Oklahoma, Tennessee, and Virginia as either being in the South or North. Respondents in the states listed above are dropped from the analysis here for 1976. We include the indicator for the South since the region has long had politics distinct from the rest of the United States, and we want to condition on any such regional effect.

9. Complete model estimation results for both demographic models are included in appendix 3.1.

We present graphical representations of the estimates of the marginal effects of each demographic variable (i.e., the magnitude of the effect of that variable, controlling for all other demographic characteristics in the model) herein, using the demographics model that excludes Hispanic ethnicity so that we can include the entire time period. The graphical presentation of the marginal effects for Hispanic ethnicity are based on the demographics model that includes indicators of Hispanic ethnicity and therefore is restricted to 1976–2008.

For each variable, we plot the marginal effects for each presidential election year. These marginal effects represent how the probability of an individual voting would increase or decrease by changing from one category of the independent variable to another category (e.g., from high school graduate to some college education, or from black to white).

3.3 Education and Income

Empirically, there is universal consensus that both education and income are independently related to individuals' decisions to vote, though in most cases researchers find that education has a stronger relationship than income. Wolfinger and Rosenstone emphasized that education and income have distinct effects, with education being much stronger, and the effects of income moderating once individuals reached a "modestly comfortable standard of living" (1980, 34).

Rosenstone and Hansen (1993), too, point to the central role of education, with evidence from models of turnout estimated using American National Election Studies (NES) data from 1956 to 1988. However, they note that, controlling for demographics *and attitudinal characteristics*, the effect of education is only slightly stronger than that of income, and more important in explaining voter turnout than other types of electoral participation (1993, chap. 5, especially 130–31).[10] Whether their findings of the importance of education relative to income would hold had they not conditioned on attitudinal characteristics in their model is not clear.

Wolfinger and Rosenstone's initial theoretical argument regarding education highlighted three mechanisms by which education increased the probability of voting: by enhancing individuals' cognitive skills (and therefore reducing information costs), by increasing the gratification that individuals receive from politics (thus increasing benefits), and

10. For studies of more recent elections, see Leighley & Nagler (1992a, 1992b, 2007); Nownes (1992); Teixeira (1992); and Timpone (1998).

by providing (bureaucratic) experience that is useful in dealing with the costs of voting such as voter registration requirements. Similarly, Verba, Schlozman and Brady (1995) emphasize the skills as well as the enhanced psychological engagement (i.e., more positive attitudes toward and interest in politics) resulting from higher education as the mechanisms linking education with voter turnout (see also Hillygus [2005]).

An alternative argument is that the empirical correlation between education and voter turnout reflects not a causal relationship between education and turnout but a self-selection process: that individuals who choose to pursue more education are also more likely to vote, independent of any civic engagement effects as argued by Wolfinger and Rosenstone (1980).[11]

Wolfinger and Rosenstone (1980, 20–22) identify five possible reasons that income might be associated with voter turnout:

- poor people have less time to devote to matters not essential to everyday existence
- wealthy people have jobs that tend to increase their political engagement, regardless of education levels
- income determines one's social context, and thus wealthy individuals are more likely to be exposed to social networks with norms of civic duty and engagement
- wealthy individuals are likely to be especially engaged and aggressive in their political and social pursuits, otherwise they would not have succeeded in terms of income, regardless of education
- wealthy individuals have a greater "stake in the system"

Wolfinger and Rosenstone conclude that "rock bottom poverty seems to depress turnout somewhat. Beyond that income does not have much effect on turnout" (1980, 26). And on the basis of this empirical evidence from 1972, they conclude that their first possible explanation for the association between income and voter turnout is most likely the correct one: poor people have less time to devote to political matters as they are managing everyday survival instead.[12]

It is important to note that Wolfinger and Rosenstone's classic finding on the key role of education as a major determinant of voter turnout, more so than income, has not been directly examined since their

11. See also Henderson & Chatfield (2011); Kam & Palmer (2008, 2011); Mayer (2011); and Tenn (2007).
12. This would be consistent with Rosenstone's (1982) analysis of "economic adversity," which suggested that poor people are less likely to vote.

initial study. Rosenstone and Hansen find that the relative importance of education and income as predictors of voter turnout may have changed over time, but this is conditioning on attitudinal variables. Since those attitudes could be intermediary variables between education and turnout, we cannot draw any inferences on the relative importance of education and income on turnout if we condition on attitudes. And it is possible that the relative import of education and income may have changed since 1972, as the level of economic inequality increased substantially.

We now turn to our empirical evidence addressing this point. Figure 3.1 shows how much less likely someone in the lowest education third is to vote than someone in the middle third, how much less likely someone in the lowest education third is to vote than someone in the top third, and how much less likely someone in the middle third is to vote than someone in the top third.[13] Each point on the graph represents our estimate of the marginal effect of being in the higher rather than lower education group in a specific year. The vertical line associated with each point represents the 95 percent confidence interval for that estimated effect. And the horizontal trend line connecting the points represents the trend over time of the effect.[14]

While the effects of education are positive, we can also see that the effect of education is substantially *higher* in 1972 and 1976 than it was for subsequent years. In 1972 someone in the middle third of the education distribution was approximately 17 percentage points more likely to vote than someone in the bottom third, ceteris paribus. However, by 1992 that effect had dropped to approximately 12 percentage points before

Figure 3.1. (facing page) Marginal Effect of Education as a Predictor of Turnout, 1972–2008.
Note: Each point in the graph represents the estimated difference in the probability of voting between an individual in the higher education group and an individual in the lower education group, holding all other variables in the multivariable model constant. Positive values indicate that, ceteris paribus, an individual with more education is more likely to vote than an individual with less education. Each vertical bar provides a 95 percent confidence interval. The trend line is an ordinary least squares regression line fitted to the points. Estimated by the authors using data from the Current Population Survey; see section 3.2 for model details.

13. The first differences in probabilities presented in the graphs are computed for a hypothetical respondent where all variables we are conditioning on are set to their mode or mean. So our hypothetical respondent is a white married woman between the ages of thirty-one and forty-five in the middle income quintile, living outside the South.
14. The horizontal line is the ordinary least squares regression of the estimated effects against a time trend.

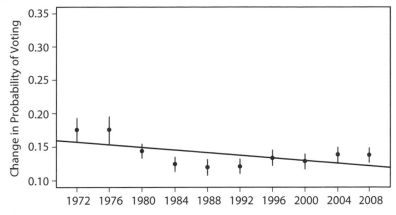

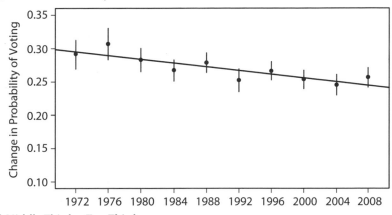

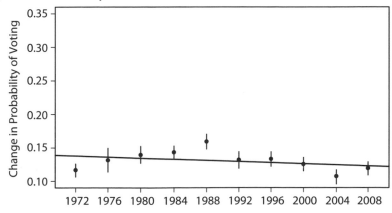

Figure 3.1.

rebounding a bit in subsequent elections. The graph clearly shows that the difference in turnout from the bottom to middle group was unusually large in 1972 and 1976. Another way to interpret the graph is to infer that respondents paid a particularly high price for being in the bottom of the education distribution in 1972 and 1976. Thus, in looking to determine the impact of education on turnout, Wolfinger and Rosenstone (1980) seem to have looked at an unusual year.

It is important to note that while the marginal effect of education has decreased, it has decreased by a comparatively small amount. The magnitude of the effect has been reasonably stable and *large*: the estimated difference in the probability of voting between otherwise similar individuals in the middle third and the bottom third of the education distribution varies from 12 percentage points to 17 percentage points. Over the entire time period, the difference in turnout between someone in the bottom education group and someone in the top education group with otherwise the same demographic characteristics never drops below 25 percentage points. And the difference in turnout between someone in the bottom education group and middle education group, ceteris paribus, never drops below 12 percentage points.

We next look at the conditional relationship between income and turnout over the time period. In figure 3.2 we show the difference in predicted turnout between persons in different pairs of income distributions. The first four graphs in figure 3.2 show the difference in predicted turnout between persons in the bottom quintile and each of the other four income quintiles, conditional on all other characteristics in our model. Comparing respondents in the bottom income quintile to respondents in the second through fourth income quintiles, we see that, conditioning on other characteristics, members of the bottom income quintile seemed to fall *farther* behind members of quintiles 2–4 from 1972 through 2000. For example, while in 1972 we predict a 4 percentage-point gap between persons in the first and second income quintile, by 1984 that gap had risen to approximately 6 percentage points. Then, in 2004 and 2008, the conditional relationships between income and turnout seem to weaken: in each of the graphs comparing the bottom quintile to the other quintiles, we see smaller effects in 2004 and 2008 than we did in earlier elections.

In contrast, when comparing respondents in the bottom quintile to those in the top quintile, the conditional relationship between income and turnout varies somewhat from election to election from 1972 to 2008, sometimes increasing and sometimes decreasing. In 2004 and 2008, however, the marginal effects actually decrease to levels *lower* than those we estimated for 1972 and 1976. The relatively flat trend

(a) Quintile 1 → Quintile 2

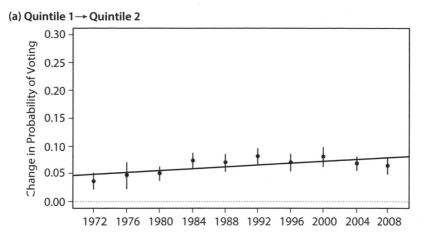

(b) Quintile 1 → Quintile 3

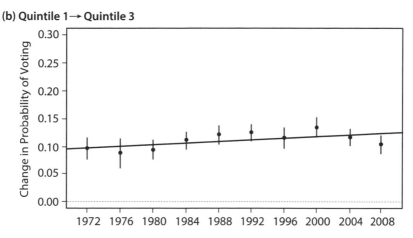

Figure 3.2. Marginal Effect of Income as a Predictor of Turnout, 1972–2008. *Note*: Each point in the graph represents the estimated difference in the probability of voting between an individual in the higher income group and an individual in the lower income group, holding all other variables in the multivariable model constant. Positive values indicate that, ceteris paribus, an individual with more income is more likely to vote than an individual with less income. Each vertical bar provides a 95 percent confidence interval. The trend line is an ordinary least squares regression line fitted to the points. Estimated by the authors using data from the Current Population Survey; see section 3.2 for model details.

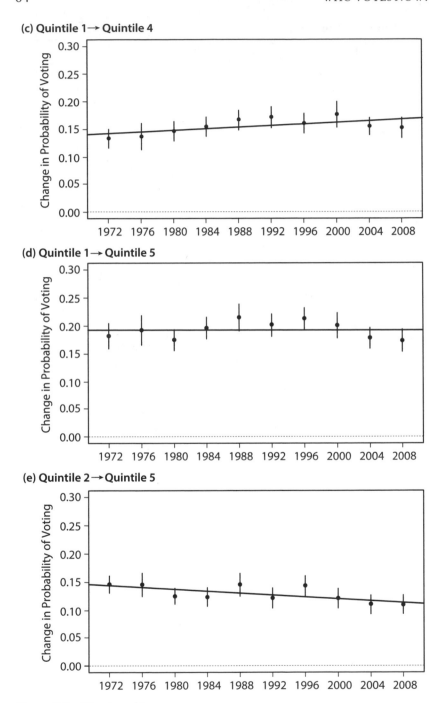

Figure 3.2. (Continued.)

(f) Quintile 3 → Quintile 5

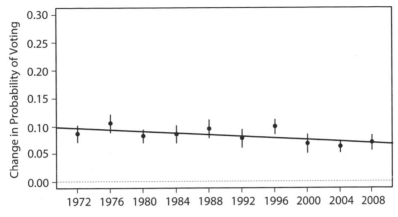

(g) Quintile 4 → Quintile 5

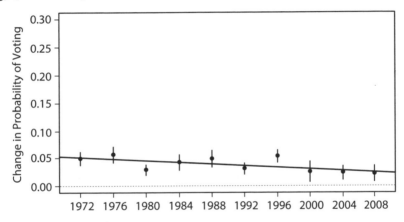

Figure 3.2. (Continued.)

lines suggest that the effects of income did not systematically increase or decrease between 1972 and 2008.

In the next two graphs of figure 3.2 we compare respondents in quintiles 2 and 3 to respondents in the top quintile, and in the last graph we compare the respondents in quintile 4 to respondents in quintile 5. In each case we see the same effect: the conditional relationship between respondents in quintiles 2–4 and respondents in quintile 5 has *decreased over time*. That is, once we condition on other observable characteristics, the gap in turnout rates between respondents in the top quintile and the other quintiles is smaller today than it was in 1972. This gap is still large, however: it is over 10 percentage points when comparing respondents in the second quintile to the top quintile, and approximately 7 percentage points when comparing the middle quintile to the top quintile. But it has been decreasing.[15]

To summarize, we find no change in income bias, conditioning for other demographics, when comparing the bottom and top quintiles. Conditional on other characteristics, respondents in income quintiles 2–4 are voting *more* relative to respondents in the very top income quintile than they were thirty years ago. Thus, while those in the top quintile have gotten a larger share of *income*, they have not gotten a larger share of *votes* conditional on their other demographic characteristics (education, ethnicity, and age). This finding of no change in share of the votes for the top income quintile when conditioning on other demographic characteristics is the same as our bivariate finding in chapter 2 comparing income and turnout directly.

Since there is particular interest in the question of whether education or income is more important to turnout, we report the predicted probability of voting for different combinations of education and income in both 1972 and 2008 (see table 3.1). Here again we are showing the predicted probability of voting for a hypothetical respondent, with other demographic characteristics set as they are for the graphs in this chapter. We discuss the results for 2008 here, but the discussion would be virtually identical for 1972 given the similar estimates.

We first consider the effect of changes in level of education. In 2008, the probability of voting for our hypothetical individual in the top income quintile increased from 0.64 to 0.87 (an increase in probability of 0.24) as her position in the education distribution improved from the bottom third to the top third. We next consider the effect of changes in level of income. The predicted probability of our 2008 hypothetical individual in the top education group but lowest income group is 0.74, and increases to 0.87 when shifted to the highest income group (an increase in probability of 0.13).

It thus appears that education still trumps income as a predictor of turnout. A hypothetical individual in the highest education group is anywhere from 23 to 30 percentage points more likely to vote than a similar individual in the lowest education group, whereas a hypothetical individual in the highest income group is anywhere from 13 to 20 percentage points more likely to vote than a similar individual in the lowest income group.[16]

---

15. We show the relationships between respondents in quintiles 2, 3, and 4 in appendix 3.2. Those relationships have been stable over time, and in the expected direction.

16. And note that this is a conservative conclusion, as the comparison is across only education thirds, but across five categories of income, which should bias our test in favor of a larger effect for income.

Table 3.1. The Relative Effects of Education and Income on Turnout for a Hypothetical Respondent, 1972 and 2008.

	1972 Income Quintile				
	Q1	Q2	Q3	Q4	Q5
Education					
Bottom Third	0.43	0.47	0.53	0.58	0.64
Middle Third	0.61	0.65	0.71	0.75	0.79
Top Third	0.76	0.78	0.83	0.85	0.88
	2008 Income Quintile				
	Q1	Q2	Q3	Q4	Q5
Education					
Bottom Third	0.43	0.50	0.55	0.61	0.64
Middle Third	0.59	0.65	0.70	0.75	0.77
Top Third	0.74	0.79	0.82	0.85	0.87

Note: Cell entries represent the probability that a hypothetical respondent with the specific combination of education and income characteristics will vote in either the 1972 presidential election (top panel) or the 2008 presidential election (bottom panel). The probabilities are computed by the authors using data from the Current Population Survey to estimate the demographic model described in section 3.2 for a married white woman, age thirty-one to forty-five, who lives outside the South.

3.4 Race and Ethnicity

Most analyses of participation that consider race and ethnicity do *not* focus on the relative turnout rates of blacks, whites, and Hispanics conditioning on the demographic characteristics of these groups. Instead, they try to explain what drives participation in the different groups, or consider the relative participation of members of the groups conditioning on different sets of political attitudes such as political interest or partisanship. We are interested in answering questions of a different type, such as: Are Anglo and Hispanic citizens of equal ages, income, and education levels equally likely to vote?

To answer these questions, we focus exclusively on demographics. If we include attitudinal factors in our model of turnout, they can mask the underlying relationship between demographic characteristics and turnout. For instance, if highly educated people are also highly interested in politics, than including interest in politics in our models will mask the true underlying relationship between education and turnout.[17] Since we are confident that the demographic characteristics precede the development of attitudes, we are not in danger of reporting spurious relationships between demographic characteristics and attitudes with our model specification.[18]

Empirical evidence on the effects of race and ethnicity on voter turnout *independent of attitudinal factors* is sparse, as many typical data sources simply contain too few African Americans, Latinos, or Asians to allow for accurate comparisons across racial/ethnic groups. Ramakrishnan (2005) points to census data from 1984 and 1994 to show that Hispanics and blacks voted at much lower rates than did Anglos in those years.

The few analyses that examine race-related differences in turnout produce mixed results, but these studies typically include political, legal, and attitudinal characteristics as predictors of turnout. As a result, their substantive conclusions regarding race-related differences solely as a result of demographics are tentative. Rosenstone and Hansen's (1993) bivariate evidence indicates that blacks are less likely than whites to vote, comparing self-reported National Election studies (NES) data from 1972 through 1988 for blacks and whites. Their multivariable analyses of changes in black turnout include other demographic variables and various attitudinal mobilization measures, and also suggest that blacks are less likely to vote than whites conditional on those attitudinal characteristics.[19] In contrast, Leighley and Nagler (1992b) find that blacks were more likely than whites to vote, based on data from the 1984 Current Population Survey (CPS), when controlling for other demographic characteristics such as education, income, and age, along with election law characteristics of the states in which citizens reside.[20]

17. Alternatively, if we consider ethnicity as the treatment, then the attitudinal variables are all posttreatment, and we do not want to consider those in examining the relationship between demographic characteristics and turnout.
18. Education attainment and income are also, of course, posttreatment here, but they are part of our question of interest.
19. They also suggest in a footnote that their estimated gap in turnout between whites and blacks may underestimate the difference due to blacks possibly overreporting at a higher rate than whites; see Rosenstone and Hansen (1993, 60n 20).
20. Also inconsistent with Rosenstone and Hansen's finding that blacks vote less than whites conditioning on attitudinal characteristics is Verba, Schlozman, Brady, and Nie's (1993) conclusion, using a cross-sectional study of political participation conducted in 1985, that any differences in African American and Anglo self-reported turnout rates in presidential elections reflect differences in civic resources (i.e., education, income, language skills, and opportunities for civic involvement).

For Hispanics, we have only a few studies of demographics and turnout, and these studies, too, reach different conclusions.[21] Wolfinger and Rosenstone (1980) report that controlling for demographics (and election laws, but not attitudes), Chicanos in 1972 were slightly more likely than Anglos to vote (by about three percentage points), while Puerto Ricans in 1974 were less likely than Anglos to vote.[22] Two more recent studies also lead to conflicting findings. Abrajano and Alvarez (2010, 79) describe how turnout rates of Hispanics have lagged behind those of blacks in every election since 1972 (though the gap narrows slightly in recent elections), and document lower levels of Hispanic turnout compared to black and Anglo turnout by education, by income, by age, and by residential mobility (separately); yet they do not consider a more complete demographic model of turnout.[23] In contrast, Highton and Burris (2002), who examine the 1996 CPS data, conclude that Hispanics vote as often as whites once demographic characteristics and region are controlled for.[24]

Hence, studies of turnout of Hispanics compared to non-Hispanics do not provide a convincing answer as to whether Hispanic turnout, independent of attitudes or context, has changed over time. That means we do not know whether—or the extent to which—the gap between the voting rates of Hispanics and Anglos has shrunk over time. Based on the few conflicting studies that we discuss above, we remain agnostic as to

21. We should note that many analyses of Latino turnout are more complex than those used in the study of African American turnout. As in studies of Asian Americans, studies of Latino turnout often include four demographic or legal characteristics other than socioeconomic status: citizenship status, immigrant status (i.e., generation), country of origin and English-language proficiency, see, for example, Arvizu & Garcia (1996); Cho (1999); DeSipio, Masuoka, & Stout (2006); Leighley & Vedlitz (1999); Ramakrishnan (2005); Rocha et al. (2010); and Wong (2006). Since being a citizen is a necessary condition for voting, our models only include citizens, and thus our analyses compare Hispanics citizens with other citizens.

22. Rosenstone and Hansen say little about Hispanic participation relative to Anglo participation, most likely due to the small sample sizes of Hispanics in the NES. Cassel (2002), who uses validated NES data, finds no statistically significant differences between Anglos and Hispanics while controlling for demographic characteristics and party contact. However, she makes this claim based on a sample of only 255 Hispanic voters from 1984 and 1988.

23. See also Bullock & Hood (2006), who report that Hispanics in several southeastern states vote at lower rates than Anglos.

24. Highton & Burris (2002) examined political participation of Hispanics in 1996 and concluded that Hispanic versus non-Hispanic turnout differences disappeared when adding state dummies to a model similar to the one we use. We added state dummies to our model, and we found this not to be the case in 1996, *and* that 1996 was an unusual year for Hispanic versus non-Hispanic turnout in that the conditional difference between the two groups reported in the CPS was noticeably less than in other years.

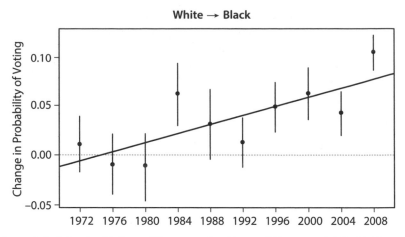

Figure 3.3. Marginal Effect of Race as a Predictor of Turnout, 1972–2008.
Note: Each point in the graph represents the estimated difference in the
probability of voting between a black individual and a white individual, holding
all other variables in the multivariable model constant. Positive values indicate
that, ceteris paribus, a black individual is more likely to vote than a white
individual. Each vertical bar provides a 95 percent confidence interval. The
trend line is an ordinary least squares regression line fitted to the points.
Estimated by the authors using data from the Current Population Survey; see
section 3.2 for model details.

what we will find regarding turnout of Hispanics in presidential elections
over this time period when focusing on demographics alone.[25]

Figure 3.3 shows the difference in voting between whites and blacks,
conditional on the other demographic characteristics (education, income,
age, and gender) in our model. Figure 3.3 shows that not only do blacks
not vote less than whites once we control for demographic factors, but
that in every election since 1984 blacks have been voting at substantially
higher rates than whites, conditioning on other demographic characteristics. The two largest black-white differences are seen in 1984 and 2008,
years when Jesse Jackson and Barack Obama ran for president, respectively. But even if we were to remove these outliers, we would still see
the same trend of a gap increasing from pre-1984 to post-1984, with the
three largest values being in the three most recent non-Obama elections.

25. We recognize, of course, that some elections might witness distinct patterns of
race-related differences in turnout. For example, Tate (1991, 1993) documents the
mobilizing effects of Jesse Jackson's presidential bids in 1984 and 1988 on the African
American community, while some recent discussions emphasize higher turnout of Latinos
in California in response to a heightened anti-immigrant (i.e., Hispanic) political climate;
see Barreto (2005).

This, of course, differs from our findings in chapter 2, where we compared the voting rates of whites and blacks, *not* conditioning on other demographic characteristics, and found that whites have voted at higher rates than blacks in every election except 2008. For questions relating to the *marginal* difference in voting rates between whites and blacks, after controlling for basic characteristics such as education and income, the evidence is clear: blacks vote at higher rates than whites. It is the other characteristics of blacks (most likely lower levels of education and income) that result in a lower overall voting rate as a group than whites.

Our analyses of Hispanic turnout are presented in figure 3.4, in which we plot the differences in the probability of voting for Hispanic whites versus non-Hispanic whites, conditioning on other demographics. Unlike the analyses in the previous figure comparing whites and blacks, here we consider only non-Hispanic whites (i.e., Anglos) rather than including Hispanics in the group of whites. And because there were so few nonwhite Hispanics in our data, we are only examining the turnout of white Hispanics here. The figure suggests that, conditioning on other

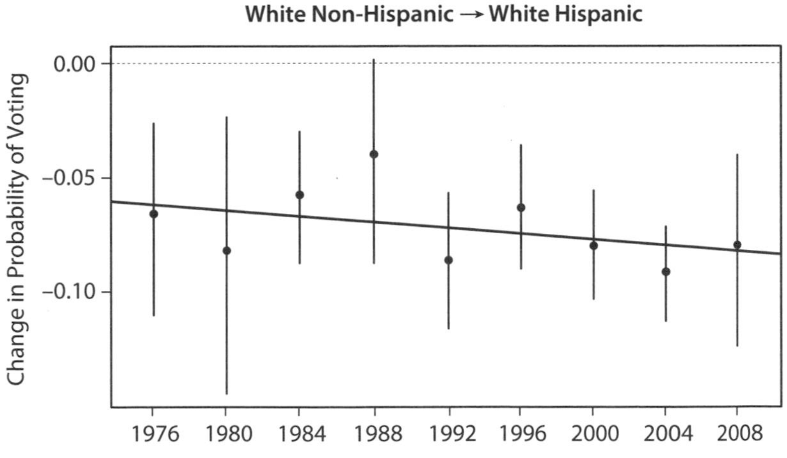

Figure 3.4. Marginal Effect of Ethnicity as a Predictor of Turnout, 1976–2008. *Note:* Each point in the graph represents the estimated difference in the probability of voting between a white Hispanic individual and a white non-Hispanic individual, holding all other variables in the multivariable model constant. Negative values indicate that, ceteris paribus, a Hispanic individual is less likely to vote than a white non-Hispanic individual. Each vertical bar provides a 95 percent confidence interval. The trend line is an ordinary least squares regression line fitted to the points. Estimated by the authors using data from the Current Population Survey; see section 3.2 for model details.

demographics, in every election since 1976 Hispanic whites were less likely to vote than non-Hispanic whites. In fact we see *no increase* in turnout of white Hispanics relative to Anglos, conditioning on demographics, in the last thirty years. Thus it would be wrong to think that participation differences between Hispanics and Anglos are disappearing. And these results suggest that the turnout gap between Hispanics and Anglos would not disappear even if Hispanic and Anglo demographic characteristics such as education, income, and age become more similar.

The implication of this is that the gap in Hispanic and Anglo turnout we observed in chapter 2 is *not* spurious. Even conditioning on demographic characteristics such as income, education, and age, white Hispanics are still substantially less likely to vote than are Anglos. That this gap has not changed over time is contrary to what we might expect based on claims made by many political consultants and activists regarding the importance of the increasingly large Hispanic electorate.

3.5 Age

Although Wolfinger and Rosenstone (1980) emphasize the importance of education and income as predictors of turnout, they also confirmed and clarified the important role of age, especially for those individuals with lower levels of education and income. They suggest that aging is a proxy for life experience, and what one does not gain in formal education can be obtained through the experiences of daily life. Moreover, they find that the conventional wisdom of the day, that there is a drop-off in turnout in old age, is incorrect: lower levels of voter turnout over the age of sixty actually reflect differences in education, income, and marital status (see also Jennings and Markus [1988]).

Similarly, Rosenstone and Hansen (1993) find that age is the only demographic characteristic estimated to have a greater (conditional) effect on voter turnout than education and income and find no evidence to suggest that the oldest age group psychologically or physically disengages from politics. They conclude that the positive effect of age on turnout reflects the reduction of information costs associated with life experience (see also Strate et al. [1989]).

Of particular interest to Wolfinger and Rosenstone was a life-cycle model of age effects that was dominant at the time. The life-cycle model posits that participation increases as individuals mature and take on adult roles, and then decreases in the later years, when the physical and psychological costs of voting are likely greater. Highton and Wolfinger (2001), however, test adult role theory using a model of participation in which residential stability, marriage, home ownership, full-time employment, being a student, and leaving home are used as indicators of taking on adult roles. Among individuals age twenty four and under, they find little support for any of these role-takings increasing turnout.[26]

They conclude that theoretical arguments regarding the differences in the turnout of the young and the elderly must look elsewhere. They provide some evidence that aging as learning or experience is likely one possibility: in their sample, the probability of voting increased by about 5 percentage points as individuals aged from eighteen to twenty four, with other roles and demographics controlled for. A second possibility they raise, but provide no evidence for, is that age-related differences reflect generational differences—that is, factors unique to the political and social context in which each generation entered the political world, and which result in high turnout among older generations and lower turnout among younger generations.[27]

Another possibility is that differences in political mobilization help to account for the relationship between age and participation. As Rosenstone and Hansen (1993) note, political elites are more likely to mobilize those who have a record of voting, and those who are easily reached and socially connected. This suggests that political elites are less likely to target younger individuals. Indeed, Beck and Jennings (1979) demonstrate that in the 1970s, the relationship between age and participation in protests was reversed, with the younger more likely to participate than the elderly, and attribute this variation to the intense mobilizing efforts of antiwar interests.

Alternatively, the critical role of political elites in structuring participation, as noted by Rosenstone and Hansen, also suggests that over the past decade, with the increasing strength and visibility of organized interests such as the American Association of Retired Persons (AARP), we should likely see less of a decline in turnout of the oldest age groups, or that such a decline, if it exists, is delayed. We examine this possibility using the marginal effects of age over time (see fig. 3.5). We compare the turnout of each age group to that of forty-six to sixty-year-olds, whom we chose as an arbitrary comparison group.

The first graph in figure 3.5 shows the marginal impact of going from ages 18–24 to ages 46–60. Whereas, conditioning for other demographic

26. There is limited and mixed evidence regarding the effects of parenthood on voter turnout. Jennings (1979) finds that being a parent increases voter turnout of women in school (but not national) elections, while Pacheco and Plutzer (2007) find that adolescents who become parents are less likely to vote.
27. Plutzer's (2002) analysis of turnout as a developmental process provides some evidence on generational differences in initial starting points. He notes that declining levels of partisanship might well result in longer-term declines in voter turnout, as youth are less likely to be exposed to partisan parents and political behaviors.

(a) 18–24 → 46–60

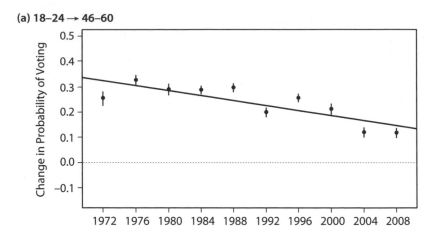

(b) 25–30 → 46–60

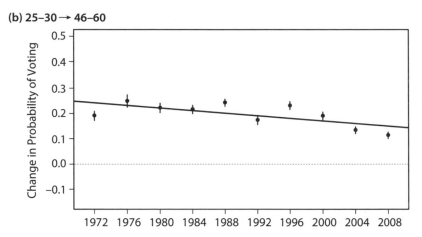

Figure 3.5. Marginal Effect of Age as a Predictor of Turnout, 1972–2008. *Note*: Each point in the graph represents the estimated difference in the probability of voting between an individual in the older age group identified and an individual in the younger age group identified, holding all other variables in the multivariable model constant. Positive values indicate that, ceteris paribus, an older individual is more likely to vote than a younger individual. Each vertical bar provides a 95 percent confidence interval. The trend line is an OLS regression line fitted to the points. Estimated by the authors using data from the Current Population Survey; see section 3.2 for model details.

(c) 31–45 → 46–60

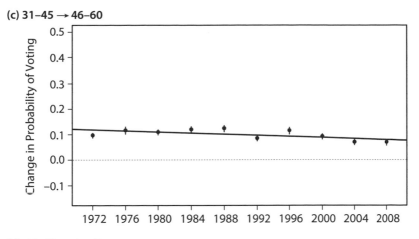

(d) 46–60 → 61–75

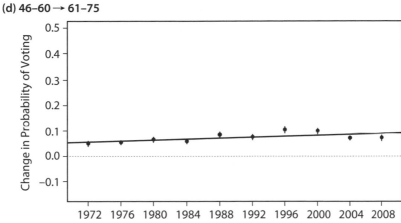

(e) 46–60 → 76–84

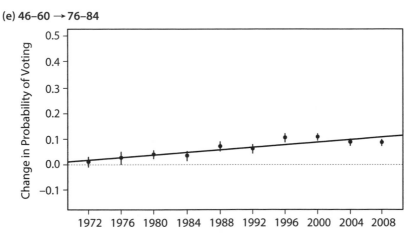

Figure 3.5. (Continued.)

characteristics in 1972 young people were almost 25 percentage points less likely than 46- to 60-year-olds to vote, that difference had dropped to approximately 12 percentage points in the 2004 and 2008 elections (though we note that it remained over 20 percentage points in each election prior to 2000).[28] At the other end of the age spectrum, the fourth and fifth graphs in figure 3.5 show that, ceteris paribus, 61- to 75-year-olds have been voting more than 46- to 60-year-olds at a fairly steady rate. What is perhaps surprising is that they also show that it is the very old, 76- to 84-year-olds, whose turnout relative to 46- to 60-year-olds has been increasing the most.

Generally, these age-related patterns in turnout affirm previous findings on the positive relationship between age and turnout. While increases in turnout rates, ceteris paribus, among the youngest age group and the oldest age group might reflect changes in the mobilization patterns of parties, candidates, or the AARP targeting these two groups, how enduring—rather than election-specific—these patterns are is not clear. Anecdotal discussions of the 2004 and 2008 elections have emphasized the importance of the Obama campaign's priority on youth mobilization, but more systematic analyses will be required to determine whether these mobilization efforts, as opposed to other differences in this youth cohort, account for the age patterns we observe.

Since mobilization by a group such as the AARP would target all respondents over 50, and we notice the turnout of the 76- to 84-year-old group increasing relative to the 61- to 75-year-old group, the higher levels of turnout of this older group, ceteris paribus, are likely *not* caused by increased mobilization efforts. It might be an increase in the physical well-being of the oldest age group, or it could be the result of reforms such as no-excuse absentee voting making it easier for the very old to vote. But the contrast in behavior between the oldest group and the second oldest group is striking.

3.6 Gender and Marital Status

Wolfinger and Rosenstone (1980, 37–39) reported that women in 1972 were only slightly (by approximately 2 percentage points) less likely than men to report having voted, and that married individuals voted

---

28. This should not be interpreted to mean that youth are better represented than they were previously. This is a ceteris paribus result, conditioning on other demographic characteristics. Also, this result is for youth turnout *relative* to the turnout of a specific age group (46- to 60-year-olds). To see if people ages 18–24 are actually more represented among the voters in 2008 than they were in previous years, one should refer to the representativeness ratios presented in chapter 2.

at substantially higher rates than single individuals.[29] According to the Center for American Women in Politics at Rutgers University, prior to 1980, a smaller percentage of women reported voting in presidential elections than did men, but since 1980, a greater percentage of women, compared to men, have reported voting. Consistent with this data on self-reported turnout rates of men and women, we have found that an important difference between the 1972 and 1984 elections in the determinants of voter turnout was the marginal effect of gender: controlling for other demographic characteristics such as education, income, and age, women were significantly more likely than men to vote in 1984 (Leighley and Nagler 1992b). What we expect to find, then, is that, controlling for other demographics, women are more likely than men to vote in presidential elections.

Differences in turnout based on marital status are typically explained as a result of the increased stability and social integration associated with marriage, or as a reflection of the social networks and information contexts introduced by a new partner (Kingston & Finkel 1987, Stoker & Jennings 1995). Stoker and Jennings (1995) conclude that marital transitions are especially important influences on voter turnout compared to other types of participation: because the decision to vote is typically made within a fixed time period and is a relatively discrete act, the decision is more likely to be a joint one, influenced by a spouse.[30] Based on this evidence, then, we expect to find a consistent (and positive) effect of being married, rather than single, on voter turnout.

In figure 3.6 we can see that the marginal difference in voting rates between women and men, conditioning on other demographic characteristics, increased sharply between 1972 and 1984—and has remained substantial ever since. The steadiness of the gap suggests that it

29. Studies examining gender differences in voter turnout explained lower levels of female voting with reference to older women being socialized prior to the adoption of the constitutional amendment granting women the right to vote (Wolfinger & Rosenstone 1980, 43). More recent studies point to the mobilizing effects of the women's rights movement and the increasing prominence of women in national government as increasing the likelihood of women's political engagement (see, for example, Atkeson 2003; Conway, Ahren, & Steuernagel 2004; Rosenstone & Hansen 2003). Other studies note the importance of women being elected to office for stimulating the political interests of women, which tends to be lower, on average, than men's (Verba, Burns, & Schlozman 1997). Finally, another factor distinguishing men and women is women's lower probability of being mobilized (Rosenstone & Hansen 1993, 140–41n15), part of which is explained by working at home or working in lower-status jobs (Schlozman, Burns, & Verba 1999).

30. We also found that married individuals were more likely than single individuals to report voting in the 1984 presidential election (Leighley & Nagler 1992b).

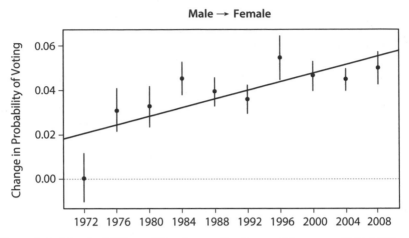

Figure 3.6. Marginal Effect of Gender as a Predictor of Turnout, 1972–2008. *Note*: Each point in the graph represents the estimated difference in the probability of voting between a woman and a man, holding all other variables in the multivariable model constant. Positive values indicate that, ceteris paribus, a woman is more likely to vote than a man. Each vertical bar provides a 95 percent confidence interval. The trend line is an ordinary least squares regression line fitted to the points. Estimated by the authors using data from the Current Population Survey; see section 3.2 for model details.

does not depend on short-term electoral context. What is interesting here is not the trend over thirty years, but the fact that there has been such a substantively large effect for the last twenty years. When we control for demographic factors women are about 4 percentage points more likely to vote than men. Given the size of the two groups in the electorate, this gap translates to a large difference in the share of total votes. Specifically, it means that, given equivalent levels of education and income, women would have 52 percent of the votes and men would have only 48 percent of the votes in a presidential election.

Figure 3.7 shows the difference in voting rates between single and married people, conditioning on other demographic characteristics. While we see no trend over time in the data, what is interesting is that married people are *substantially* more likely to vote than single people, with the difference generally within the range of 8 to 10 percentage points. In 2008, a married person was over 7 percentage points more likely to vote than a single person with otherwise similar demographic characteristics. While we see year-to-year variation in the magnitude of this effect, it is nonetheless large and positive in every election.

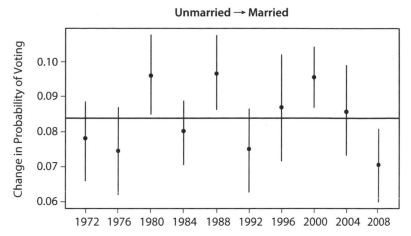

Figure 3.7. Marginal Effect of Marital Status as a Predictor of Turnout, 1972–2008.

Note: Each point in the graph represents the estimated difference in the probability of voting between a married individual and an unmarried individual, holding all other variables in the multivariable model constant. Positive values indicate that, ceteris paribus, a married individual is more likely to vote than a single individual. Each vertical bar provides a 95 percent confidence interval. The trend line is an ordinary least squares regression line fitted to the points. Estimated by the authors using data from the Current Population Survey; see section 3.2 for model details.

3.7 Conclusion

The analyses we report in this chapter assess whether what we have observed in the bivariate cases (chapter 2) also holds when we control for other demographics characteristics. The demographics of interest here— education, income, age, race, ethnicity, gender, and marital status— are all highly correlated. Thus, as a precursor to even thinking about any causal connection, we need to know if each variable is related to turnout *when* we condition on other demographics, or if any of these variables are instead reflecting other important characteristics of the demographic subgroup. As an important example, education and income are the canonical pair of variables that are highly correlated with each other, *and* with many outcome variables of interest to political scientists. We naturally want to know if the relationship between education and turnout is spurious, merely an artifact of education's correlation with income. And conversely, we want to know the same about the relationship between income and turnout, as well as the relationships between ethnicity and turnout, age and turnout, and gender and turnout.

The overall pattern of our results is consistent with the relationships we observed in chapter 2, and so we conclude that these bivariate findings were *not* spurious. Even conditioning on other characteristics, the rich vote more than the poor, the better educated vote more than the less educated, the old vote more than the young, Hispanics vote less than Anglos, women vote more than men, and married individuals vote more than singles.

One notable exception in which the marginal effects we report in this chapter differ from the bivariate results reported in chapter 2 is the turnout of blacks. Blacks vote less than whites, but the multivariable analysis shows that all of this difference can be accounted for by the other demographic characteristics of blacks compared to whites. Blacks as a group have overall lower levels of income and education than whites. But when we condition on our other demographic characteristics, we see that blacks are *more* likely to vote than whites, and have been since 1984.

With a few exceptions, these relationships (again, conditioning on the other demographic characteristics included in our model) have generally been stable from 1972 through 2008. The effect of income and education remain most striking. The gap in turnout between an individual in the bottom third of the education distribution and an individual in the top third is approximately 25 percentage points once we condition on other demographic characteristics. That is a chasm in expected turnout rates for otherwise demographically similar individuals. For income, the relationship between the bottom fifth and top fifth of the income distribution once we condition on other demographic characteristics is approximately 20 percentage points. The stability of this relationship affirms one of Wolfinger and Rosenstone's (1980) central findings: education is a more influential predictor of turnout than is income.

In our bivariate comparisons in chapter 2 we saw a stable relationship between income and turnout. The rich vote more than the poor, and that relationship has not changed substantially. In the multivariable context, we see that, conditional on our other demographic measures, the same conclusion holds for the most part. Yes, turnout of the bottom quintile has dropped somewhat over time, but the increase in turnout for moving from quintiles 2, 3, or 4 into quintile 5 (the top quintile) has decreased somewhat. And moving from the bottom of the education distribution to the middle third is not worth as much as it used to be, nor is a move from the middle to the top. But the magnitude of these changes—which cut in different directions as to the import of education and income in predicting turnout—is quite small. We conclude that the most important findings regarding education and income from the multivariable analysis is that they remain critical and overwhelming in their roles as correlates of turnout.

We discuss the broader implications of these findings in chapter 7. But here we note that the stability of education and income as predictors of turnout over a period of tremendous changes in inequality of income is striking. We find that conditional income bias remains essentially the same over the entire period. To the extent that institutional stability is important to a functioning democracy, this is may be perceived as good news. The concern, of course, is that it may suggest something about the unresponsiveness of American electoral politics.

Another surprising finding of stability between 1972 and 2008 is that of the lower turnout rates of Hispanics relative to Anglos, even when controlling for demographic differences between the two groups. We saw in chapter 2 that Hispanic turnout was substantially lower than Anglo turnout (figs. 2.3 and 2.4). But we would expect much of that gap to be explained by the demographic differences between the two groups (levels of education and income, as well as age). Popular commentary suggests that Hispanics comprise a group that has potential political power because of its size and mobilization potential, especially in light of the salience of immigration as a political issue over the past decade. Yet the persistent gap in turnout between Hispanics and Anglos, even after conditioning on demographic characteristics, is not easily explained despite its political and normative importance.[31]

An important exception to patterns of stability that we have identified is that of gender. In chapter 2 we found that women vote more than men, and that this gap has been increasing steadily over time. In this chapter we have seen that the magnitude of the difference in turnout between men and women, when conditioning on other demographic characteristics, is striking. According to our estimates, since 1996 a woman is 5 percentage points more likely to vote than a man of comparable income, education, and age.[32] That is an extremely large difference. To put that

31. Our model omits factors that others have argued explain Hispanic political behavior, such as national origin, language, and generational differences. Including these could reduce our estimate for the ceteris paribus difference in Hispanic and Anglo turnout.
32. We use the phrase "5 percentage points more likely" to indicate an increase of 0.05 in the probability of an individual voting. While the graphs in this chapter represent the change in the probability of voting for a single hypothetical individual, we discuss percentage point increases in the text to maintain comparability with discussions of increases in group turnout.

in perspective, a woman in the third income quintile is approximately as likely to vote as a man of similar age and education in the fourth income quintile.

3.7.1 A Note on Bivariate and Multivariable Results

In chapters 2 and 3 we have represented the turnout of different demographic groups in three different ways: (1) the level of turnout of the group (figs. 2.1–2.7); (2) the representativeness ratio for the group (figs. 2.8–2.11 and appendix figs. A2.2.1–2.2.6; and in the chapter appendix table A2.2.1); and (3) the marginal difference in turnout between each group and other groups, *conditional* on all other observed demographic characteristics (figs. 3.1–3.7 and chapter appendix fig. A3.2.1). Each representation of turnout tells a different story. The graphs of the level of turnout for a demographic group over time show whether turnout for the group has been increasing or decreasing over time, as well as how much it varies from election to election. And since each demographic group's level of turnout is graphed along with the level of turnout of other groups based on the same demographic characteristic (e.g., the bottom education group compared to the middle education group), these graphs show the difference in turnout over time across different subgroups of each demographic characteristic that we measure.

The representativeness graphs show whether a group is over- or underrepresented among the voters relative to its share of the population or to its share of the citizen population. The representativeness ratios are the statistics that indicate the over- or underrepresentation of each group.

Note that the representativeness ratio is different from a group's *share* of the votes, as the latter depends not just on the turnout rate for the group but also on the group's size. This means that a group can maintain the same turnout rate while also gaining or losing in the share of votes if its group size changes. We generally do not focus on a group's share of the votes. But table 2.2 lists the vote shares for each group (the percentage of voters) for 1972 and 2008. Here we can see that whereas in 1972 the eighteen- to twenty-four-year old age group had 14.3 percent of the votes, the group's share of the votes had shrunk to 9.3 percent in 2008. This is not because the members of the group were voting less but because the group had simply decreased in size as a proportion of the electorate.

Finally, the graphs of conditional differences between groups presented in this chapter show how much, if any, of the bivariate relationships presented in chapter 2 remain after we condition on other observable demographics. So while in chapter 2 we saw difference in turnout rates between the bottom and top income quintile of almost

30 percentage points, in the present chapter we see that the difference in turnout rates for two *otherwise similar* people from the bottom income quintile versus the top income quintile was less than 20 percentage points in most years.

Having extensively examined the demographics of turnout, we shift now to investigating several other factors associated with voter turnout. Chapter 4 focuses on changes in election laws governing registration and election administration. Changes in these laws since 1972 have been immense, yet few studies offer definitive, national-level evidence as to whether these legal changes have influenced turnout in presidential elections. Chapter 5 then considers one aspect of the political determinants of turnout: the policy choices offered by candidates. Demographics aside, if "there's not a dime's worth of difference" between presidential candidates, citizens might reasonably and rationally choose to stay home. These analyses offer some insight as to what candidates offer citizens as policy choices, and whether citizens recognize these choices as they decide whether to vote or not. These chapters are especially important in light of the findings of the centrality and stability of demographics as predictors of turnout, for if these relationships rarely change, the question is when, and if, they might. Perhaps changes in electoral laws and changes in policy choices offered by candidates could provide a mechanism for change.

Appendix 3.1: Estimation Results for the Demographic Models of Voter Turnout

Table A3.1.1. Logit Estimates of Demographic Model without Hispanic Variables, 1972–1988.

Variable	1972 coef	1972 t-stat	1976 coef	1976 t-stat	1980 coef	1980 t-stat	1984 coef	1984 t-stat	1988 coef	1988 t-stat
Constant	−0.06	−1.53	−0.07	−1.18	0.04	0.98	0.08	2.00	0.12	3.10
Education—Middle Third	0.76	37.06	0.78	26.66	0.64	36.35	0.55	29.80	0.51	27.33
Education—Top Third	1.42	62.05	1.48	45.52	1.44	72.84	1.35	64.76	1.35	63.24
Income—2nd Quintile	0.16	6.39	0.20	5.61	0.22	10.00	0.32	13.80	0.30	12.47
Income—3rd Quintile	0.43	16.54	0.40	10.78	0.42	18.44	0.50	20.82	0.52	20.97
Income—4th Quintile	0.61	22.60	0.64	16.43	0.68	28.43	0.71	28.14	0.73	27.92
Income—5th Quintile	0.89	30.63	0.94	23.03	0.84	33.51	0.94	34.97	0.98	35.08
Age 18–24	−1.27	−27.97	−1.70	−26.06	−1.65	−40.94	−1.62	38.75	−1.82	42.69
Age 25–30	−1.01	−21.44	−1.39	−20.73	−1.37	−33.32	−1.33	31.43	−1.59	37.42
Age 31–45	−0.59	−13.11	−0.82	−12.81	−0.87	−21.91	−0.90	22.15	−1.10	27.30
Age 46–60	−0.07	−1.49	−0.20	−3.20	−0.29	−7.21	−0.27	−6.52	−0.49	11.72
Age 61–75	0.28	6.39	0.18	2.82	0.20	4.94	0.17	4.04	0.10	2.39
Women	0.00	0.06	0.14	6.18	0.15	10.35	0.20	13.21	0.17	10.85
Married	0.35	19.19	0.32	12.56	0.42	26.50	0.36	21.32	0.40	23.41
Living in the South	−0.46	−25.61	−0.28	−10.36	−0.23	−13.52	−0.27	15.15	−0.24	13.83
Black	0.05	1.84	0.00	0.05	−0.01	−0.25	0.35	13.48	0.17	6.66
Number of Observations	83,322		41,604		106,695		94,692		88,449	
Percent Correctly Predicted	70.0		70.1		70.5		70.9		70.5	

Note: Entries are estimated logit coefficients followed by the associated t-statistic. See text for a description of variable coding. Estimated by the authors using data from the Current Population Survey.

Table A3.1.2. Logit Estimates of Demographic Model without Hispanic Variables, 1992–2008.

Variable	1992		1996		2000		2004		2008	
	coef	t-stat	coef	t-stat	coef	t-stat	coef	t-stat	Coef	t-stat
Constant	0.11	2.88	0.07	1.59	0.09	1.88	0.24	5.71	0.18	4.13
Education—Middle Third	0.55	30.11	0.55	27.47	0.55	26.37	0.64	32.51	0.62	30.70
Education—Top Third	1.32	62.11	1.19	53.28	1.20	50.80	1.30	57.28	1.31	55.26
Income—2nd Quintile	0.35	15.02	0.29	11.17	0.34	12.41	0.32	12.46	0.29	10.96
Income—3rd Quintile	0.57	23.44	0.49	18.03	0.59	20.63	0.56	21.30	0.48	17.59
Income—4th Quintile	0.81	31.16	0.68	24.33	0.79	26.32	0.77	27.62	0.73	25.36
Income—5th Quintile	0.97	35.07	0.94	31.32	0.91	29.03	0.92	30.64	0.85	27.45
Age 18–24	−1.43	34.37	−1.79	38.17	−1.71	35.00	−1.38	30.40	−1.25	26.76
Age 25–30	−1.32	31.46	−1.69	36.09	−1.62	32.59	−1.45	31.04	−1.23	25.90
Age 31–45	−0.91	23.38	−1.21	28.02	−1.20	26.53	−1.13	26.59	−1.01	23.28
Age 46–60	−0.47	11.57	−0.68	15.28	−0.76	16.45	−0.73	17.10	−0.63	14.63
Age 61–75	0.08	1.97	−0.03	−0.63	−0.10	−1.99	−0.18	−3.98	−0.13	−2.94
Women	0.16	10.71	0.23	13.66	0.20	11.41	0.21	12.85	0.23	13.08
Married	0.35	20.24	0.36	19.50	0.41	21.16	0.41	21.68	0.33	16.77
Living in the South	−0.22	12.30	−0.17	−8.63	−0.13	−6.11	−0.21	10.36	−0.13	−5.97
Black	0.13	4.90	0.26	9.30	0.37	12.59	0.32	10.87	0.66	21.06
Number of Observations	90,783		73,750		67,366		77,843		72,927	
Percent Correctly Predicted	71.4		68.8		69.5		72.1		72.1	

Note: Entries are estimated logit coefficients followed by the associated t-statistic. See text for a description of variable coding. Estimated by the authors using data from the Current Population Survey.

Table A3.1.3. Logit Estimates of Demographic Model with Hispanic Variables, 1976–1988.

Variable	1972		1976		1980		1984		1988	
	coef	t-stat	coef	t-stat	coef	t-stat	coef	t-stat	coef	t-stat
Constant	—	—	-1.01	-8.12	-0.43	-7.38	-0.45	-7.43	-0.51	-8.31
Education—Middle Third	—	—	0.74	24.98	0.62	34.64	0.53	28.77	0.50	26.27
Education—Top Third	—	—	1.45	43.82	1.41	70.62	1.35	63.67	1.34	62.19
Income—2nd Quintile	—	—	0.20	5.50	0.21	9.66	0.31	13.22	0.29	11.83
Income—3rd Quintile	—	—	0.38	10.01	0.41	17.64	0.48	19.87	0.51	20.02
Income—4th Quintile	—	—	0.61	15.47	0.67	27.49	0.68	26.95	0.71	27.08
Income—5th Quintile	—	—	0.92	22.11	0.83	32.55	0.92	33.82	0.96	34.15
Age 18–24	—	—	-1.65	-25.07	-1.62	-39.71	-1.59	-37.47	-1.80	-41.68
Age 25–30	—	—	-1.34	-19.73	-1.34	-32.18	-1.30	-30.31	-1.58	-36.73
Age 31–45	—	—	-0.77	-11.86	-0.85	-21.04	-0.87	-21.12	-1.08	-26.47
Age 46–60	—	—	-0.17	-2.67	-0.27	-6.67	-0.24	-5.65	-0.48	-11.28
Age 61–75	—	—	0.20	3.11	0.21	5.09	0.19	4.40	0.10	2.44
Women	—	—	0.14	6.06	0.15	10.43	0.20	13.44	0.17	10.98
Married	—	—	0.33	12.60	0.42	26.27	0.35	20.81	0.41	23.37
Living in the South	—	—	-0.26	-9.57	-0.23	-13.04	-0.27	-14.84	-0.25	-13.72
White Non-Hispanic	—	—	0.97	8.89	0.50	11.29	0.55	12.01	0.67	13.95
White Hispanic	—	—	0.68	5.70	0.14	2.47	0.29	5.02	0.49	7.94
Black Non-Hispanic	—	—	0.93	8.15	0.45	9.15	0.87	16.73	0.82	15.19
Number of Observations			40,854		104,834		93,135		87,116	
Percent Correctly Predicted			70.2		70.6		71.0		70.6	

Note: Entries are estimated logit coefficients followed by the associated t-statistic. See text for a description of variable coding. Estimated by the authors using data from the Current Population Survey.

Table A3.1.4. Logit Estimates of Demographic Model with Hispanic Variables, 1992–2008.

Variable	1992 coef	1992 t-stat	1996 coef	1996 t-stat	2000 coef	2000 t-stat	2004 coef	2004 t-stat	2008 coef	2008 t-stat
Constant	−0.65	−11.75	−0.48	−8.18	−0.60	−9.86	−0.42	−7.97	−0.42	−7.83
Education—Middle Third	0.53	28.76	0.55	26.93	0.54	25.46	0.63	31.77	0.60	29.86
Education—Top Third	1.30	60.68	1.18	52.77	1.19	49.80	1.29	56.34	1.30	54.48
Income—2nd Quintile	0.34	14.44	0.28	10.65	0.33	11.79	0.30	11.73	0.28	10.57
Income—3rd Quintile	0.55	22.15	0.47	17.35	0.56	19.55	0.53	20.09	0.46	16.85
Income—4th Quintile	0.78	29.81	0.66	23.51	0.75	25.00	0.74	26.33	0.71	24.43
Income—5th Quintile	0.95	34.02	0.92	30.56	0.88	27.85	0.88	29.33	0.83	26.72
Age 18–24	−1.37	−32.58	−1.76	−37.21	−1.67	−33.79	−1.32	−28.95	−1.19	−25.33
Age 25–30	−1.26	−29.91	−1.66	−35.28	−1.58	−31.44	−1.39	−29.54	−1.17	−24.62
Age 31–45	−0.86	−21.79	−1.18	−27.23	−1.16	−25.44	−1.08	−25.22	−0.96	−22.00
Age 46–60	−0.42	−10.22	−0.65	−14.66	−0.72	−15.55	−0.69	−16.08	−0.60	−13.90
Age 61–75	0.11	2.64	−0.01	−0.31	−0.08	−1.57	−0.16	−3.47	−0.12	−2.53
Women	0.17	10.84	0.23	13.79	0.20	11.62	0.22	13.05	0.23	13.45
Married	0.34	19.75	0.36	19.29	0.41	20.83	0.41	21.52	0.32	16.57
Living in the South	−0.23	−12.34	−0.18	−9.13	−0.14	−6.73	−0.22	−10.73	−0.13	−6.15
White Non-Hispanic	0.80	20.10	0.59	14.15	0.75	17.72	0.73	21.97	0.67	19.90
White Hispanic	0.41	7.81	0.33	6.00	0.41	7.67	0.30	6.67	0.30	6.86
Black Non-Hispanic	0.86	18.67	0.81	16.48	1.05	20.93	0.97	22.60	1.26	28.32
Number of Observations	89,643		73,536		66,832		77,843		72,927	
Percent Correctly Predicted	71.6		68.8		69.7		72.1		72.3	

Appendix 3.2: Additional First Differences for Income

(a) Quintile 2 → Quintile 3

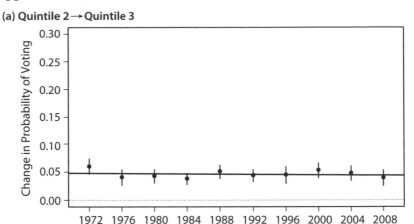

(b) Quintile 2 → Quintile 4

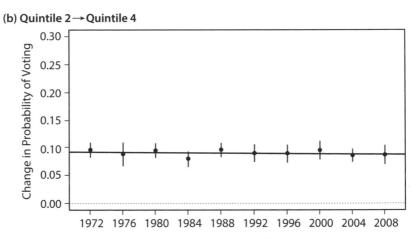

Figure A3.2.1. Marginal Effect of Income Using Different Income Comparisons, 1972–2008.

Note: Each point in the graph represents the estimated difference in the probability of voting between an individual in the higher income group identified and an individual in the lower income group identified, holding all other variables in the multivariable model constant. Positive values indicate that, ceteris paribus, an individual in the higher income group is more likely to vote than an individual in the lower income group. Each vertical bar provides a 95 percent confidence interval. The trend line is an ordinary least squares regression line fitted to the points. Estimated by the authors using data from the Current Population Survey; see section 3.2 for model details.

(c) Quintile 3 → Quintile 4

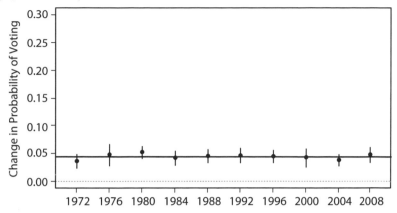

Figure A3.2.1. (Continued.)

Four

· ·

The Legal Context of Turnout
Voter Registration and Voting Innovations

W*ho Votes?* (Wolfinger & Rosenstone 1980) provided new evidence of the effects of registration rules on the probability of voting. Examining numerous characteristics of state registration laws and their implementation, Wolfinger and Rosenstone's results underscored the critical negative effect of the registration closing date in the 1972 election: the greater the number of days prior to the election that voter registration closes, the lower an individual's probability of voting in presidential elections. This finding has been confirmed in subsequent analyses over the past several decades.[1]

However, since 1972 the states have engaged in a wide variety of policy innovations governing presidential elections, including, for example, election day registration, registering and voting by mail, increased access to absentee voting, and early voting. Many of these innovations were adopted with the explicit intention of increasing voter turnout, and often with the intention of increasing voter turnout of traditionally underrepresented groups (e.g., the poor or racial and ethnic minorities).

While some of these reforms—in particular, absentee voting and early voting—have been quite popular with voters, existing research provides no evidence that they have actually raised turnout or affected the disparities in voting rates between different groups of voters. Most research on the topic has concluded that voters using these methods of voting are simply switching the way in which they vote; were these new modes of voting not available, they would vote by other (i.e., traditional) means (Fitzgerald 2005; Gronke, Galanes-Rosenbaum & Miller 2007).

1. See Leighley and Nagler 1992a, Nagler (1991; 1994), and Rosenstone and Hansen (1993).

In this chapter we return to these fundamental questions, considering the electoral impact of this new, wider array of voter registration and election administration laws using a new data set we collected on state electoral rules between 1972 and 2008. We first describe the major features of changes in electoral laws during this period, and then use two analytical approaches to examine whether states that adopt easier registration and voting laws subsequently witness higher aggregate turnout. We first provide standard bivariate intervention analyses, comparing changes in turnout in states that adopted reforms with changes in turnout over the same period in states that did not adopt the same reforms. If a costs and benefits theory of the demographics of turnout is correct, then we should see that making voting easier should make those individuals with fewer demographic resources such as education (or, more broadly, traditionally underrepresented groups) more likely to vote, and therefore reduce group-based differences in turnout. Lowering the costs should allow more people with fewer resources to clear the cost hurdle. We examine this proposition with respect to election day registration.

Second, we also estimate cross-sectional time series models at the state level. This allows us to test whether these policy innovations are associated with increases in turnout once we condition on other factors related to turnout.

4.1 Electoral Innovation in the United States

The United States is unique among modern democracies in the burden it puts on citizens seeking to exercise their right to vote. Much of this burden over the past several decades has resulted from state voter registration rules that require citizens to formally apply for voting eligibility certification prior to election day. In contrast, citizens in most other democracies are automatically registered to vote through other identification or residential registration procedures (often borne by the national or local government), or indeed may even be *required* to vote by national compulsory voting laws. Thus the costs of voting are higher in the United States, and this simple observation is often used to explain lower levels of voter turnout in the United States compared to other Western European democracies (Blais 2006; Franklin 2004; Jackman 1987; Powell 1986).[2]

---

2. The centrality of registration to the act of voting is underscored by Erikson's (1981) study equating registration with voting, but more recent analyses have challenged this concept; see Lloyd (2001) as well as Brown & Wedeking (2006); Fitzgerald (2005).

Yet the last thirty years have seen substantial reductions in restrictions on registration and voting. States have eased the registration process in response to the 1993 National Voter Registration Act (NVRA), which mandated that they make available the opportunity to register to vote wherever drivers licenses were issued and wherever states provide public benefits. At the same time, many states have independently adopted election reforms intended to make voting easier. Early voting, where citizens may vote in person before election day, is now available in numerous states, as is the option of voting at locations other than traditional precinct polling places. And many states now allow citizens to vote without going to any polling place by returning an absentee ballot, independent of whether or not the voter is in the state and would have no serious impediment to voting in person on election day.

With the support of the Pew Charitable Trusts, we compiled data on voter registration and election administration statutes in the states for all presidential election years between 1972 and 2008; details about this data collection are provided in appendix 4.1 and can also be found in Cemenska, et al. (2009). These data show a diversity in the complex set of election laws adopted by the state since 1972, and they underscore how many of the states have adopted laws to make registering to vote and casting a ballot easier for citizens.

Table 4.1 lists the number of states in which various registration laws enacting these reforms had been adopted in each year since 1972: election day registration, availability of registration at departments responsible

Table 4.1. State Adoption of Registration Reforms, 1972–2008.

		Number of States with:		
	EDR	DMV Reg	Closing GE 30 days	Closing GE 25 days
1972	0	2	28	33
1976	3	2	23	32
1980	3	3	22	31
1984	3	5	20	29
1988	3	8	20	29
1992	3	18	19	31
1996	6	50	15	31
2000	6	50	14	30
2004	6	50	14	28
2008	9	50	13	25

Note: Entries are number of states in which the indicated registration provision was in effect in the given year. See appendix 4.1 for source and coding details.

for motor vehicle and drivers licenses (DMV), and the number of days before an election that registration closes. Being able to register on election day, register at public agencies, and register closer to election day are considered legal features that reduce the costs of voting. They are also the registration reforms that have received the greatest amount of attention by lawmakers and the media.

As shown in table 4.1, between 1972 and 1976 three states (Maine, Minnesota, and Wisconsin) adopted election day registration (EDR), and this basically remained constant until three additional states (Idaho, New Hampshire, and Wyoming) adopted EDR between 1992 and 1996 rather than comply with the NVRA requirement that state agencies provide registration materials.[3] Between 2004 and 2008 an additional three states adopted it, resulting in nine states offering election day registration in 2008.

A more dramatic increase is seen in the availability of DMV registration by 2008, largely due to the requirement being imposed by passage of the NVRA. Prior to the 1980s, only two states provided any sort of voter registration when citizens applied for drivers licenses. Between 1980 and 1992 this number rose to eighteen, and basically became universal (if one excludes the EDR states) with the passage of the NVRA.

In contrast, reforms associated with reducing the number of days prior to election day by which citizens must register to vote (i.e., the registration closing period) are far from universal, and changes in these laws are more accurately described as modest. In 1972, 28 states required citizens to be registered to vote 30 days or more before election day. While this number dropped to 13 by 2008, this does not mean that states have substantially reduced the registration closing period. Instead, what has happened is that many states with registration closing periods longer than 30 days have reduced that requirement to somewhere between 25 and 30 days, as suggested in the last column in table 4.1 (the number of states with registration closing period greater than or equal to 25 days). In 1972, 33 states required registration 25 or more days prior to the election. By 2008 this number had only dropped to 25 states. So many of the legal changes consisted in moving states to a registration deadline of within 30 days of the election but not to a deadline of closer than 25 days.

Perhaps the most dramatic change in state electoral laws over the past several decades has been in rules regarding when or where individuals (once registered) may vote. While absentee voting for citizens meeting certain requirements (such as being out of state or being physically unable

---

3. The NVRA relieved states of the obligation to provide registration materials at state agencies offering public services if they adopted election day registration.

to get to the polls on election day) has long been available in many states, since 1972 a large number of states have relaxed absentee voting requirements, effectively providing absentee voting on demand (no-fault absentee voting). Usually such ballots can be returned by mail or in person a certain number of days prior to election day.

Early voting is another electoral reform that has been adopted by many states in the post-1972 period. Like absentee voting, early voting reduces the costs of balloting for registered voters. Early voting periods in most states last up to two weeks, and close several days prior to election day. During this period citizens can go to the polls (sometimes traditional polling places, sometimes at fewer, yet more centralized, locations) to cast their votes in person. According to the U.S. Election Assistance Commission,[4] nearly one third of ballots in the 2008 presidential election were cast prior to election day.[5]

Table 4.2 presents the number of states allowing two forms of alternative voting: no-fault absentee voting and in-person early voting. Here we see striking change. In 1972 only 2 states allowed no-fault absentee voting, in contrast to 27 states in 2008. While in 1972 only

Table 4.2. State Adoption of Early and Absentee Voting Reforms, 1972–2008.

	No-Fault Absentee Voting	In-Person Early Voting
1972	2	5
1976	3	6
1980	6	7
1984	6	7
1988	6	9
1992	12	11
1996	16	14
2000	22	22
2004	24	27
2008	27	31

Note: Entries are number of states in which the indicated voting provision was in effect in the given year. See appendix 4.1 for source and coding details.

4. U.S. Election Assistance Commission. "Ballots Cast Before Election Day Expected to Increase as Early Voting Trend Continues," September 30, 2012; available at http://www.eac.gov/ballots_cast_before_election_day_expected_to_increase_as_early_voting_trend_continues_/.
5. While absentee votes are also cast early (i.e., before election day), we use the term *early voting* to refer to voting that occurs in person prior to election day.

5 states allowed early voting, that number increased to 31 by 2008. Of course, neither of these reforms do anything to reduce the costs associated with registration, but they do reduce the costs associated with having a specified day and finite time period in which a registered citizen must appear to cast a ballot.

4.2 Previous Research on Electoral Rules and Turnout

The increasing diversity and popularity of these alternative voting procedures does not, of course, demonstrate that their adoption has increased voter turnout. Without exception, reformers have argued that decreasing the costs of voting by adopting these reforms will increase the number of citizens casting ballots. And nearly as often, supporters seeking the adoption of such reforms have claimed that individuals least able to bear the costs of voting and thus those typically underrepresented among voters (i.e., the poor, the less-educated, and minorities) benefit more than those most able to bear such costs. And so adopting these electoral reforms should lead not just to a larger but also to a more representative electorate.

These arguments were clearly evident in the protracted debates and political maneuvering preceding passage of the National Voter Registration Act of 1993. The NVRA required states to provide the opportunity for citizens to register to vote at all state agencies dispensing public benefits, including state agencies providing drivers' licenses. While the latter provision is the best known of the bill (and generates its common name, "motor voter") the bill's provision requiring states to provide voter registration assistance in agencies providing aid to poor people generated much of the political conflict. Hence, the normative claims of a larger and perhaps more representative electorate were often met with concerns over the partisan implications of the bill's passage.

Once these substantial political hurdles were overcome, the states had some time before being required to implement various aspects of the legislation. At the same time the NVRA was being adopted, other electoral innovations that we have described—absentee voting and early voting—were being adopted by the states. However, most of the empirical studies evaluating whether these reforms have increased turnout or made the electorate more representative have focused on only one reform at a time, often looking at only brief time periods. The conclusion drawn from many of these existing studies is that these reforms have had at best a modest effect on turnout levels, and that they have either had no effect on the representativeness of the electorate or possibly made it slightly less representative.

Using aggregate-level data, a number of scholars have investigated the effects of motor voter on registration, turnout, and the composition of the electorate (Brown & Wedeking 2006; Franklin & Grier 1997; Hanmer 2007; Hill 2003; Knack 1995). While the particular estimates vary a bit, many of these studies suggest that this reform significantly increased registration in the states but did not increase turnout substantially. Knack (1995) is an exception to this set of null findings. Looking at data for 1976 through 1992, and estimating a multivariable model of turnout that considered how long motor voter implementation had been in effect, Knack concluded that motor voter *did* increase turnout. None of these studies find any significant group-specific differences in turnout as a consequence of the law. Hence, motor voter was modestly effective in two of its initial goals, to increase registration and to reduce the costs of registration to underrepresented groups, but possibly ineffective in increasing turnout.

Most studies of the impact of EDR suggest that being able to register at the polls on election day increases turnout by about 3 to 5 percentage points, with the early adopting states experiencing a greater boost (Brians & Grofman 1999; Fenster 1994; Fitzgerald 2005; Hanmer 2007; Highton 1997; Knack 2001; Knack & White 2000). Fenster (1994) estimated the effect EDR had on aggregate turnout in the three early adopters—Maine, Minnesota, and Wisconsin—to be about 5 percentage points by comparing the change in turnout in those states to the change in turnout in other states preadoption and postadoption. Knack (2001) has estimated the change for the second wave of states—Idaho, New Hampshire, and Wyoming—to be about 3 percentage points using a similar technique.

Hanmer (2007) and Knack and White (2000) conclude that the adoption of EDR has had limited effects on the representativeness of the electorate. Hanmer does report that the effect of EDR is larger for persons with lower levels of education than those with higher levels. Knack and White (2000) report that the greatest effects of EDR are evidenced for younger citizens and recent movers, and only slight effects are shown across income groups. They find no effect on turnout differences, however, across education groups. Brians and Grofman (1999) are a bit more optimistic about group-related differences in turnout as a result of EDR, but their analysis is based on comparing only two elections. Hence, this evidence suggests that class effects of EDR on the composition of the electorate are likely minimal.

Research on absentee voting has also produced somewhat inconsistent findings on whether this electoral reform actually increases overall turnout. Demographically, absentee voters tend to be more educated and older than election day voters (Barreto et al. 2006; Karp & Banducci

2000, 2001). And because absentee voters tend to be more politically active, partisan, and psychologically engaged in politics than election day voters, these studies also suggest that absentee voting does not increase turnout overall but instead makes it more convenient for those who would have otherwise voted on election day to vote at another time. Consistent with this interpretation, Fitzgerald (2005), Giammo and Brox (2010), and Gronke et al. (2007) conclude that absentee voting does not increase turnout. The only studies to conclude that absentee voting increases turnout, Francia and Herrnson (2004) and Oliver (1996), do so based only on cross-sectional analyses.

Studies of early voting also suggest that the individuals who are most likely to take advantage of this electoral innovation are those who would otherwise vote on election day: those who are politically engaged and highly partisan (Neeley & Richardson 2001; Stein 1998; Stein & Garcia-Monet 1997). These studies, as well as Francia and Herrnson (2004) and Gronke et al. (2007), are all limited by research design in time, location, or both. Yet they are consistent with Fitzgerald's (2005) more comprehensive analysis of turnout between 1972 and 2002, which indicates that early voting has no significant effect on overall turnout. Only two studies conclude that early voting increases turnout, but these findings are somewhat tentative. Giammo and Brox (2010) find that early voting leads to greater turnout when first adopted, but that the effect disappears within two elections, while Lyons and Scheb (1999) claim that early voting increases turnout, using evidence based on early voting in one county in Tennessee in one year.

In sum, there is no causal evidence that the two electoral reforms adopted by approximately half the states and used by approximately a third of voters has actually affected net turnout. Below we provide a more definitive answer to the question of the effects of these electoral reforms. Our findings show that absentee voting *has* in fact increased turnout, and suggest that early voting *can* increase turnout when implemented aggressively, both of which are important advances in what we know about the consequences of electoral reforms in the United States

4.3 Research Design and the Search for Effects

We begin with a discussion of research design issues, for even the modest effects of election law reforms identified in some previous research might be questioned due to concerns regarding how previous studies have drawn causal inferences and how they have estimated these causal effects. Many studies either utilize a single cross-section (using either individual or aggregate data based on either national-, state-, or county-level data) or change over time in a single state (again, using either individual or aggregate data based on either national- or state- or county-level data). But when we ask whether election laws affect turnout, we consider this to be a causal question. That means that our research designs should maximize our ability to draw causal inferences about the relationship between the adoption of an electoral reform and the level of voter turnout.

A standard and common approach to establishing causality in contemporary social science research examines variations in individual behavior using cross-sectional, multivariable models, where the dependent variable of interest (voter turnout) is modeled as a function of a set of independent variables (demographics and state election laws). Many studies examining the turnout effects of in-person early and absentee voting use this approach. But the causal inferences we can draw from this approach are limited because we do not necessarily know why some states have adopted these measures (while others have not), or whether those states are as a group different from the states that have not adopted the election reforms. If we were to compare turnout in states with in-person early voting to turnout in states that do not have it, the comparison would only be valid for drawing an inference on the effect of early voting *if the adoption of in-person early voting were not correlated with other factors related to turnout.* This means that the causal inferences from any cross-sectional analysis are suspect. It may be that states where turnout is higher independent of the electoral rules also choose to adopt reforms designed to increase turnout.

An alternative approach to assessing the effects of an electoral reform on voter turnout is to analyze it as a policy innovation problem, comparing turnout in a state before the innovation to turnout in a state after the adoption of the electoral reform. But because turnout varies from election to election, comparing turnout in a single state in a single year to turnout in the same state in the first election after reform, we would not know if we were observing the impact of the electoral reform or instead observing a secular (independent) change in turnout that affected all states in that election year.

Solving this latter problem requires using a *difference-in-difference* approach—that is, comparing the change in turnout for the state adopting the reform to the change in turnout of other states that did not adopt the reform. Provided that other things have remained constant, the difference between the differences would reflect the impact of the reform. We begin our analyses below using this difference-in-difference approach.

However, if other factors affecting turnout change across the states, and those changes are correlated with adoption of reforms, then the changes observed via the difference-in-difference approach could be the result of changes in those other factors and not the result of the electoral reform of interest. This possibility also leads us to believe that the most robust approach is to combine the cross-sectional and difference-in-difference analyses into a cross-sectional time series (CSTS) approach. Thus, our second analytical approach treats the adoption of absentee voting and the adoption of in-person early voting as interventions, and assesses whether such interventions raised or lowered turnout in the states. This approach allows us to condition on the values of other observable factors known to influence turnout, such as the closeness of elections, and demographic characteristics.

In this model, the unit of analysis is the state-year; the dependent variable is turnout percentage in the state-year; and independent variables include demographic and political characteristics argued to affect voter turnout, along with variables for each state-year indicating whether the state had in that year adopted either absentee or in-person early voting. The model thus incorporates both changes over time and differences across states. The strength of the CSTS approach is that we are able to condition on observable factors and avoid drawing inferences that require the assumption that no other factors related to turnout changed in ways correlated with the adoption of electoral reforms. However, the cost of more thoroughly isolating the causal impact of electoral reforms is that we lose statistical power.

In principle, we can use both of our approaches to determine the impact of reforms on different demographic groups. The difference-in-difference model can be used by examining differences in turnout before and after electoral reform adoptions by different education, income, or age groups, for example. Unfortunately, while disaggregating by demographic groups could be accomplished with the cross-sectional time series model, when we did this we were not able to recover precise enough estimates to distinguish effects between different demographic groups. Thus, in the demographic-specific analyses below, we only present the difference-in-difference estimates, and only for the effect of EDR.

We use the difference-in-difference estimates to compare the effects of election day registration across the five income groups to determine whether EDR has differential effects across these age, income, and education-level groups. This allows us to test whether the claims of supporters of this electoral reform—that it would increase the turnout of underrepresented groups and therefore make the electorate more representative—are substantiated. While the CSTS estimates would offer more robust estimates of effects, that the difference-in-difference estimates are similar to the CSTS estimates in the aggregate data gives us some confidence that the demographic estimates hold as well.

Our data are drawn from three sources: the Current Population Survey (CPS), official vote returns and census population estimates (as described in appendix 4.2), and a new data set on state registration and election administration laws (as described in appendix 4.1). We use the CPS (as described in appendix 2.1), and compute a measure of voter turnout that is the proportion of the citizen voting age population in each state that casts a vote for president. We also use CPS data for measures of turnout in each state for distinct demographic groups of the population. We supplement the CPS data with our state voter registration and election administration data (as described in appendix 4.1).

4.4 The Effects of Electoral Reforms: Difference-in-Difference Estimates

We first perform several difference-in-difference tests to examine the impact of election day registration (EDR) for the three states that first adopted it—that is, wave 1 states, and then analyze the later adopters (i.e., wave 2 and wave 3 states) separately to avoid contaminating the effects estimates due to differences in the timing of the adoptions over a thirty-five-year period. If EDR really raises turnout, then we should see a larger increase in turnout from pre–EDR adoption (i.e., 1972) to post–EDR adoption (i.e., 1976 through 2008) for the three states that adopted it prior to 1976 than for the states that did not adopt it. Since the CPS did not include a state variable in 1976, we compare 1972 turnout to turnout in the postadoption period of 1980–2008 with CPS data. But to utilize 1976, and extend our baseline comparison beyond one election, we also do the comparison using turnout based on official vote tabulations, comparing 1960–72 turnout to 1976–2008 turnout for the EDR states and the non-EDR states.[6]

Table 4.3 reports turnout for two groups of states, EDR wave 1 states (Maine, Minnesota, and Wisconsin) and non-EDR states, for two periods for each group. Prior to the adoption of EDR, the three EDR states had substantially higher turnout than the non-EDR states (69.9 percent compared to 64.1 percent). But what matters here is that adoption of EDR *increased* this advantage even more. The key columns are the increases in turnout from 1972 to the postadoption period of 1980–2008. If EDR is effective, we should see larger increases in the first

6. Since the non-EDR states were affected by a major institutional change during the 1960–72 period, the Voting Rights Act of 1965, we only used non-Southern states for this analysis.

column of one-time increases in turnout (EDR states) than for the second column of one-time increases in turnout (non-EDR states). That is exactly what we see. Since 1980 the EDR states have had turnout on average 3.0 percentage points higher than their 1972 turnout, whereas turnout in the non-EDR states has decreased by 1.5 percentage points since 1972.[7]

However, we note that we are only using one election year, 1972, as our pre-EDR baseline here. To avoid an error in inference that might be caused if 1972 was an unusual year for the three EDR states, we also average over the 1960–1972 presidential elections to create an alternative pre-EDR baseline for comparison. These numbers are reported in the second row of the table.[8] Here we see that for the three EDR states, turnout averaged 69.1 percent for the four presidential elections from 1960–1972, whereas it averaged 68.5 percent for the presidential elections from 1976–2008. Thus these states saw a drop in turnout of 0.6 percentage points. However, the corresponding figures for the comparison set of non-EDR states are 63.8 percent and 57.2 percent, a drop in turnout of 6.7 percentage points. Thus, the net effect on turnout that can be attributed to EDR here is a 6.1 percentage-point *increase*.

Having concluded that EDR does in fact raise turnout, the question remains as to *who* is voting more. To address this question, we use measures of turnout of different demographic groups for each state in each election and repeat the difference-in-difference analysis we initially did for overall turnout. Rows 3 through 7 in table 4.3 report the change in turnout for citizens in different income groups. EDR increased the turnout of the second and third income quintiles by 5.8 percentage points and 4.7 percentage points, respectively, while only increasing turnout for the bottom income quintile group by 0.6 percentage points. EDR increased the turnout of the top two income quintile groups by 2.3 percentage points and 2.2 percentage points, respectively. So it appears that EDR has almost twice as large an impact on the second and third income quintiles as on the top two income quintiles; the smallest effect is for those in the first income quintile. Thus, these results suggest that adoption of EDR leads to an increase in the representation of voters in the second and third quintiles relative to the fifth (i.e., wealthiest) quintile, while harming the representation of voters in the first quintile (i.e., the poorest).

7. We note that our unit of analysis here is *the state*; thus we average over states, not over population. This difference between the increase for the EDR states and the non-EDR states is the net effect of adoption of EDR on turnout, and is reported in column 7 (Net EDR Effect) of table 4.3.
8. Here we only use non-Southern states to avoid conflating increases in turnout in Southern states due to the passage of the 1965 Voting Rights Act with increases in turnout caused by the electoral reforms we are studying.

Table 4.3. The Effect of the Adoption of Election Day Registration on Turnout (Wave 1 EDR States).

	EDR Wave I States			Non-EDR States			Net EDR Group Effect[a]	At-Individual risk Effect[b]
	1972	1980–2008	Increase, 1972 to 1980–2008	1972	1980–2008	Increase 1972 to 1980–2008		
Aggregate CPS	69.9	72.9	3.0	64.1	62.5	−1.5	4.5	15.0
Aggregate (1960)[c]	69.1	68.5	−0.6	63.8	57.2	−6.7	6.1	19.7
Income—1st Quintile	62.4	59.9	−2.5	51.8	48.7	−3.0	0.6	1.5
Income—2d Quintile	60.5	68.5	8.0	55.6	57.8	2.2	5.8	14.6
Income—3rd Quintile	70.9	74.8	3.8	64.7	63.9	−0.8	4.7	16.1
IIncome—4th Quintile	79.0	81.3	2.2	70.9	70.8	−0.0	2.3	11.1
Income—5th Quintile	85.6	85.2	−0.4	80.1	77.6	−2.5	2.2	15.1
Education—Less than High School	60.0	54.1	−5.9	52.2	43.3	−8.9	3.0	7.4
High School Grad	69.2	68.3	−0.9	65.4	56.9	−8.5	7.6	24.7
Some College	81.0	77.6	−3.4	75.7	68.1	−7.6	4.3	22.5
College Grad and Above	91.7	89.1	−2.6	84.6	82.1	−2.6	0	0.1

Table 4.3. (Continued.)

Age 18–24	51.6	55.3	3.7	49.9	41.7	−8.2	11.9	24.7
Age 25–30	66.4	65.4	−1.0	60.5	51.9	−8.6	7.6	22.5
Age 46–60	76.1	79.5	3.4	71.4	71.3	−0.1	3.5	14.8
Age 61–75	77.5	81.2	3.7	70.8	74.7	3.9	−0.2	−0.9
Single	60.8	62.1	1.3	54.0	52.3	−1.6	30.0	7.5
Married	73.6	80.0	6.4	68.4	69.5	1.1	5.2	19.8

Notes: Except for row 2, entries are computed by the authors using self-reported turnout from the Current Population Survey, or increase in reported turnout, for states that adopted EDR between 1972 and 1976, or for states that have never adopted EDR. The wave 1 EDR states are: Maine, Minnesota, and Wisconsin.

[a] Entries are the post-1972 change in turnout for the three EDR wave 1 states minus the post-1972 change in turnout for the non-EDR states.

[b] Entries are the percentage of nonvoters converted to voters based on the net effect of EDR. See the text for a discussion of at-risk effects.

[c] Entries in this row compare change in turnout from the period 1960–72 in the EDR states to changes in turnout over the same period in non-Southern, non-EDR states. Turnout figures used in this row are actual aggregate turnout figures from public sources (not reported turnout from the Current Population Survey); see appendix 4.2 for details.

However, it is important to realize that these are results about *groups* of voters, not inferences about individuals. While the adoption of EDR may result in a larger percentage increase in turnout among persons in the second income quintile than the fifth income quintile, that does *not* mean that a given individual in the second quintile is more likely to vote because of EDR than is a given individual in the fifth quintile. One reason for the lower percentage-point increase for the fifth quintile is that there are simply not many nonvoting persons in the fifth quintile available to become voters—that is, to be receptive to the treatment of EDR.

Prior to the introduction of EDR we can think of the nonvoters as the people at risk of being converted to voters via the treatment of EDR. The eighth column of table 4.3 gives the impact of EDR on the at-risk population of citizens among any group. This is the set of people who could be converted to voters based on the availability of EDR. We can think of this as an individual-level average treatment effect. The at-risk effect is really an individual-level effect; this gives the increased likelihood that a single nonvoting person would become a voter based on adoption of EDR. These are the estimates that provide the most direct evidence regarding individual differences in the effects of electoral reforms across demographic subgroups.

Consider aggregate turnout first. In 1972, aggregate reported turnout was 69.9 percent in EDR states; thus, 31.1 percent of citizens were not voting. These are the citizens who were at risk to be converted to voters by EDR. Since EDR had a net impact of 4.5 percentage points on turnout, the effect on at-risk voters was that 4.5 out of 31.1 were converted to voters by EDR. Thus, the effect on at-risk voters was 15.0 percent (i.e., $4.53 \div 31.1$). In other words, between one out of six and one out of seven nonvoters was converted to voting via EDR.

Now consider the at-risk effects for the different quintiles. If we look at the last column in table 4.3 we see that persons in quintile 5 were slightly *more* likely to take advantage of EDR (15.1 percent) than were citizens in quintile 2 (14.6 percent). Thus, the increased net group turnout effect of EDR for quintiles 2 and 3 over quintiles 4 and 5 is *not* because any individual person in income quintiles 2 or 3 is more likely to take advantage of EDR than any individual person in income quintile 4 or 5. It is simply because there are more persons eligible for the treatment. For the purpose of understanding the effect of EDR on income bias in turnout, the net group effect is what we care about. But if we want to understand individual behavior, it is the at-risk effect that we need to look at.

The next four rows in table 4.3 give the change in turnout for persons of different levels of education. For citizens with different levels of education, we see the largest net group effect for the middle two groups:

aggregate turnout of citizens with a high school degree or some college goes up by 7.6 and 4.3 percentage points, respectively, while turnout of those with college degrees or higher barely changes. For the least educated, those with less than a high school degree, aggregate turnout only rose 3.0 percentage points. In the last column of the table, we see huge differences between the at-risk effect on individuals in the bottom group and the at-risk effect on individuals in the two middle groups. Whereas 7.4 percent of those eligible in the bottom group become voters through EDR, fully 24.7 percent and 22.5 percent of previously nonvoting members of the middle education group become voters. This challenges previous assertions that people with low levels of education do not vote because the process is too confusing for them. Here we see that a change designed to make registration easier is more likely to be taken advantage of by non-voters with a high school education than by nonvoters without a high school education.

The next four rows of table 4.3 give the corresponding values of people in different age groups. In contrast to the relatively small variation in the net group effect of EDR we see across socioeconomic classes, we see stark differences across age groups: younger citizens receive a much greater benefit from EDR than do older voters. Whereas the aggregate turnout of eighteen- to twenty-four-year-olds rose 11.9 percentage points based on the adoption of EDR, we cannot even observe a positive effect for those ages sixty-one through seventy-five, and the net group effects decrease as we look at older citizens.[9] These comparisons hold for both the net group benefit of EDR being larger for younger than older age groups, *and* for the at-risk effect being largest for younger individuals. Younger nonvoters are simply much more likely to become voters from EDR than are older nonvoters.

Table 4.4 reports similar analyses for the wave 2 EDR states (Idaho, New Hampshire, and Wyoming). These states adopted EDR between 1992 and 1996. Here the results are much less impressive. There has in fact been a decrease in turnout of 3 percentage points in the elections since adoption of EDR for the wave 2 states, and a similar decrease of 3.1 percentage points for the non-EDR states during this period. This suggests a net group EDR effect of just 0.1 percentage points. Of course, these are small states, but more important while they were adopting EDR, the non-EDR states were following the mandates of the NVRA and adopting other reforms intended to increase turnout. Thus, the correct

9. Note, however, 1972 was the first election following adoption of the twenty-sixth Amendment which gave eighteen-year-olds the right to vote, so the comparisons at the very bottom of the age distribution should be interpreted with caution.

Table 4.4. The Effect of the Adoption of Election Day Registration on Turnout (Wave 2 EDR States).

	EDR Wave 2 States			Non-EDR States			Net EDR Group Effect[a]	At-Individual risk Effect[b]
	1972–1992	1996–2008	Increase, post-EDR	1972–1992	1996–2008	Increase, same period		
Aggregate CPS[c]	67.3	64.3	–3.0	64.1	61.0	–3.1	0.1	0.4
Income—1st Quintile	54.2	49.8	–4.5	49.8	48.2	–1.6	–2.9	–6.3
Income—2nd Quintile	63.5	59.8	–3.6	57.4	57.7	0.2	–3.9	–10.6
Income—3rd Quintile	67.1	67.0	–0.1	64.1	63.8	–0.3	0.1	0.4
Income—4th Quintile	74.2	73.1	–1.1	71.1	70.5	–0.6	–0.5	–1.9
Income—5th Quintile	76.3	81.0	4.8	78.6	77.0	–1.6	6.4	27.2
Education—Less than High School	51.5	40.2	–11.4	48.8	38.7	–10.1	–1.3	–2.6
High School Grad	62.7	55.5	–7.2	61.6	53.2	–8.4	1.2	3.1
Some College	73.3	68.4	–4.9	71.7	65.6	–6.1	1.2	4.7
College Grad and Above	87.9	83.6	–4.2	85.0	79.1	–5.8	1.6	13.0
Age 18–24	41.7	44.1	2.4	44.4	40.4	–3.9	6.3	10.9
Age 25–30	56.3	54.5	–1.8	55.4	49.7	–5.7	3.9	8.9
Age 46–60	78.9	73.4	–5.5	73.5	68.5	–5.0	–0.5	–2.6
Age 61–75	82.0	74.6	–7.4	75.4	73.0	–2.4	–5.0	–27.7
Single	55.4	52.6	–2.7	53.7	51.0	–2.7	0.0	–0.0
Married	72.9	71.9	–1.0	70.1	68.5	–1.6	0.5	2.0

Notes: Entries are computed by the authors using self-reported turnout from the Current Population Survey, or increase in reported turnout, for states that adopted EDR between 1992 and 1996, or for states that have never adopted EDR. The wave 2 EDR states are: Idaho, New Hampshire, and Wyoming.
[a] Entries are the post-1992 change in turnout for the three EDR wave 2 states minus the post-1992 change in turnout for the non-EDR states.
[b] Entries are the percentage of nonvoters converted to voters based on net effect of EDR. See the text for a discussion of at-risk effects.

inference here is not that EDR had no effect for these states but that it did not have a substantially larger effect than did the adoption of NVRA provisions in the other states.[10]

In table 4.5 we report the effect of EDR for the wave 3 states (Iowa, Montana, and North Carolina), which first used EDR in the 2008 presidential election. Obviously these results are based on only one election, and generalizing from them should be done with extreme caution. But these states did experience an increase of 1.5 percentage points relative to the non-EDR states.

We next turn to an analysis of early voting and absentee voting. As we documented in table 4.2, states adopted these two reforms over an extended period. The adoption of election reforms by so many states over such a long period makes it reasonably straightforward to determine the impact of the reforms. For each state that adopted no-fault absentee voting between the years 1976 and 2008, we looked at the change in turnout for the state from the election immediately preceding adoption of no-fault absentee voting to the election immediately following its adoption.[11] To control for any nationwide changes in turnout between elections, we also compute the matching change in turnout between the same election years for the set of states that did not change their no-fault absentee voting laws between the relevant elections. Thus, in the election of 1980, we compare the change in turnout of the three states that adopted no-fault absentee voting between 1976 and 1980 to the change in turnout of the forty-seven states that did not alter their absentee voting laws between 1976 and 1980.

Table 4.6 presents these results. For 1980, the states that adopted no-fault absentee voting had an average increase in turnout of 0.2 percentage points, while the forty seven states that did not adopt no-fault absentee voting between 1976 and 1980 had an average *decrease* in turnout of 0.4 percentage points. Thus, the difference between them, or the estimate of the impact of adoption of no-fault absentee voting, was 0.6 percentage points. We then compute a weighted average of these comparisons for each election from 1976 to 2008, and estimate the impact of adoption of no-fault absentee voting to be 1.4 percentage points.[12]

---

10. We also note that these three states appear to have had relatively high registration rates prior to adoption of EDR. Thus, the impact of adoption of EDR could be mitigated, though we would not expect it to be zero.
11. Since our initial year of data is 1972, we do not know if states with no-fault absentee voting in 1972 also had it in 1968, so we cannot use turnout in 1972 as a measure of the impact of adoption of no-fault absentee voting. Also note that we are only considering elections in presidential years. So for a state that adopted no-fault absentee voting in 1979, the election preceding adoption would be 1976, not 1978.
12. We weight each year by the number of states adopting no-fault absentee voting for that year.

Table 4.5. The Effect of the Adoption of Election Day Registration on Turnout (Wave 3 EDR States).

	EDR Wave 3 States			Non-EDR States			Net Group EDR Effect[a]	At-risk Effect[b]
	1972–2004	2008	Increase, post, EDR	1972–2004	2008	Increase, same period		
Aggregate CPS[c]	65.2	67.7	2.2	62.6	63.3	0.7	1.5	4.3
Income—1st Quintile	49.9	53.3	3.4	48.6	53.0	4.4	-1.0	-2.0
Income—2nd Quintile	61.4	68.0	6.6	57.1	61.5	4.4	2.2	5.6
Income—3rd Quintile	67.9	74.1	6.1	63.5	67.7	4.2	2.0	6.2
Income—4th Quintile	74.9	78.7	3.8	70.5	73.7	3.3	0.5	2.1
Income—5th Quintile	81.2	80.5	-0.1	77.7	79.1	1.3	-2.1	-11.2
Education—Less than High School	46.5	38.9	-7.6	45.0	38.7	-6.3	-1.3	-2.5
High School Grad	61.5	60.0	-1.4	58.3	54.5	-3.7	2.3	6.0
Some College	73.3	71.2	-2.1	69.1	67.4	-1.7	-0.4	-1.6
College Grad and Above	86.0	83.7	-2.3	82.7	80.1	-2.4	0.2	1.2
Age 18-24	45.3	52.8	7.5	42.1	46.8	4.7	2.7	5.0
Age 25-30	54.0	60.3	6.3	52.7	54.2	1.6	4.7	10.3
Age 46-60	73.7	72.3	-1.4	71.6	68.8	-2.8	1.4	5.3
Age 61-75	74.6	76.9	2.3	74.4	73.2	-1.2	3.5	13.8
Single	53.5	58.3	4.8	52.2	54.8	2.6	2.2	4.7
Married	71.9	74.6	2.6	69.3	70.2	1.0	1.7	6.0

Notes: Entries are computed by the authors using self-reported turnout from the Current Population Survey, or increase in reported turnout, for states that adopted EDR between 2004 and 2008, or for states that have never adopted EDR. The wave 3 EDR states are: Iowa, Montana, and North Carolina.
[a] Entries are the post-2004 change in turnout for the three EDR wave 3 states minus the post-2004 change in turnout for the non-EDR states.
[b] Entries are the percentage of nonvoters converted to voters based on the net effect of EDR. See the text for a discussion of at-risk effects.

Table 4.6. The Effect of the Adoption of No-Fault Absentee Voting, 1972–2008.

Year[a]	Change in Aggregate Turnout		
	States Adopting No-Fault Absentee Voting[b]	Other States[c]	Difference[d]
1976 (1)	−3.3	−1.0	−2.3
1980 (3)	0.2	−0.4	0.6
1984 (0)	—	—	—
1988 (1)	−2.1	−2.1	0.1
1992 (6)	6.5	5.3	1.2
1996 (5)	−5.2	−7.0	1.8
2000 (6)	4.0	2.2	1.8
2004 (2)	9.4	6.0	3.4
2008 (3)	2.4	1.2	1.2
Weighted Average:			1.4
Pre and Postadoption Comparison[e]	1.6	1.6	0.0

Notes: See appendix 4.2 for data sources.
[a] Numbers in parentheses are the number of states adopting no-fault absentee voting in that year.
[b] Entries are the average change in actual turnout from the previous presidential election to the current (row) election in those states adopting no-fault absentee voting between the previous presidential election and the current (row) year.
[c] Entries are the average change in actual turnout from the previous presidential election to the current (row) election in those states that had no change in their absentee voting laws between the two elections.
[d] Entries are the difference in change in turnout experienced by states adopting no-fault absentee voting between elections and those states that did not change absentee voting laws between elections.
[e] See text for explanation of pre- and postadoption comparison involving all election results from 1972–2008.

We performed an identical analysis for the adoption of early voting by the states. The results are reported in table 4.7. Here the weighted average of the effects over the years is only a 0.4 percentage-point difference in turnout between states adopting no-excuse early voting and the comparison set of states. Thus these two sets of analyses suggest that the states adopting no-fault absentee voting and those adopting no-excuse early voting had small increases in turnout relative to those states that did not.

These comparisons are very direct analyses of the effect of no-fault absentee voting and early voting. We are using all the data from the election immediately preceding a state's adoption of early or absentee voting and the election immediately following the state's adoption of early or absentee voting. The values we present are then basic statements

Table 4.7. The Effect of the Adoption of Early Voting, 1972–2008.

Year[a]	Change in Aggregate Turnout		
	States Adopting Early Voting[b]	Other States[c]	Difference[d]
1976 (1)	−9.1	−0.9	−8.2
1980 (1)	2.1	−0.4	2.5
1984 (0)	—	—	—
1988 (2)	−1.6	−2.2	0.6
1992 (2)	8.2	5.3	2.8
1996 (3)	−4.8	−7.0	2.2
2000 (8)	2.6	2.4	0.2
2004 (5)	7.1	6.0	1.1
2008 (4)	0.5	1.3	−0.9
Weighted Average:			0.4
Pre- and Postadoption Comparison[e]	1.3	3.4	−2.1

Notes: See appendix 4.2 for data sources.

[a] Numbers in parentheses are the number of states adopting no-excuse early voting in that year.

[b] Entries are the average change in actual turnout from the previous presidential election for those states adopting no-excuse early voting between the previous presidential election and the current (row) year.

[c] Entries are the average change in actual turnout from the previous presidential election for those states that had no change in their early voting laws between the two elections.

[d] Entries are the difference in change in turnout experienced by states adopting no-excuse early voting between elections, and those states that did not change early voting laws between elections.

[e] See the text for an explanation of the pre- and postadoption comparison involving all election results from 1972 to 2008.

of fact: states adopting absentee voting and states adopting early voting experienced an increase in turnout in the elections immediately following compared to states that did not adopt these reforms.

However, while the comparisons we report above are perfectly valid, we note that they are limited in that they only utilize one pair of elections per state that adopted a reform: the election immediately prior to reform, and the election immediately after the reform. Since either of those elections may have been unusual for the state, we might ask a more comprehensive question: if we compare all elections from 1972 to the year prior to adoption, to all elections from the year of adoption to 2008, was the increase in turnout higher for those states that adopted no-fault absentee voting (or early voting) than for those states that did not adopt these measures in the entire period?

Thus, for each state that adopted no-fault absentee voting, we calculated average turnout for the state for each election since 1972 *prior* to adoption, and for each election *since* adoption of no-fault absentee voting up to 2008. We look at the change in average turnout for the state between the two periods—preadoption versus postadoption—and compare it to the change in turnout *averaged over those same two periods* for the set of states that never adopted no-fault absentee voting. We performed an identical analysis for states that adopted early voting. The results of these calculations are reported in the final rows of tables 4.6 and 4.7.

Here we get slightly different answers. Over the entire period from 1972 to 2008, the states that adopted no-fault absentee voting during this period had an average turnout increase of 1.6 percentage points, considering all preadoption elections versus all postadoption elections. However, over the same period the control group of states also had a turnout increase of 1.6 percentage points when we compare the same turnout in the same time periods. For early voting, the comparable figures are a 1.3 percentage-point increase for the states that adopted early voting, but a 3.4 percentage-point increase over the same time period for states that did not adopt early voting.

Thus, either absentee voting and early voting have led to initial increases in turnout that then subside, or they simply have not led to any increases in turnout in the states that have adopted them. Again, this is based on looking at all the votes cast and not cast, in presidential elections since 1972. Thus we can concur with conventional wisdom that suggests that the vast majority of votes cast by either of these methods simply represent voters switching their mode of casting a ballot, not additional votes.

An additional observation we would add to these results is that while we have shown that states adopting no-fault absentee voting and early voting did *not* experience an increase in turnout relative to states that did not adopt these reforms, this does not answer the counterfactual question as to what would have happened had these states *not* adopted no-fault absentee voting or early voting. While it is tempting to infer that no-fault absentee voting and no-excuse early voting do not raise turnout, it may be the case that the set of states adopting them were not random, and that other factors were at work to depress turnout in those states, thus masking the impact of the reforms.

The simple conjecture is that it is possible that the states adopting these reforms did so in order to combat other trends negatively affecting turnout. Or, in a less nefarious conjecture, it is possible that the states adopting these reforms may have been states that had less competitive elections postadoption, or changes in other turnout-related characteristics, leading to lower turnout. The data presented here simply do not control for other things that could be happening to affect turnout in both states that adopted and states that did not adopt these reforms. Thus, to draw a causal inference about the effect of these reforms on turnout, we next present a cross-sectional time-series analysis to control for observable characteristics of the states—such as demographic characteristics, other elections laws, and competitiveness of elections—that were changing over this period.

4.5 Cross-Sectional Time Series Analysis of Aggregate Turnout

Our second analytical approach is to estimate a multivariable cross-sectional time series model of turnout where we condition the effect of the institutional changes on observable characteristics of the states known to affect turnout. By including year-specific fixed effects and state-specific fixed effects we are only measuring the impact of variables that change over time in the model while allowing for unobserved factors (incorporated in the year fixed effects) leading to secular changes in turnout for each year. Assuming our model is well specified, we will have measures of the causal impact of the institutional variables of interest on turnout.[13]

We estimate aggregate turnout in each election as a function of aggregate turnout in the previous presidential election, the presence or absence of the five registration or election administration characteristics of interest (EDR, absentee voting, early voting, the number of days before the election that registration closes, and whether voter registration is available in motor vehicle offices), demographic characteristics of the state, and measures of electoral context. To condition on the demographic characteristics of the state we include the state per capita income, the age distribution of the citizens as measured by the proportion of citizens in each of six age categories, and the education distribution of the state as measured by the proportion of citizens in each of four

---

13. We attempted to use this methodology to estimate the effects of the reforms on different demographic groups, and we explain the result of that separately below. Our estimation strategy for the group-specific effects differs from previous research in that we estimate the turnout rates of different subgroups separately rather than relying on model specifications that include interaction terms between the demographic characteristic of interest (e.g., registration income) and the electoral reform of interest (e.g, registration closing).

education categories. To condition on the electoral context, we include a measure for the closeness of the presidential race in the state, and dummy variables for the presence of a gubernatorial or senate race in the state, as well as measures of the closeness of those races.[14]

To allow for the effect of EDR to be contingent on how soon before election day registration closes, we include an interaction term between the two variables. We expect EDR to have less of an effect in states where registration has closed well before the election than in states where registration is available until very close to the election.[15] We also allow for the effect of early voting to depend on the length of the early voting period by including the length of the period.

Thus, we estimate a model of the following form, where s and t index state and time, respectively:

$$
\begin{aligned}
T_{s,t} = {} & \beta_0 + \beta_1 T_{s,t-1} \\
& + \beta_2 \, \text{DaysToClosing}_{s,t} + \beta_3 \, \text{EDR}_{s,t} \\
& + \beta_{23} \, (\text{EDR}_{s,t} * \text{DaysToClosing}_{s,t}) \\
& + \beta_4 \, \text{NoFaultAbsentee}_{s,t} \\
& + \beta_5 \, \text{EarlyVoting}_{s,t} + \beta_6 \, \text{EVPeriod}_{s,t} \\
& + \sum_{d=1}^{d=3} \beta_{7d} \, \text{EducDUMMIES}_{d,s,t} + \sum_{d=1}^{d-5} \beta_{8d} \, \text{AgeDUMMIES}_{d,s,t} \\
& + \beta_9 \, \text{MeanPerCapitaIncome}_{s,t} + \beta_{10} \, \text{PresMargin}_{s,t} \\
& + \beta_{11} \, \text{SenMargin}_{s,t} + \beta_{12} \, \text{GovMargin}_{s,t} \\
& + \Gamma \, (\text{StateDummies}_{s}) \\
& + \Psi \, (\text{YearDummies}_{t}) \\
& + \epsilon_{s,t}
\end{aligned}
$$

We estimated the model above using data for turnout in the fifty states from 1972 to 2008. We measured aggregate state turnout

14. We measure closeness of an election as the reciprocal of the absolute value of the difference between the two-party vote shares. For closeness of senate and gubernatorial elections when there was no election, we assign a closeness value corresponding to an extremely uncompetitive race. We experimented with different values of closeness for non-races, and the results are not sensitive to the value chosen.

15. A common misperception is that states with EDR have no closing of registration (i.e., a closing period of zero). That is not the case. States with EDR typically close normal registration anywhere from seven to fifteen days *prior* to election day, and then allow unregistered persons to register on election day itself.

as the proportion of the voting-age citizen population casting votes for the highest office. Since turnout is bounded between 0 and 1, we used the log-odds ratio of turnout as the dependent variable, and we compute panel corrected standard errors. In table 4.8 we report the parameter estimates for the model; we do not report the estimated coefficients for the year or state fixed effects.

Because of the inclusion of several interactive terms, and the nature of the model with log-odds of turnout as the dependent variable, we do not discuss these coefficients but instead focus our discussion on the

Table 4.8. Cross-Sectional Time Series Model of Turnout by State, 1972–2008.

	Coefficient	T-statistic
Log-odds Turnout (t − 1)	0.553**	(6.74)
Registration Closing Period	−0.0018*	(−1.81)
Early Voting	−0.075**	(−2.54)
Early Voting Period	0.0028**	(2.15)
No-fault Absentee Voting	0.056**	(3.38)
Election Day Registration (EDR)	−0.025	(−0.38)
EDR × Registration Closing Period	0.0049	(1.45)
DMV Registration	0.001	(0.04)
State Per-Capita Income	−4.08e-06	(−0.59)
Proportion of Citizens Age 25–30	0.258	(0.38)
Proportion of Citizens Age 31–45	0.843	(1.64)
Proportion of Citizens Age 46–60	0.429	(0.76)
Proportion of Citizenss Age 61–75	0.758	(1.37)
Proportion of Citizens Age 76–89	0.518	(0.70)
Proportion of Citizens with High School Degree	0.366	(1.40)
Proportion of Citizens with Some College	−0.049	(−0.14)
Proportion of Citizens with College Plus	0.837**	(2.42)
Closeness of Presidential Election	0.0035	(0.67)
Closeness of Gubernatorial Election	0.0055	(0.79)
Closeness of Senate Election	−0.0000	(−0.05)
Gubernatorial Election in State	0.050	(1.40)
Senate Election in State	0.013*	(1.92)
Constant	−0.548	(−0.98)
Observations	450	
R^2	0.92	

Notes: Table entries are cross-sectional time series coefficient estimates of voter turnout by state in each year, where the dependent variable is the log-odds of turnout. We use panel-corrected standard errors and report the associated t-statistics. State and year fixed effects are included but not reported here. See appendix 4.2: for data sources.
*p < 0.01; **p < 0.05.

first differences below. However, note that the coefficients generally have the expected sign. The specification we use implies that the impact of early voting is contingent on the length of the early voting period, and that the impact of EDR depends upon the number of days to closing of registration.

According to the estimates in table 4.8, an early voting period of twenty-seven days is required for early voting to increase turnout. Also note that while we found no differences in aggregate turnout based on absentee voting using the difference-in-difference estimates reported in table 4.6, in the multivariable model we see that when controlling for the state-level characteristics listed above, no-fault absentee voting has a statistically significant, positive impact on turnout.

To gauge the magnitude of the effects of the institutional reforms, we estimated the long-run impact on turnout in a state with a 50 percent turnout rate if the state adopted a reform, and all other variables were held constant. Thus, we incorporate both the immediate impact of the change in each institutional reform on turnout as well as the long-run impact picked up through the lagged log-odds turnout term in the model. These first differences are presented in table 4.9. These are the most precise estimates we have of the real causal effect of these reforms, they make use of data from all fifty states over ten presidential elections. And these are not based on samples, but on actual recorded votes.

According to our estimates, adoption of no-fault absentee voting leads to a 3.2 percentage-point increase in turnout. We note that this estimate is quite different from the conventional wisdom, which claims that absentee voting has had no appreciable impact on turnout. However, this finding, reflecting a more rigorous analytical approach than previous studies, suggests that no-fault absentee voting is one of—if not *the*—single most important of the changes made to election laws since the Civil Rights Act. We also note that this finding comports more with the reality of millions of votes cast via absentee voting than a finding that *all* of those votes would have been cast by other means if absentee voting were not available.

As reported in table 4.9, the adoption of early voting is estimated to lead to a 3.1 percentage-point increase in turnout if the early voting period were as long as forty-five days. Since this is a longer voting period than states allow, we have less confidence that early voting is actually increasing turnout. As we indicated above, our estimates suggest that a voting period of as long as twenty-seven days is required to see any positive effect of early voting.

Consistent with previous estimates on the effect of EDR, we estimate that EDR leads to an increase in turnout of 2.8 percentage points in a

Table 4.9. The Marginal Effect of Legal Reforms as Predictors of Turnout, 1972–2008.

Change in Law	Effect on Turnout	95% CI
Absentee Voting	3.2	[1.7, 5.1]
Early Voting with a 45-Day Period:	3.1	[−1.5, 8.1]
Registration Closing Period (10-Day Decrease, no EDR):	1.0	[0.1, 2.1]
EDR (Registration Closing Period = 15 days):	2.8	[−0.8, 6.5]
EDR (Registration Closing Period = 29 days):	6.6	[1.1, 12.3]

Note: Entries are the long-run expected percentage-point increase in turnout for the adoption of the indicated reform, with 95 percent confidence intervals in brackets. Estimates are based on the model reported in table 4.8.

state with a fifteen-day registration closing period.[16] The estimated effect would be higher in states with longer registration closing periods, and lower in states with shorter registration closing periods. These estimates bolster our earlier conclusion that the adoption of EDR does indeed increase turnout.

Finally we estimate that a ten-day decrease in the length of the registration closing period itself would lead to a 1.0 percentage-point increase in turnout (for states without EDR). Again, this is broadly consistent with previous work going all the way back to Wolfinger and Rosenstone (1980) that has suggested that the length of the registration period is crucial to turnout. Registration is a prerequisite for voting, and having to register further in advance of election day predictably decreases turnout.

We also estimated our cross-sectional time series model on data disaggregated by demographic groups. Here the unit of analysis is turnout *of persons with particular demographic characteristics* by state and year. We did this for persons in each of five quintile groups, each of four education categories, and each of six age groups. We were not able to distinguish between the impact of the reforms on different groups with any reasonable level of precision (though it does appear that EDR is more important for younger voters than for older voters).[17]

16. These estimates are based on the adoption of EDR by all nine current EDR states.
17. The CSTS model we are using is saturated with year and state-level fixed effects, making it difficult to get statistically significant estimates of the parameters of interest for the electoral reforms we are studying (e.g., early voting, etc.). We also attempted to estimate an individual level model that included an imputed value for the likelihood that

4.6 Conclusion

Our analyses in this chapter have focused primarily on three different electoral reforms—EDR, absentee voting, and early voting—and advances what we know about them in important ways. First, we provided a comprehensive set of tests regarding the effects of the adoption of EDR over the past forty years and concluded that EDR has an important effect on turnout in the states that adopt it.

Second, we estimated these effects by considering the impact of EDR on the entire state population, but also on the at-risk population—the set of nonvoters. This is a major modification to prior approaches to estimating the impact of electoral reforms. In order to understand the impact of electoral reforms it is important to develop an understanding of the behavioral mechanism through which they operate. Authors of previous work have inferred that larger net effects of EDR on the turnout of people with low levels of education mean that such people have a harder time dealing with registration barriers than people with higher levels of education. However, our difference-in-difference analysis as presented in table 4.3 suggests that the net effect of EDR on the probability of poorly educated individuals voting is not larger than for highly educated individuals, *and* that the individual-level at-risk effect of EDR on poorly educated individuals is substantially less than it is for individuals in the two middle education categories. The evidence in table 4.3 suggests that inability to deal with registration barriers is *not* what accounts for the lower turnout of poorly educated individuals, given that a higher proportion of nonvoting higher-educated people become voters when the advance registration restriction is lifted than do nonvoting lower-educated people. But we caution that further analysis using a multivariable approach is required to confirm this.

Third, confirming differences in the impacts of EDR in the wave 1, wave 2, and wave 3 states, our results suggest that variation in implementation of EDR, as well as variation in the strategic use of EDR by the parties and candidates, can determine how effective EDR is at increasing turnout.

Our empirical evidence also strongly refutes most earlier research on the effect of absentee voting. Identifying a positive, substantial, and statistically significant effect of no-fault absentee voting adds substantially to what we know about electoral reforms and their effects.

---

the respondent voted in the previous election to take advantage of the intervention of the state law change and attempted to compare behavior before and after the change. This also did not yield sufficiently precise estimates to distinguish between demographic groups, though we think the method could prove fruitful in future work.

Our finding on the effect of early voting is more tenuous. Early voting could increase turnout, given a long enough voting period. However, the length of the period required suggests that previous scholars who inferred that early voters are individuals who simply shifted the day on which they voted—rather than new voters who cast early ballots instead of staying home and not voting—may have been correct. The sensitivity of the result to the length of the early voting period suggests that we may need to more accurately model other aspects of implementation, such as the number and location of polling places available, to have a better understanding of the impact of early voting on turnout.

Our evidence also demonstrates the importance of state laws on the closing of registration prior to the election. Previous research on the effects of registration laws yielded fairly consistent conclusions: the longer the period, the lower the turnout, but this cross-sectional research could not make strong claims as to the causal relationship between closing days and turnout. Our analyses provide original and persuasive evidence showing that the relationship between the length of the registration period and turnout is a true causal effect. By isolating the effects of the length of the registration closing period on turnout in a well-specified model with data over time and including a variety of more contemporary reforms, we are far more confident that we have identified a true causal effect of these laws on turnout, thus validating inferences drawn from earlier, more limited, analyses.

Our findings suggest where those interested in increasing voter turnout might find some hope. Increasing the number of states with no-fault absentee voting, decreasing the registration closing period to fifteen days, and increasing the number of states with EDR could all increase turnout in presidential elections. Whether voters, candidates, or parties think that the efforts devoted to accomplishing these policies changes are worth it or not is, of course, a different question.

Taken together, our results confirm the cost part of a cost and benefit theory of voting: if the cost of voting is lowered, more people will vote. This does not contradict the claim that many people will not vote even if costs are zero. Nor does it suggest that the entire difference between the level of turnout in the United States and the level of turnout in other countries can be explained by differences in the cost of registering and voting. But we would be foolish to deny that costs influence the turnout decision.

We would also be foolish to ignore the *benefit* part of the cost and benefit theory of voting, which we consider more fully in chapter 5.

Appendix 4.1: Voter Registration and Election Law Data Set

Our data set on voter registration and election administration in the states, 1972–2008, was made possible with a generous grant from the Pew Charitable Trusts to Daniel Tokaji, Nathan Cemenska, Jan Leighley, and Jonathan Nagler. The data set of laws is available from the Pew Trusts as both a spreadsheet and a Stata document. The details that follow are drawn from our 2009 report (Cemenska et al. 2009).

Our documentation of state laws included whether election day registration was available in a state; how many days prior to the election registration closed; and whether voter registration was available in motor vehicle agencies. In addition, we focused on two types of nonprecinct voting available: absentee voting and in-person early voting. These terms are sometimes used interchangeably by policy makers as well as academics, and state legislative statutes governing their availability sometimes overlap as well. Consequently, it was necessary to first clearly define each term so that states could be accurately categorized on various dimensions of these policies. We define *absentee voting* as the option of requesting, completing, and returning a ballot prior to election day, and being able to do so without being present in person at an election office or precinct.

We define *in-person early voting* as a one-stop transaction in which the voter requests a ballot, completes it, and returns it. If any portion of this three-part transaction does not occur simultaneously, or if it occurs at another location, it is not in-person early voting by our definition. Therefore, states were only classified as allowing early voting if the relevant statutory language explicitly permitted the voter to complete the ballot in the presence of election officials. This definition may exclude some states in which early voting takes place where those operations are not explicitly described in state statutes. We use the terms *in-person early voting* and *early voting* interchangeably.

One case that often causes confusion in the use of the terms *absentee voting* and *early voting* is that of Oregon, which conducts all statewide elections primarily by mail (both ballot delivery and ballot returns). Because voting by mail can be done before election day and does not take place in traditional precincts, the state might be considered as having a form of early or absentee voting. In our data set, however, we code Oregon (like the other states) based on the above definitions of absentee and in-person early voting. Under these definitions, voting by mail is neither early nor absentee voting. Instead, in accordance with our definitions, we code Oregon's absentee and early voting rules based on state laws specific to those individuals who do not vote via the regular vote-by-mail system rules, for example, those individuals who will be away from their residence during the voting period.

The primary research method used to produce this data set was review of relevant state statutes and administrative codes (hereinafter referred to simply as laws) identified using standard search procedures in LexisNexis and Westlaw. The goal was to identify the contours of the laws according to their plain meaning, even if other sources suggested that actual practice may sometimes deviate from that meaning. The review did not take into account any case law that might have interpreted these laws in a way that deviated from their plain meaning. We emphasize that the data we have collected are based entirely on state statutes and administrative law. We have no data on how state or local officials implement these state laws.

After identifying the relevant laws, researchers coded each state on fifty three variables associated with state absentee and early voting laws. For a description of each variable and its values, see Cemenska et al. (2009).

Appendix 4.2: Sources of State-Level Turnout and Demographic Data

For analyses that use state-level turnout data by a specific demographic group, we have aggregated reported turnout rates from U.S the Census Bureau's Current Population Survey. For overall state turnout rates we have relied on two sources. For the period 1972 through 1980 we use figures on turnout reported by the Congressional Research Service (Crocker 1996). We combine this with data for 1980 through 2008 with figures for turnout made available by Michael McDonald (2011). Splicing the two series together gives a value for turnout for highest office in each state, with the best available estimate of the citizen voting age population for 1980 through 2008 as the denominator, and an estimate of the voting-age population of the state as the denominator for 1972 and 1976. In analyzing the series where overlap was available, we do not think this is a significant source of error. In the one case in which we use data for the 1960–68 period, we also use aggregate turnout data reported by the CRS.

State-level demographic data was estimated from the Census Bureau Current Population Survey for each year (with 1976 interpolated).

Five

·· ·

Policy Choices and Turnout

A fundamental shift in the study of political participation since Wolfinger and Rosenstone's classic study (1980) has been to acknowledge the role of political elites in stimulating (or at times, depressing) voter turnout. Rosenstone and Hansen (2003) offered a theoretical interpretation of the role of elites in affecting turnout similar to that of the demographics model of turnout: in some circumstances political elites reduce or subsidize the costs of participating, and this is likely to increase turnout. Their evidence that the activities of party elites (such as contacting voters) and election characteristics (such as competitiveness) account for more than half of the decline of voter turnout since 1960 sustains their more fundamental claim: "Explanations of political involvement that have focused exclusively on the personal attributes of individual citizens—their demographic characteristics and political beliefs—have missed at least half the story" (2003, 213).[1]

Existing research has shown that contextual factors such as electoral competitiveness (Cox & Munger 1989) and unionization (Leighley & Nagler 2007) affect turnout. In this chapter we address a relatively overlooked aspect of this other half of the story: candidate position-taking in presidential elections. As Key (1966) famously observed, "Voters are not fools." But they are constrained by the electoral choices that they are offered. And it would be more foolish to sit out an election where the choices differ than to sit out an election in which the choices are not choices, but echoes.

1. A renewed wave of research focusing on field experiments has demonstrated anew the role of elite and nonelite contacting activity in stimulating turnout. See Green and Gerber (2008) for an introduction to this work.

Zipp (1985) was perhaps the first to empirically document the importance of candidates' relative policy positions as determinants of voter turnout, but little research has been done more recently to assess whether the choices that candidates offer voters in presidential elections matter. Consistent with a cost and benefit framework of voter turnout, we argue that individuals will be more likely to vote when offered more distinctive positions between the candidates. To test this claim, we add to our basic individual-level demographic model the relative policy positions of the leading presidential candidates in each election year from 1972 through 2008. These analyses demonstrate whether the choices elites offer to individuals matter as they decide to vote or not.

We also consider how these choices have changed over time, and whether the nature of the choices is equally important to the turnout decisions of people in different positions of the income distribution. That is, do the policy positions offered by elites have a larger influence on the turnout of poor people than rich people? Our evidence on this question allows us to determine whether the policy choices offered by candidates affect who votes as well as influence the representativeness of voters.

5.1 Policy Choices and the Costs and Benefits of Voting

Discussions of *why* elite activities and characteristics such as party competitiveness, union mobilization, and voter contact increase turnout typically emphasize how such factors reduce the costs associated with voting. More generally, most theoretical interpretations likewise focus almost exclusively on the costs rather than the benefits of voting. Certain demographic characteristics, such as higher levels of education and income, for example, are often interpreted as reducing information costs, while research on electoral reforms focusing on voter registration requirements and election administration frames these legal restrictions as increasing the costs of voting.

In a review of some of this work, Aldrich (1993) suggests that one of the fundamental assumptions motivating many rational choice models of voter turnout—that voter turnout is an example of a collective goods problem—approaches being incorrect. Or, at least, he portrays voter turnout as so low-cost and so low-benefit that it likely takes little in the way of reduced costs *or* enhanced benefits to get voters to the polls.

Aldrich suggests the reason turnout appears higher in close elections is that strategic politicians invest more heavily in close races, and that citizens respond to these mobilization efforts.[2] Most aggregate-level studies,

---

2. See Jackman (1993) for a commentary on Aldrich's essay.

and many individual-level studies, report significant effects of competitiveness on voter turnout (see, for example, Cox & Munger [1989], Endersby, Galatas, & Rackaway [2002], Leighley & Nagler [1992b], and Rosenstone and Hansen 2003]). But as Aldrich suggests, the causal mechanism remains uncertain: do competitive races yield high turnout because voters calculate that they are more likely to be decisive in such contests, or because elites invest more heavily in mobilization activities?

Discussions of benefits as integral to the decision to vote are few, in part due to the basic logic of the calculus of voting, where one's benefit must be discounted by the probability that one casts the decisive ballot; because this probability is so small, the benefits approach zero (Riker & Ordeshook 1968). Alternatively, several different types of psychological benefits associated with voting, such as feelings of civic duty or partisan loyalty, as well as benefits associated with the social rewards from voting, would not depend on the perceived probability of being pivotal. Yet interpretations of these factors as benefits are often discounted for they seem to be posthoc adjustments to the formal model.

Several scholars, however, have considered a different type of benefit in empirical analyses of voter turnout: the choices that are available to voters, as represented by the candidates. Zipp (1985) argues that individuals' decisions to *not* vote likely reflect the choices that they are offered as opposed to any particular individual characteristics typically used to explain not showing up at the polls.[3] Zipp's empirical analysis of voter turnout in presidential elections from 1968 to 1980 confirms this argument, as do numerous more recent studies of turnout in legislative elections (see, for example, Adams, Dow, & Merrill [2006], Adams & Merrill [2003]; Ashenfelter & Kelley [1975]; and Plane & Gershtenson [2004].

Zipp conceptualizes individuals' distance from candidates in each presidential election as resulting in alienation (i.e., the distance between the individual's preferred policy position and the closest candidate's policy position) and indifference (i.e., the difference in distance between the respondent's preferred policy position and the policy position of each of the candidates). Estimating cross-sectional models of turnout consisting of demographic characteristics along with measures of issue-specific alienation and indifference, Zipp finds that both alienation and indifference significantly influence individuals' decisions to vote. Though which particular issue-based measures of indifference and alienation are significant varies each election year, he concludes that indifference has a slightly larger effect on turnout than alienation.

---

3. Implicitly Zipp assumes, as do we, that voters are behaving as if they are pivotal, or as if they are not completely discounting the likelihood of being pivotal.

Using similar measures of candidate issue positions in the 1988–92 Senate elections, Plane and Gershtenson (2004) find that individuals are less likely to vote when they feel indifferent to or alienated from candidates' ideological positions. They report that alienation has a greater potential effect on citizens' turnout decisions than does indifference. Analyzing presidential elections from 1980 to 1988, Adams, Dow, and Merrill (2006) suggest that the effect of alienation on turnout is slightly larger than the effect of indifference on turnout.

Following Zipp (1985) we argue that an individual will be more likely to vote when candidates take policy positions providing the voter with more distinct choices, and when candidates offer policy choices that more closely match the individual's preferences. The hypothesized relationships we examine are the same as what these previous studies have examined. First, when one candidates' policy positions are more appealing to an individual than the other candidates' policy positions, the resulting perceived policy difference increases the probability of voting. Second, when candidates' policy positions are distant from those of the individual, then the resulting perceived policy alienation of the individual decreases the probability of voting.

Our evidence in this chapter begins with descriptive data on individuals' perceptions of candidates' policy positions, and how these change over time and vary by income group. We then report multivariable tests of the relationships between these perceived policy choices and voter turnout. Our interest in evaluating possible differences across income groups is motivated by our broader interest in understanding the political consequences of economic inequality. An increase in economic inequality is likely accompanied by an increasing divergence in the economic needs and priorities of poorer and wealthier individuals, and this divergence might well be reflected in increasingly distinctive policy preferences across income groups (Schlozman et al. 1999). A critically important empirical question over a period of increasing economic inequality, then, is whether citizens both poor and rich are offered equally satisfying policy options by presidential candidates as they decide whether to vote or not.

5.2 Policy Choices: Conceptualization and Measurement

In our analyses below, we use data from the American National Election Study to test the effects of policy choices on voter turnout in each presidential election year from 1972 to 2008. Our measures of policy choices are similar to those used by Zipp (1985), who derived measures of indifference and alienation based on the individual's self-reported policy positions on 7-point scales on a variety of issues (e.g., urban unrest, the Vietnam War, government guarantee of jobs, minority rights, the role of women, and ideology) compared to the individual's perception (i.e., placement) of each candidate's location on the same set of 7-point scales. Our analysis includes measures based on ideology and the government guaranteeing jobs issue.

To avoid confusion with psychological approaches to alienation and mass political behavior, we have adopted different terminology for the policy-based concepts of indifference and alienation introduced by Zipp.[4] Instead of using the term *indifference* we use the term *perceived policy difference* (PPD), and instead of using *alienation*, we use *perceived policy alienation* (PPA).

Our measures of perceived policy difference and perceived policy alienation are based on the two 7-point scales that are available in every presidential election year between 1972 and 2008: ideology and government guaranteeing jobs. For each topic, respondents are asked to identify their preferred position on the 7-point scale. They are also asked to identify the positions of the presidential candidates. The two endpoints of the ideology scale are "extremely liberal" and "extremely conservative"; the two endpoints for the government guaranteeing jobs scale are "Some people feel that the government in Washington should see to it that every person has a job and a good standard of living" and "Others think that the government should just let each person get ahead on his/her own." (For complete question wording, see appendix 6.1.)

Our measure of perceived policy difference on each question is the absolute value of the *difference* in the distance between a respondent's own placement and her placement of each of the candidates. A perceived ideology/jobs policy difference score of 0 thus means that a respondent is equidistant from both candidates, and a positive perceived policy difference score of high magnitude suggests that the respondent is substantially closer to one candidate than the other.[5] To illustrate: if the respondent places herself at 2, and places the candidates at 1 and 5, then the perceived policy difference score is 2 ($||2 - 1| - |2 - 5||$).

Our measure of perceived policy alienation on each question is the minimum of the absolute value of the distance from the respondent to each candidate. A score of 0 indicates that one of the candidates

---

4. See, for example, Dennis & Owen (2001), Gibson (1991); Schildkraut 2005; Theiss-Morse (1993); and Weatherford (1991; 1992).

5. We also computed additional measures of perceived policy alienation and perceived policy difference, reflecting differences in how the candidate's ideology/jobs policy position was computed (e.g., the individual's perception vs. the mean placement of a candidate based on the entire sample's reported perception) and differences in the voter's utility function (i.e., quadratic vs. linear vs. log). These results and the details on the different measurement decisions are presented in appendix 5.1.

is placed at the same point as the respondent's preferred position on the ideology/jobs scale, while a positive perceived alienation scores means that the closest candidate's position is farther way from the respondent's preferred position. Using the same scenario as described above, if the respondent places herself at 2 on the 7-point scale, and places the candidates at 1 and 5, the perceived policy alienation score is 1 ($\mathbf{min}(|2 - 1|,|2 - 5|)$).

5.3 Perceived Policy Choices, 1972–2008

We begin with a preliminary description of individuals' perceptions of presidential candidates from 1972 to 2008 by graphing (in figs. 5.1 and 5.2) the average placement of Republican and Democratic candidates by each income group, first for ideology and then for government jobs. We provide the graphs broken down by income group because we ultimately want to investigate how the impact of candidate choice varies by income. As the lines represent equal portions of respondents, the aggregate placement would just be the average of the five lines. This descriptive detail provides some useful information about how policy choices vary by election as well as whether the poor and the rich see the same or different policy options over time.

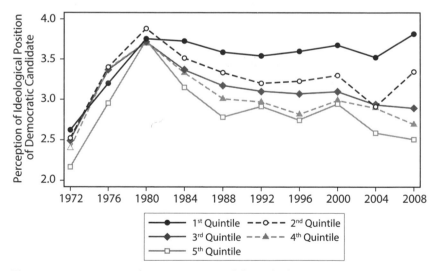

Figure 5.1. Perception of Democratic Candidate Ideology.
Note: Higher values indicate more conservative perceptions. Computed by the authors using data from the American National Election Studies Time Series Cumulative File, 1972–2008.

What we see is *substantial* divergence over time between the placement of the candidates by the different groups of respondents. Whereas from 1972 through 1980 the groups basically agreed on the placement of the Democratic and Republican candidates, they diverged quite sharply and systematically thereafter. After 1980, respondents in the lower-income quintile consistently saw the Democratic candidate as less liberal than did respondents in the upper-income quintiles. At the same time, respondents in the lower-income quintile consistently saw the Republican candidate as less conservative than did respondents in the upper-income quintiles.[6]

Respondents in the lower-income groups were also less likely to be able to offer a placement of the candidates. The nonresponse rates for the bottom quintile for placing the Democratic candidate and the Republican candidate on the ideology scale ranged between 12 and 17 percent in the three most recent elections, while the nonplacement rate ranged between only 2 and 6 percent in the three most recent elections for respondents

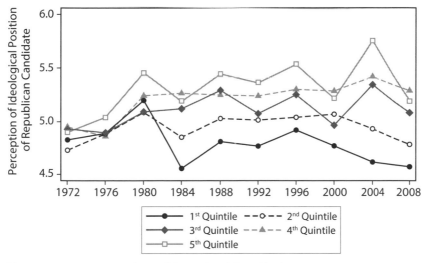

Figure 5.2. Perception of Republican Candidate Ideology.
Note: Higher values indicate more conservative perceptions. Computed by the authors using data from the American National Election Studies Time Series Cumulative File, 1972–2008.

6. We note that this is also consistent with respondents in the lower-income quintile as seeing *both* candidates as being more centrist, which could be observed if these respondents are simply guessing the midpoint more often than are respondents in higher-income quintiles.

in the top quintile. For placement of candidates on the guaranteed jobs scale, the nonresponse rate for those in the bottom quintile is again substantially higher than those in the top quintile, ranging from 8 to 24 percent over the last three elections for the bottom quintile but only 5 to 11 percent for those in the top quintile. Those respondents in the bottom income quintile who do not know where the candidates stand on issues will not be motivated to vote by a perception that the candidates offer distinct choices. Failure to place the candidates is equivalent to seeing both candidates as having identical positions for the purposes of motivating turnout.

It is well documented that the parties have become polarized in Congress over this time period.[7] But what has not been documented is whether these elite-level changes are recognized equally among various demographic groups. Our evidence shows that those in the lower-income groups are much less aware of this than those in the higher-income groups. Regardless of the reasons for this gap in perceptions, we want to examine how individuals' perceptions of the policy choices offered them in presidential elections influence whether they decide to vote or not.

5.4 Multivariable Analysis: Perceived Policy Alienation and Perceived Policy Difference

To test for the effects of perceived policy difference and perceived policy alienation on voter turnout, we estimate an individual-level multivariable logit model of turnout for each presidential election year from 1972 to 2008, using data from the American National Election Study. Our primary interest focuses on the estimated effect of our four measures: two of perceived policy difference (one based on ideology, one based on government guaranteeing jobs) and two of perceived policy alienation (one based on ideology, one based on government guaranteeing jobs).

We refer to the perceived policy difference measure based on ideology as $PPD^{Ideology}$ and the perceived policy difference measure based on government guaranteeing jobs as PPD^{Jobs}. Similar terms are used for the measures of perceived policy alienation: $PPA^{Ideology}$ and PPA^{Jobs}.

We condition on the demographic characteristics of respondents by including a series of dummies for the level of education of the respondent; the position in the income distribution of the respondent; the age of the

---

7. See Poole & Rosenthal (1997) and Han & Brady (2007) for evidence on polarization over time in Congress.

respondent, and the respondent's gender, marital status, and race.[8] We also include a dummy variable for respondents living in the South.

We estimate the model using logit for each of the ten election years, including in each year the four measures of perceived difference and perceived alienation described above, as well as the control variables listed above. We provide graphs of the estimates for the effect of the two PPD and two PPA variables in figures 5.3 through 5.6. We expect to see that increases in perceived policy difference will lead to higher turnout (positive effects), and that increases in Perceived Policy alienation will lead to lower turnout (negative effects). Figure 5.3 graphs the effect of one-standard-deviation change in perceived policy difference, measured on ideology ($PPD^{Ideology}$), on turnout for each election from 1972 through 2008.

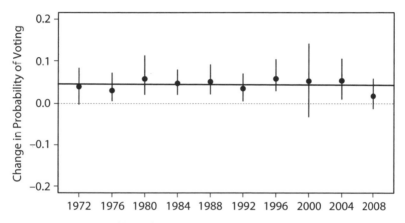

Figure 5.3. Marginal Effect of Perceived Policy Difference (Ideology) on Turnout, 1972–2008.
Note: The vertical axis represents the effect of a one-standard deviation change in perceived policy difference (ideology) on the probability of voting. The vertical line through each point gives a 95 percent confidence interval about the estimate. The probabilities are calculated using the demographic model described in section 5.4 for a hypothetical respondent who is a middle-income, married, white woman, a high school graduate, age thirty-one to forty-five, who lives outside the South. Computed by the authors using data from the American National Election Studies Time Series Cumulative File, 1972–2008.

8. Education was coded as less than high school, high school graduate, some college, and college and beyond. Income was coded based on the income quintile the respondent was in. Age was coded as: 18–24, 25–30, 31–45, 46–60, 61–75, and 76–89.

The solid dot in the figure represents the estimated magnitude of the marginal effect of a one-standard-deviation change in $PPD^{Ideology}$, while the vertical line represents the 95 percent confidence interval for the estimated effect in each year.[9] The effect is estimated conditional on all other demographic characteristics included in the model.[10] The figure shows that respondents who have a perceived policy difference one standard deviation higher on ideology, ceteris paribus, are approximately 5 percentage points more likely to vote in each election from 1972 to 2008.[11] The estimated effect is quite stable and in nearly every election reaches traditional levels of statistical significance.

That the estimated effect does not reach traditional levels of statistical significance in two of the ten elections does not suggest that the hypothesized effect is not confirmed at the 95 percent confidence level. It is true that we are not 95 percent confident that perceived policy difference affected turnout *in the 2008 election* based on our estimate for that year. However, given the distribution of p-values for our ten estimated coefficients, we can reject the null hypothesis that perceived policy difference does not affect turnout at well over the 99 percent confidence level. In other words, the probability that we would observe the distribution of estimates we do (with the ratio of positive to negative estimates, and associated standard errors) if the hypothesized relationship did not exist is less than 1 percent.

Figure 5.4 graphs the effect of a one-standard-deviation change in perceived policy difference, measured this time on the respondent's view of the role of government in guaranteeing jobs (PPD^{Jobs}) on turnout. The effect of perceived policy difference based on the jobs question does not seem as large as the effects of perceived policy difference based on ideology until the most recent elections. In 2004 and 2008 the estimated effect of perceived policy difference on government jobs on turnout was *larger* than the estimated effect of perceived policy difference on ideology on turnout.

---

9. If any one vertical line (i.e., the estimated effect in any one election) does not cross zero, then the interpretation is that we are 95 percent sure that the the hypothesized effect is larger than zero.

10. The graph shows the first difference estimated for a single hypothetical respondent who is a high school graduate in the middle income quintile, age thirty-one to forty-five, a married white woman not living in the South.

11. We use the phrase "5 percentage points more likely" to indicate an increase of 0.05 in the probability of an individual voting. While the graphs in this chapter represent the change in the probability of voting for a single hypothetical individual, we discuss percentage-point increases in the text to maintain comparability with discussions of increases in group turnout.

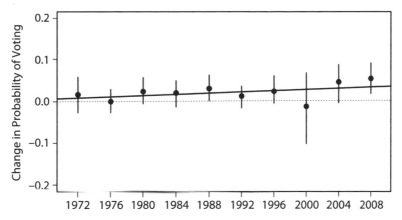

Figure 5.4. Marginal Effect of Perceived Policy Difference (Government Jobs) on Turnout, 1972–2008.

Note: The vertical axis represents the effect of a one-standard-deviation change in perceived policy difference (government jobs) on the probability of voting. The vertical line through each point gives a 95 percent confidence interval about the estimate. The probabilities are calculated using the demographic model described in section 5.4 for a hypothetical respondent who is a middle-income, married, white woman, a high school graduate, age thirty-one to forty-five, who lives outside the South. Computed by the authors using data from the American National Election Studies Time Series Cumulative File, 1972–2008.

Having shown that increases in perceived policy differences between the candidates lead to increases in turnout, we next look at the effect of perceived policy alienation. Figure 5.5 graphs the effect of one-standard-deviation change on the level of perceived policy alienation, measured on ideology (PPA^{Ideology}), on turnout for each election from 1972 through 2008. Here we expect that higher levels of alienation would lead to *lower* levels of turnout. But we see almost no relationship between levels of alienation on ideology and turnout in each election. Each estimated effect is very close to zero, or statistically indistinguishable from zero.

Figure 5.6 graphs the effect of one-standard-deviation change in perceived policy alienation on the respondent's view of the role of government in guaranteeing jobs. Here we see, in contrast to the results based on the perceived policy alienation measure based on ideology, that for most elections prior to 1996, increases in alienation did indeed lead to lower levels of turnout. However, in each election from 1996 through 2008 it appears that there was no effect of PPA^{Jobs} on turnout; each dot for those years is extremely close to zero.

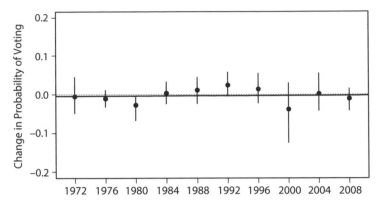

Figure 5.5. Marginal Effect of Perceived Policy Alienation (Ideology) on Turnout, 1972–2008.
Note: The vertical axis represents the effect of a one-standard-deviation change in perceived policy alienation (ideology) on the probability of voting. The vertical line through each point gives a 95 percent confidence interval about the estimate. The probabilities are calculated using the demographic model described in section 5.4 for a hypothetical respondent who is a middle-income, married, white woman, a high school graduate, age thirty-one to forty-five, who lives outside the South. Computed by the authors using data from the American National Election Studies Time Series Cumulative File, 1972–2008.

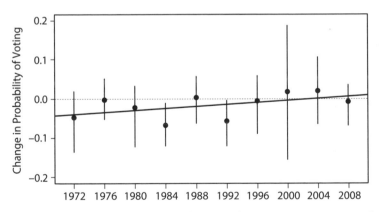

Figure 5.6. Marginal Effect of Perceived Policy Alienation (Government Jobs) on Turnout, 1972–2008.
Note: The vertical axis represents the effect of a one-standard-deviation change in perceived policy alienation (government jobs) on the probability of voting. The vertical line through each point gives a 95 percent confidence interval about the estimate. The probabilities are calculated using the demographic model described in section 5.4 for a hypothetical respondent who is a middle-income, married, white woman, a high school graduate, age thirty-one to forty-five, who lives outside the South. Computed by the authors using data from the American National Election Studies Time Series Cumulative File, 1972–2008.

We note that the estimated effects above actually understate the potential impact of perceived policy difference as we are showing the effect of changing only one of our two measures of PPD at a time. However, respondents' views of government jobs and ideology, as well as candidate placement on the issues, are likely to be highly correlated. And the estimates above are holding one issue fixed as we estimate the effect of change on the other issue alone. So a more realistic exercise is to see what would happen if a respondent perceived larger levels of policy difference on *both* issues simultaneously. Thus, in figure 5.7 we show what would happen if a respondent's level of perceived policy difference on *both* ideology and government job guarantees increased by one standard deviation each. As we can see, the estimated cumulative effect on a single respondent is between 5 and 10 percentage points, substantially larger than we saw for each issue alone.

We also looked at the effect of the respondent's level of perceived policy alienation changing on *both* ideology and government job guarantees, again moving the respondent on both issues simultaneously by

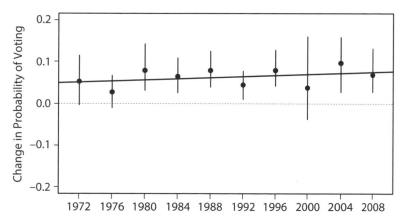

Figure 5.7. Marginal Effect of Perceived Policy Difference (Ideology and Government Jobs) on Turnout, 1972–2008.

Note: The vertical axis represents the effect of a one-standard-deviation change in perceived policy difference (ideology) and a one-standard-deviation change in perceived policy difference (government jobs) on the probability of voting. The vertical line through each point gives a 95 percent confidence interval about the estimate. The probabilities are calculated using the demographic model described in section 5.4 for a hypothetical respondent who is a middle-income, married, white woman, a high school graduate, age thirty-one to forty-five, who lives outside the South. Computed by the authors using data from the American National Election Studies Time Series Cumulative File, 1972–2008.

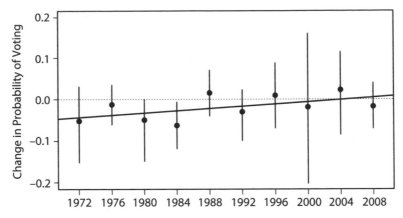

Figure 5.8. Marginal Effect of Perceived Policy Alienation (Ideology and Government Jobs) on Turnout, 1972–2008.
Note: The vertical axis represents the effect of a one-standard-deviation change in perceived policy alienation (ideology) and a one-standard-deviation change in perceived policy alienation (government jobs) on the probability of voting. The vertical line through each point gives a 95 percent confidence interval about the estimate. The probabilities are calculated using the demographic model described in section 5.4 for a hypothetical respondent who is a middle-income, married, white woman, a high school graduate, age thirty-one to forty-five, who lives outside the South. Computed by the authors using data from the American National Election Studies Time Series Cumulative File, 1972–2008.

one standard deviation. Here we see in figure 5.8 that the impact of alienation appears to be decreasing over time, mirroring our finding for the individual estimates above.

The size of the effects of increased perceived policy differences based on both ideology and government guaranteeing jobs is striking. To put this in a broader context, a 5 to 10 percentage-point impact is larger than our estimates of the impact of any legal change that we observed in chapter 4. We emphasize that is likely a conservative estimate of the effect of perceived policy difference. We are only looking at the perception of the candidates on two issues. If we included more measures of candidate positions, we might well see an even larger effect. This suggests that choices offered by candidates matter for elections, and that strategic decisions by candidates to try to alter voter perceptions of them can have significant effects on turnout (if such attempts at altering perceptions are successful).

Thus, our analyses confirm the theory that respondents' perceptions of the policy differences between candidates do influence turnout.

Respondents who perceive a greater difference between the candidates, and presumably have a stronger preference for one over the other, are more likely to vote. And the difference in the findings between perceived policy difference on ideology, and perceived policy difference on the government role in guaranteeing jobs, is suggestive. The recent increase in the effect of perceived policy difference on the government's role in guaranteeing jobs suggests that economic concerns could be becoming more important, and that respondents could be putting more emphasis on candidates' positions on economic issues.

5.5 Perceived Policy Difference and Perceived Policy Alienation across Income Groups

Our initial evidence, then, suggests that levels of perceived policy difference and perceived policy alienation do affect voter turnout. Yet we also observed differences in the perceptions of the poor and wealthy as to where they place Republican and Democratic candidates on ideology and the government guaranteeing jobs. Our interest in the political consequences of increasing economic inequality thus leads us to consider whether levels of perceived policy difference and perceived policy alienation vary across income groups over time, as well as whether perceived policy difference and perceived policy alienation influence individuals' turnout decisions differently depending on income levels.

Above we have shown that perception of candidate positions on issues varies across income groups. In figure 5.9 we graph the level of perceived policy difference for respondents in each of the five income quintiles on ideology ($PPD^{Ideology}$) from 1972 through 2008. For the period 1972 through 2000 the levels of perceived policy difference reported by each quintile group basically move together. The gap between the groups is never very large, nor is the level of perceived policy difference generally monotonically related to income. However, in 2004 and 2008 we see a divergence between the groups. In both of those years, the perceived policy difference between the two candidates for the top quintile is substantially higher than that of the bottom quintile. Note what this means: those in the top income quintile see a *larger* difference between the candidates on ideology than do those in the bottom quintile.

Figure 5.10 graphs the level of perceived policy difference for respondents in each of the five income quintiles on the government's role in guaranteeing jobs for 1972 through 2008. We see a similar pattern here in 2008: respondents in the highest income quintile see a much

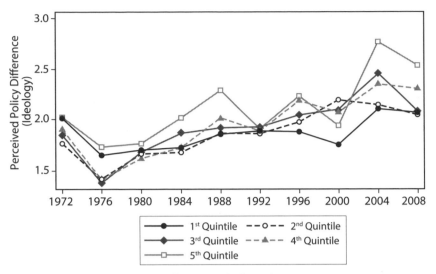

Figure 5.9. Perceived Policy Difference (Ideology) by Income, 1972–2008.
Note: Computed by the authors using data from the American National
Election Studies Time Series Cumulative File, 1972–2008.

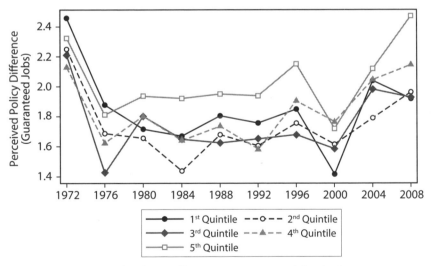

Figure 5.10. Perceived Policy Difference (Government Jobs) by Income,
1972–2008.
Note: Computed by the authors using data from the American National
Election Studies Time Series Cumulative File, 1972–2008.

larger difference between the candidates on the government jobs issue than do respondents in the lowest income group. Since respondents in the top income quintile observe larger policy differences between candidates than those in the low income quintile observe, we would expect an increase in income bias in 2008. Since we did not see such an increase in 2008, this suggests that other election-specific factors worked to mitigate income bias.

We also examined the levels of perceived policy alienation of respondents for each income group. Figure 5.11 graphs the mean level of perceived policy alienation on ideology for each quintile, and figure 5.12 graphs the mean level of perceived policy alienation on guaranteed jobs for each quintile. Here we see that respondents in the highest income quintile are almost always the least alienated on ideology, and that those in the bottom income quintile generally are more alienated on guaranteed jobs than are respondents in the other income quintiles.

But differences in the impact of perceived policy difference and perceived policy alienation across income groups on turnout can come from two causes: different *levels* of perceived policy difference and perceived policy alienation, or varying magnitudes of *the effects* of perceived policy difference and perceived policy alienation on turnout. We now turn to examine the possibility that aside from differences

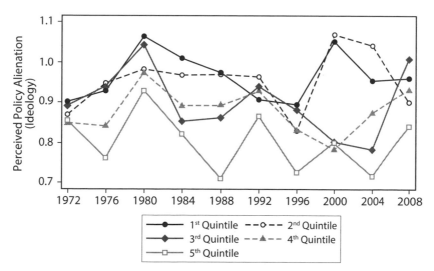

Figure 5.11. Perceived Policy Alienation (Ideology) by Income, 1972–2008.
Note: Computed by the authors using data from the American National Election Studies Time Series Cumulative File, 1972–2008.

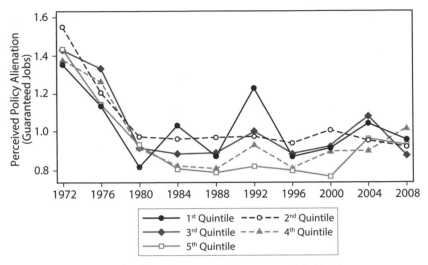

Figure 5.12. Perceived Policy Alienation (Government Jobs) by Income, 1972–2008.
Note: Computed by the authors using data from the American National Election Studies Time Series Cumulative File, 1972–2008.

in *levels* of perceived policy difference and perceived policy alienation between the poor and wealthy, the *effects* of these two predictors of turnout may be greater for the poor than for the wealthy. We anticipate that it is the poor for whom distinctive policy positions on redistribution will have the greatest appeal as a benefit of voting. We test this possibility by estimating the multivariable model used above, disaggregated by income group. This allows the effects of perceived policy alienation and perceived policy difference to vary by the income of the respondent.[12]

Figure 5.13 provides the estimates of the effect of a one-standard-deviation change in the level of perceived policy difference on ideology on turnout for respondents in each of the five income quintiles, for each election from 1972 through 2008. We are not able to estimate the effect of perceived policy difference on ideology for each income group very precisely for each election. But we do observe that when averaging the estimates for any one group over time, the effects do not differ substantially across the income groups.

12. We are thus allowing all the parameters in the model to vary over both income quintile, and year. We are generating fifty (10 years × 5 income groups) distinct sets of estimates here.

Figure 5.14 provides similar estimates for the effect of a one-standard-deviation change in the level of perceived policy difference on government's role in guaranteeing jobs on turnout. Once again, we cannot estimate effects precisely enough to make meaningful comparisons of the effects across the quintile groups for each election, but the graphs do suggest that the role of the perceived policy differences between the candidates on government jobs as a predictor of turnout is likely larger for both the first, and especially the fifth, quintile in the last three elections.

We also present estimates of the effect of perceived policy alienation on ideology and perceived policy alienation on guaranteed jobs by income quintile in figures 5.15 and 5.16. Again, our caveats about the precision of the estimates apply.

However, while we could not determine that equal levels of perceived policy difference and perceived policy alienation would have different effects on rich and poor individuals, we note that we *did* see above in figures 5.9 and 5.10 that poorer respondents have perceived less of a difference between candidates in recent elections. To examine the effects of these differences across the income groups, we simulated what turnout would be for the bottom quintile in 2008 if members of the bottom quintile perceived the same differences that the top quintile perceived. We adjusted the perceived policy difference on ideology and guaranteed jobs for each member of the bottom quintile to achieve mean perceived policy differences on ideology and guaranteed jobs equal to the mean perceived policy differences on both issues for the top quintile. We then computed the probability of voting for each respondent in the bottom quintile under the hypothetical scenario. According to our estimates, turnout of the bottom quintile would have risen by 3.5 percentage points under this scenario. This is a substantial effect, similar to the effects we estimated for several electoral reforms in the chapter 4. But it would still leave turnout of the bottom quintile approximately 20 percentage points below the turnout of the top income quintile.

5.6 Conclusion

Our interest in this chapter was to make more prominent the role of policy choices as a determinant of turnout in presidential elections. The blur of modern campaign politics often seems to overlook, or even forget, that elections are choices not just between candidates or parties, but also between issue positions.

Our evidence affirms that the policy choices offered by candidates matter for voter turnout. We have shown that the choices offered

(a) 1ˢᵗ Quintile

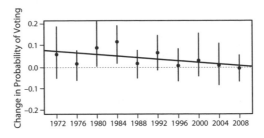

(b) 2ⁿᵈ Quintile

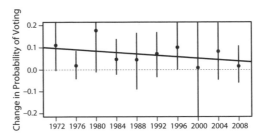

(c) 3ʳᵈ Quintile

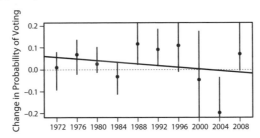

Figure 5.13. Marginal Effect of Perceived Policy Difference (Ideology) by Income, 1972–2008.
Note: The vertical axis represents the effect of a one-standard-deviation change in perceived policy difference (ideology) on the probability of voting. The vertical line through each point gives a 95 percent confidence interval about the estimate. The probabilities are calculated using the demographic model described in section 5.4 for a hypothetical respondent who is of given income, a married, white woman, a high school graduate, age thirty-one to forty-five, who lives outside the South. Computed by the authors using data from the American National Election Studies Time Series Cumulative File, 1972–2008.

(d) 4th Quintile

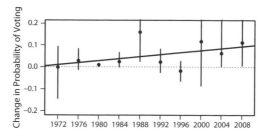

(c) 5th Quintile

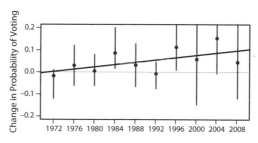

Figure 5.13. (Continued.)

individuals affect their likelihood of voting. Citizens who perceive a substantial difference between the candidates are more likely to vote than are respondents who are indifferent between the candidates.

Our analyses of the role of policy choices also included comparisons of perceived policy difference, perceived policy alienation and perceptions of candidate policy positions across income groups. We found that respondents in the bottom income quintile had substantially lower levels of perceived policy difference than did respondents in the higher-income quintiles in the 2004 and 2008 elections. This suggests that theoretical expectations that people at the bottom of the income distribution will be motivated to vote by a desire for economic redistribution are not likely to be met, as those persons are precisely the ones least likely to see the candidates as offering meaningful choices on issues.

(a) 1ˢᵗ Quintile

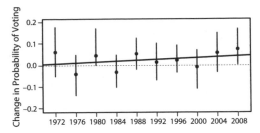

(b) 2ⁿᵈ Quintile

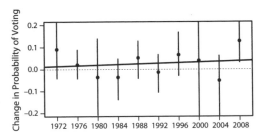

(c) 3ʳᵈ Quintile

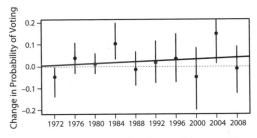

Figure 5.14. Marginal Effect of Perceived Policy Difference (Government Jobs) by Income, 1972–2008.
Note: The vertical axis represents the effect of a one-standard-deviation change in perceived policy difference (government jobs) on the probability of voting. The vertical line through each point gives a 95 percent confidence interval about the estimate. The probabilities are calculated using the demographic model described in section 5.4 for a hypothetical respondent who is of given income, a married, white woman, a high school graduate, age thirty-one to forty-five, who lives outside the South. Computed by the authors using data from the American National Election Studies Time Series Cumulative File, 1972–2008.

(d) 4th Quintile

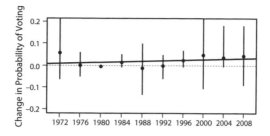

(e) 5th Quintile

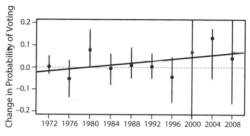

Figure 5.14. (Continued.)

Previous theories and research on the political implications of economic inequality have ignored the key role of whether parties or candidates offer relevant choices to those hurt by increasing inequality. Our answer to this point for the United States over the past decade is that the poor are less likely to perceive these differences than are the wealthy—and the poor cannot respond to policy choices they do not see. As a result, increasing economic inequality is unlikely to be met by increased turnout on the part of the poor unless one or both of the major parties offers a distinctive and compelling policy choice.

(a) 1st Quintile

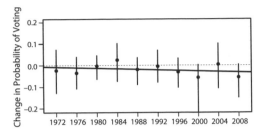

(b) 2nd Quintile

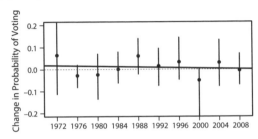

(c) 3rd Quintile

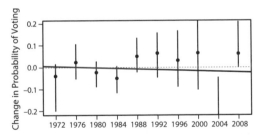

Figure 5.15. Marginal Effect of Perceived Policy Alienation (Ideology) by Income, 1972–2008.
Note: The vertical axis represents the effect of a one-standard-deviation change in perceived policy alienation (ideology) on the probability of voting. The vertical line through each point gives a 95 percent confidence interval about the estimate. The probabilities are calculated using the demographic model described in section 5.4 for a hypothetical respondent who is of given income, a married, white woman, a high school graduate, age thirty-one to forty-five, who lives outside the South. Computed by the authors using data from the American National Election Studies Time Series Cumulative File, 1972–2008.

(d) 4ᵗʰ Quintile

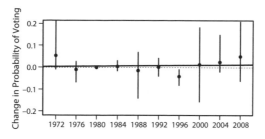

(e) 5ᵗʰ Quintile

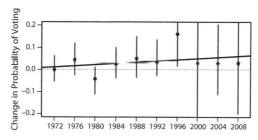

Figure 5.15. (Continued.)

(a) 1ˢᵗ Quintile

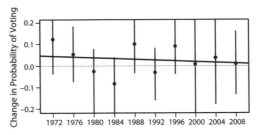

(b) 2ⁿᵈ Quintile

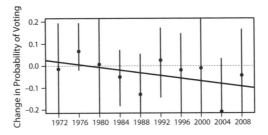

(c) 3ʳᵈ Quintile

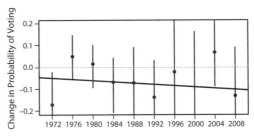

Figure 5.16. Marginal Effect of Perceived Policy Alienation (Government Jobs) by Income, 1972–2008.
Note: The vertical axis represents the effect of a one standard deviation change in perceived policy alienation (government jobs) on the probability of voting. The vertical line through each point gives a 95 percent confidence interval about the estimate. The probabilities are calculated using the demographic model described in section 5.4 for a hypothetical respondent who is of given income, a married, white woman, a high school graduate, age thirty-one to forty-five, who lives outside the South. Computed by the authors using data from the American National Election Studies Time Series Cumulative File, 1972–2008.

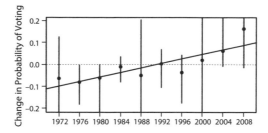

(d) 4ᵗʰ Quintile

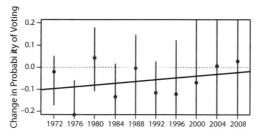

(e) 5ᵗʰ Quintile

Figure 5.16. (Continued.)

Appendix 5.1: Comparing Alternative Measures of Alienation and Indifference

When trying to measure alienation and indifference one is faced with (at least) one measurement choice and (at least) one modeling choice. We define a respondent as being indifferent between two candidates if his utility for each candidate is equal. If we restrict ourselves to spatial (proximity) models of utility, this means that we need to place the respondent and the candidates on an issue scale and come up with a functional form for utility.

In the NES surveys, respondents are asked to place themselves on the issue scale. If we take this as a starting point, the question becomes where to place the candidates. We have two choices: the respondent's placement of each candidate, or some external measure of placement such as the mean placement by all respondents of the candidate or expert placement of the candidates. Using self-placement can be problematic because (1) many respondents simply fail to place one or more candidates; and (2) respondents may place their most preferred candidate closer to themselves (or vice versa, place themselves closer to their most preferred candidate) than they would otherwise do in order to minimize cognitive dissonance. They might simply be rationalizing their voting decision.

While the second problem could jeopardize the validity of estimates of the impact of issue positions on vote choice, we argue that it should not affect estimates of the impact of issue positions on turnout. The decision to turn out to vote is, after all, based on the voter's perception of indifference between the candidates. However, we find it unlikely that the voter feels any need to justify the decision to turn out by rigging the placement of candidates to suggest a large preference for one candidate over the other. Thus, even if the respondent is minimizing cognitive dissonance in vote choice, this is what we would want to take into account in measuring his level of indifference between candidates.

However, we are still left with the problem when using the respondent's placement of the candidates that many respondents simply fail to place the candidates. This means that we could (1) impute the respondents' placement of the candidate; (2) assume that respondents who cannot place either candidate are indifferent between them; (3) use the mean placement of the candidate given by all respondents who can place the candidate; or (4) omit the respondents from the analysis who cannot place the candidates. Imputation is obviously problematic here because the failure to place the candidate is almost certainly not done at random; presumably people who cannot place the candidate fail to do so because they do not know where the candidate is in the issue space. Imputing an opinion to the respondent that the respondent has explicitly denied having is probably not a good idea.

If respondents cannot place either candidate, they might be indifferent between them. However, the failure to place the candidates might be because they find the task of placement on the 7 point scale cognitively challenging. Or, perhaps they really are indifferent?

Using the mean placement of the candidate generates measurement error in two ways. First, of respondents who can place the candidate, we are replacing their own placement with a mean of placement by others, and not all respondents interpret the scale the same way. Thus, if a respondent places himself at 2, and the candidate at 3, we *know* the respondent believes himself to be one unit from the candidate. However, the mean placement of the candidate could represent a mean given by respondents who interpret the scale differently from this respondent.

Second, for respondents who could not place the candidate we have the same problem we would with imputation—we are giving the respondent an opinion that the respondent has explicitly denied having. Omitting the respondents who fail to place the candidates from the analysis means that our analysis only generalizes to respondents able to place the candidates, and thus limits its usefulness. In the analysis presented here we have chosen the third option—omitting these respondents.

But even after measuring respondent placement and candidate placement, we still need to relate those positions to utility and indifference, and to alienation. When specifying the actual utility function for the voter, there are two common Euclidean choices we can make. First, we can specify utility as a quadratic loss function of the distance between the voter and each candidate. This is the most commonly used function. And it has a very real substantive implication. It suggests that voters put a greater value on the difference in distances between candidates going from 3 to 4 than from 1 to 2. Or, we can use a linear loss function of the distance between the voter and each candidate.

Consider how utility is measured: Define [13]

- X_i = Respondent Position
- D_i = Democratic Candidate Position
- R_i = Republican Candidate Position

- U_{iD} = $-(X_i - D_i)^2$
- U_{iR} = $-(X_i - R_i)^2$

- $U_{iD} - U_{iR}$ = $-(X_i - D_i)^2 + (X_i - R_i)^2$
- $Pr(Vote)$ = $F(abs(U_{iD} - U_{iR}))$

- $U_{iD} - U_{iR}$ = $-(X_i - D_i)^2 + (X_i - R_i)^2$
- Indifference = $- abs(-(X_i - D_i)^2 + (X_i - R_i)^2)$

The equations below give an example of the implication of a quadratic loss function for indifference.

Case 1:

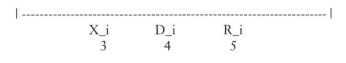

|--|
X_i   D_i   R_i
3   4   5

Case 2:

|--|
X_i   D_i   R_i
3   5   6

13. Note that in the definition here we use *indifference*, rather than perceived policy *difference*, to be consistent with standard notation on loss functions in spatial utility models.

In the case above, with quadratic utility, for case 1: Indifference = $-\mathbf{abs}((3-4)^2 - (3-5)^2) = -\mathbf{abs}(1-4) = -3$. For case 2, Indifference $= -\mathbf{abs}((3-5)^2 - (3-6)^2) = -\mathbf{abs}(4-9) = -5$. Thus, with quadratic utility the respondent is *less* likely to vote in case 1 than in case 2, as they have a higher value of indifference (the closer the value of indifference is to zero, the less likely someone is to vote). This does *not* seem to be intuitively appealing: in case 2 the Republican candidate is only 50 percent farther from the respondent than the Democratic candidate is, whereas in case 1 the Republican candidate is twice as far from the respondent as the Democratic candidate is. Thus, it is appealing to think that the respondent is more likely to vote in case 1 than in case 2, not less likely. If we are to make these proportional comparisons, it suggests taking the log of the squared distances.

Now consider alienation.

Case A1:

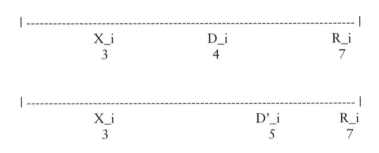

Case A2:

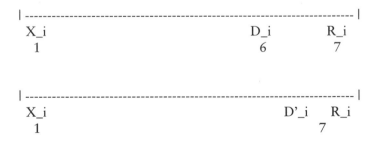

In case A1, the respondent is at position 3, and the Democratic candidate is initially at position 4. Using quadratic distance, the alienation for the respondent is $(3-4)^2 = 1$. If the Democratic candidate moved to 5, the level of alienation would then be $(3-5)^2 = 4$, for an increase of 3 units of alienation. If we consider case A2, the Democratic candidate is again going to move 1 unit. But here, the level of alienation goes from $(1 - 6)^2 = 25$ to $(1 - 7)^2 = 36$, for an increase of 11 units of alienation. However, we might logically think that whereas in case A1 the Democratic candiate moved to being *twice* as far from the respondent as he started, and in case A2 the distance between the Democratic candidate and the respondent only went up by 20 percent, that alienation should have increased more in the first case. We could capture this notion of proportional increases in distance being equivalent by simply taking the log of the squared distance.

We opt for brute force empiricism: we estimate four sets of models of turnout. In one model we use absolute value of distances and respondent placement of candidates; in the second model we use squared value for distances, and respondent placement of candidates; in the third model we use squared values for distances, and the mean placement for candidates; and in the fourth model we use the squared values for distance for indifference but take the log of the squared value for alienation and use respondent placement of candidates.

One of our measures is thus what was used by Zipp (1985). Using American National Election Study data from 1968 to 1980, Zipp derives measures of alienation and indifference based on the individual's self-reported position on 7-point scales on a variety of issues (e.g., urban unrest, the Vietnam, War, government guarantee of jobs, minority rights, the role of women, and ideology) compared to the individual's placement of where each candidate was located on the same set of 7-point scales. The alienation measure is the absolute value of the minimum distance between the individuals' issue position and either of the candidate's issue positions. Higher values thus represent greater alienation.

The indifference measure Zipp used is the absolute value of the difference of the distance between the respondent's self-placement and the perceived location of the Democratic candidate, and the distance between the respondent's self-placement and the perceived location of the Republican candidate, with this value being reversed in sign so that higher values represent greater indifference. That is, if individuals are equally close to both candidates, regardless of the direction of the preferred policy differences, then they should be more indifferent to which candidate is selected; but if individuals are quite close to one candidate and very far away from the other, then they should have a strong preference as to who is elected, and thus have low levels of indifference.

We computed the same measures of alienation and indifference used by Zipp for each election year from 1972 to 2008. As described above, we also computed three additional measures of alienation and indifference, reflecting differences in how the candidate's policy position

Table A5.1.1. Alternative Model Specifications and Measures: Goodness-of-Fit Estimates.

Year	N	Percent Voted	Log Likelihood					ePCP				
			Abs Resp[a]	Sq Resp[b]	Sq Mean[c]	Sq/log Resp[d]	Sq/LL Resp[e]	Abs Resp[a]	Sq Resp[b]	Sq Mean[c]	Sq/log Resp[d]	Sq/LL Resp[e]
1972	530	82.6	−212.71	−213.43	−216.78	−213.67	−212.00	75.1	75.0	75.0	74.9	75.2
1976	1036	71.9	−563.23	564.44	−562.43	−564.43	−563.19	63.7	63.6	63.7	63.6	63.7
1980	583	81.6	−217.13	−216.60	−231.61	−218.91	−221.05	76.5	76.5	74.9	76.3	76.1
1984	1158	74.2	−583.36	−583.58	−589.64	−587.48	−587.46	66.9	66.9	66.5	66.6	66.6
1988	904	73.2	−438.91	−441.30	−445.37	−440.96	−439.50	68.1	67.9	67.6	67.0	68.1
1992	1216	77.6	−574.79	−573.65	−580.30	−574.08	−576.19	69.6	69.7	69.3	68.0	69.6
1996	1046	75.3	−503.48	−503.63	−500.93	−503.48	−503.07	68.7	68.7	68.9	70.0	68.8
2000	231	73.2	−110.91	−111.12	−111.42	−111.36	−110.08	68.9	68.8	68.7	68.7	69.2
2004	551	75.1	−271.11	−271.27	−275.6	−271.78	−272.02	68.1	68.1	67.4	68.0	68.0
2008	611	75.0	−307.33	−309.09	−318.24	−308.31	−309.31	67.0	66.7	65.5	66.8	66.7

Note: The dependent variable is self-reported voter turnout. Each model includes demographic characteristics of respondents and perceived policy difference and perceived policy alienation for two issues: ideology and government jobs. Estimated by the authors using data from the American National Election Studies Time Series Cumulative File, 1972–2008. Goodness-of-fit measures are reported for five models.

[a] Absolute Value-Respondent Placement of Candidates: Uses respondent placement of candidates, with the absolute value of the difference in perceived policy placements on the seven-point scale as the functional form for measuring perceived policy difference and perceived policy alienation.

[b] Squared Distance—Respondent Placement of Candidates: Uses respondent placement of candidates, with the squared value of the difference in perceived policy placements on the seven-point scale as the functional form for measuring perceived policy difference and perceived policy alienation.

[c] Squared Distance—Mean Placement of Candidates: Uses the mean sample placement of candidates, with the squared value of the difference in perceived policy placements on the seven-point scale as the functional form for measuring perceived policy difference and perceived policy alienation.

[d] Squared/Log(Squared) Distance—Respondent Placement of Candidates: Uses respondent placement of candidates, with the squared value of the difference in perceived policy placements on the seven-point scale for perceived policy difference, and the log of squared values of difference in perceived policy alienation as the functional forms.

[e] Log(Squared)—Respondent Placement of Candidates: Uses respondent placement of candidates, with the log of squared values of difference in perceived policy placements on the seven-point scale as the functional form for perceived policy difference and perceived policy alienation.

was computed (e.g., the individual's perception vs. the mean placement of a candidate based on the entire sample's reported perception) and differences in the voter's utility function (i.e., quadratic vs. linear).

Table A5.1.1 presents the log-likelihood values and measures of fit (ePCP) for a model of turnout estimated on each presidential election from 1972 to 2008, but using the four different sets of measures we describe above. The model includes basic demographic variables for each respondent—education, income, and age—as well as a dummy variable for living in the South. Education is included as a series of dummy variables (high school graduates, some college, and college and beyond—with no high school degree being the omitted category). Income is also measured by a series of dummies for which income quintile the respondent is in, with the bottom quintile being the omitted category. Age is also measured as a series of dummies, with the oldest group being the omitted category. Gender, marital status, and race are included. Finally, there is a dummy variable for living in the South.

Looking across the rows, one can see almost no difference in fit in any year between the models. Clearly whether one chooses to use the respondent placement of the candidate (the Squared-Resp column) versus the mean placement of the candidate (the Squared-Mean column) makes no difference for the fit of the model. The log likelihood values and ePCP values barely change.[14] Similarly, comparing the models using squared distance versus linear (absolute value) distance, there is again virtually no difference in model fit. We do note that in only two years do the models based on mean placement of the candidate, rather than respondent placement of the candidate, fare better. Thus, consistent with our theoretical view, the model using respondent placement appears to be preferred. However, this model has a severe practical shortcoming as many voters cannot place the candidate on the issues. Examining how to treat respondents who cannot place one or both of the candidates remains an ongoing research question.

14. See Herron (1999) for a discussion of ePCP.

Six
· ·

On the Representativeness of Voters

In this chapter we consider what we believe is a critical aspect of the potential *consequences* of turnout, and that is whether voters are representative of nonvoters with respect to their preferred policy positions. Most discussions of the consequences of turnout focus on whether changes in the partisanship of the voters lead to changes in who wins the election. We believe it is also important to consider the governance consequences of turnout. Who wins an election is obviously important in a representative democracy. But once elected, officials have some flexibility to define their policy agendas and their policy priorities in ways that go beyond partisanship. We have argued that elected officials respond to their electoral constituencies by pursuing the issues or policy preferences of those who cast ballots for them. In this respect, presidents respond not only to fellow partisans, but also to the more specific policy preferences of their supporters. This argument shifts the focus from how representative voters are of nonvoters with respect to demographic characteristics to how representative voters are of nonvoters with respect to policy preferences.[1]

The empirical evidence presented in the last several chapters suggests that the relative turnout rates of the wealthy and poor have been fairly constant over the past several decades, with perhaps a slight decrease in the relative turnout of the poor in the 1990s that has recovered since 2000. As we pointed out at the beginning of this book, theory suggests that poor individuals (specifically those below the median income level)

---

1. See Erikson and Tedin (2011, fig. 7:1) for a simple demonstration of the differences between the preferences of voters and nonvoters on economic issues.

will be inclined to favor policies that redistribute income, whereas rich voters (those above the median income level) will be opposed to policies that redistribute income. Given that nonvoters are disproportionately poor relative to voters, and have been since 1972, we expect to find sustained differences in the policy preferences of voters and nonvoters in presidential elections since 1972 on redistributive issues.

We briefly review the handful of studies that have addressed the question of the representativeness of voters, and then replicate some of Wolfinger and Rosenstone's (1980) evidence for 1972 with 2008 data. We then test our expectations regarding the distinctiveness of voters' preferences using data from the 1972–2008 American National Election Studies (NES), as well as the 2004 National Annenberg Election Study (NAES), comparing the policy preferences of voters and nonvoters on redistributive issues, as well as a variety of other policy issues.

6.1 The Conventional Wisdom

The centrality of elections to representative democracy—along with concerns regarding low turnout in American elections—would suggest that scholars might well pay special attention to whether voters' policy positions are representative of nonvoters'. Yet aside from Wolfinger and Rosenstone (1980), we have identified few studies that consider this key question, and their conclusions are fairly consistent with each other: there are surprisingly few and, in any case, only modest, differences in the policy preferences of voters and nonvoters.[2]

Conventional wisdom seems to have interpreted those findings as indicating that there are no differences between voters and nonvoters. This strict interpretation certainly emerges from Wolfinger and Rosenstone's (1980) description of their data from 1972. After reporting a "slight" overrepresentation of Republicans among the voters, Wolfinger and Rosenstone examine citizens' preferences on seven issues (government guaranteeing jobs, medical insurance, bussing, abortion, legalizing marijuana, the role of women, and ideology) and observe, "All other political differences between voters and the general population are considerably smaller than this [partisan] gap of 3.7 percentage points. Moreover, these other differences, as slight as they are, do not have a consistent bias toward any particular political orientation. . . . In short, on these issues voters are virtually a carbon copy of the citizen population" (1980, 109).

---

2. We emphasize that we are considering policy preferences here, not candidate preferences. See Bennett & Resnick (1990); Ellis, Ura, & Ashley-Robinson (2006); Shaffer (1982); and Studlar & Welch (1986).

Bennett and Resnick's (1990) analysis of General Social Survey (1985), Gallup poll (1987), and American National Election Studies (1968–1988) data mirrors these conclusions for the most part, though they offer some evidence that conflicts with Wolfinger and Rosenstone's (1980) observations of "small and statistically insignificant" differences between voters and the citizen population. Bennett and Resnick's analysis considers a broader range of the attitudinal characteristics of voters, such as patriotism and other measures of system support, attitudes toward political and social groups, and levels of political information. On these items, they too report that there are few differences and that nonvoters thus do not represent a threat to democracy.

However, on some of the same issue positions that Wolfinger and Rosenstone examined, as well as some additional policy preference measures, they note that findings are mixed. Few differences are observed on partisanship, ideology, and foreign policy positions. But on some domestic policies, "nonvoters and voters do not see eye to eye. Nonvoters are slightly more in favor of an increased government role in the domestic arena. They are more likely to oppose curtailing government spending for health and education services, and they are more likely to support government guarantees that everyone has a job and a good standard of living" (Bennett & Resnick 1990, 789–94).

In addition, Bennett and Resnick's analyses of voters' and nonvoters' opinions on spending for a set of eight domestic programs indicates that nonvoters are significantly more likely than voters to favor spending. Thus, the conventional wisdom that who votes does not matter in the representation of citizens' policy views to elected officials is clearly situated in a substantial amount of data and in the analyses of Wolfinger and Rosenstone's (1980) work, with the refinements provided by Bennett and Resnick (1990) somewhat obscured.

We find these somewhat inconsistent conclusions—coupled with the common claim that voters are representative of nonvoters—to be troubling. The substantive conclusion that it does not matter who votes seems especially inconsistent with our basic beliefs about how representative politics work: it is not just that these differences in policy preferences *should* matter in a normative sense but also that common political sense suggests that they *must* matter to some degree for policy outcomes.

Moreover, these conclusions (based on the policy preferences of voters vs. nonvoters) that who votes does not matter contrast with several studies that argue that who votes *does* matter in terms of policy benefits. Hill and Leighley (1992), for example, find that states in which the poor vote as frequently as the wealthy provide significantly higher welfare benefits. Similarly, Martin (2003) finds that members of

Congress allocate federal grant awards to areas where turnout is highest. And, Bartels (2008) finds that elected officials pay more attention to the preferences of the wealthy than the poor, suggesting there is not anonymity among the electorate: not everyone's preferences count the same (see also Gilens [2012]; and Soroka & Wlezien [2010]). It would not be a great leap to suggest that elected officials pay less attention to the preferences of nonvoters than the preferences of voters.

But the key point is that the elected officials are aware of the preferences of their supporters. As we suggested in chapter 1, the poor and the wealthy might well support the same candidate and elect her; but when in office, she will pursue the policies preferred by voters (who are disproportionately wealthy) rather than those preferred by nonvoters (who are disproportionately poor). That means that for poor nonvoters; to achieve substantive representation it is not sufficient for rich voters to prefer the same *candidate* as poor nonvoters. they must also share the same *issue positions*. This possibility demands that we clearly understand whether voters hold the same policy positions as nonvoters if we are to understand the representational consequences of turnout.

We underscore the importance of this argument by noting that significant differences between voters and nonvoters have important electoral consequences even if voters and nonvoters have identical distributions of preferences across *candidates*. Imagine a world with two dimensions, and that voters who prefer the Republican candidate to the Democratic candidate do so based on economic issues, and voters who prefer the Democratic candidate to the Republican candidate do so based on social issues; but non-voters who prefer the Republican candidate to the Democratic candidate do so based on social issues, and nonvoters who prefer the Democratic candidate to the Republican candidate do so based on economic issues. Assuming that equal proportions of voters and nonvoters prefer Republican candidates to Democratic candidates, it would make no difference to the *electoral outcome* whether the nonvoters stay home or whether they choose to become voters. But if we assume that elected officials know the preferences of those who vote for them and respond to those preferences, then it would make a tremendous difference to *governing outcomes* if the nonvoters choose to vote.

Below we address the question of whether who votes matters, first assessing the representativeness of the policy preferences of voters in the 1972 and the 2008 elections to provide an initial assessment of the extent to which Wolfinger and Rosenstone's classic findings (1980) remain true. We then provide a more detailed assessment regarding trends in the representativeness of voters by examining the policy differences between voters and nonvoters in each presidential election year since 1972. These analyses provide some insight as to whether such representation varies by issue type and whether any variations we observe reflect election-specific factors or instead reflect more enduring compositional characteristics of voters relative to nonvoters. The latter is especially important from a normative perspective given the notable changes in inequality since the 1980s, while the former is valuable as well in terms of identifying contextual sources—such as candidate positions or the varying salience of different issues over time—of the representativeness of the policy preferences of voters.

We also consider additional data on the representativeness of the policy preferences of voters, relying on the 2004 National Annenberg Election Survey (NAES). This analysis complements our findings based on the time series available in the American National Election Studies (NES) in that it focuses on an additional set of more contemporary policy issues than what the NES time series allows. Our analyses of NES policy positions are drawn from the standard set of 7-point issue scales, along with questions on party identification, political ideology, and presidential candidate thermometer scores available in the NES. Our analyses of the NAES data focus on the set of policy issues asked in the postelection wave of the general election panel survey. In categorizing voters and nonvoters, we rely on the postelection self-report for the NES and on NAES respondents' self-reports on whether they voted in the 2000 election.[3] Specific question wording for both the NES and the NAES policy questions is provided in appendix 6.1.

6.2 Political Differences between Voters and Nonvoters: 1972 and 2008

We begin our comparison of the preferences of voters and nonvoters by considering attitudes on party identification and ideology, and then consider citizens' attitudes on specific issues. Table 6.1 reports the distributions of partisanship for 1972 and 2008 for nonvoters and voters using both the traditional 7-point party identification scale and a collapsed, 3-point scale.[4] Wolfinger and Rosenstone's basic observations (1980) for 1972 remain, with the most notable points being the underrepresentation of independents and the overrepresentation of Republicans among voters

---

3. We also conducted these analyses using the validated vote for those years when it is available for the NES data, 1976–88, and discuss these results below.
4. Note that the distribution for 1972 is not precisely the same as that reported by Wolfinger & Rosenstone (1980, table 6.2) because we compare the distribution of partisanship among voters with its distribution among nonvoters (rather than the entire population).

Table 6.1. Political Attitudes of Nonvoters and Voters, 1972 and 2008 (NES).

	1972			2008		
	% of Nonvoters	% of Voters	Difference[a]	% of Nonvoters	% of Voters	Difference[a]
Party ID—7-point Scale						
Strong Democrat	11.1	15.8	4.7	10.6	22.6	12.0
Weak Democrat	29.1	25.1	−4.0	18.5	15.9	−2.6
Lean Democrat	11.6	10.5	−1.1	25.0	13.2	−11.8
Independent	22.0	9.1	−12.9	18.9	5.6	−13.3
Lean Republican	9.9	11.3	2.4	13.3	10.8	−2.5
Weak Republican	11.1	15.4	4.3	9.8	15.3	5.5
Strong Republican	5.2	13.0	7.8	3.8	16.6	12.8
Party ID—3-point Scale						
Democrat	51.8	51.4	−0.5	54.1	51.7	−2.4
Independent	22.0	9.1	−12.9	18.9	5.6	−13.3
Republican	26.2	39.6	13.4	26.9	42.7	15.8
Number of Respondents	595	1,651		397	1,509	
Respondent Ideology[b]						
Liberal	22.8	26.6	3.8	23.5	29.5	6.0
Moderate	45.3	35.4	−9.9	41.0	26.8	−14.2
Conservative	31.8	38.0	6.2	35.5	43.7	8.2
Number of Respondents	311	1,237		297	1,188	

Notes: Entries in the first two columns for each year are column percentages. Entries in the "Difference" column are the difference between the group's share of voters and nonvoters. Computed by the authors using data from the American National Election Studies Time Series Cumulative File, 1972 and 2008; see appendix 6.1 for question-wording details.

[a] Positive numbers indicate overrepresentation among voters, while negative numbers indicate underrepresentation among voters.

[b] The moderate category includes only respondents who place themselves at the midpoint of the ideology scale.

relative to nonvoters. More specifically, while independents comprised 22 percent of nonvoters in 1972, they comprised only about 9 percent of voters; Republicans comprised about 26 percent of nonvoters and almost 40 percent of voters; and Democrats comprised about 52 percent of both nonvoters and voters.

In 2008, these same patterns can be observed. Independents represented almost 19 percent of nonvoters but only 5.6 percent of voters; Republicans represented nearly 27 percent of nonvoters but over 42 percent of voters; and Democrats comprised between 50 and 55 percent of both voters and nonvoters. Thus, the underrepresentation of independents and overrepresentation of Republicans is slightly greater in 2008 than in 1972.

Turning to a comparison of the distributions of ideology in 1972 and 2008 we see that moderates are underrepresented among voters in both years, though the underrepresentation is greater in 2008 than in 1972. Liberals and conservatives are overrepresented in both elections, with the overrepresentation of conservatives increasing somewhat more than overrepresentation of liberals in 2008.

To begin our analysis of voters and nonvoters on specific attitudes, in table 6.2 we reexamine the preferences of voters and nonvoters on the four issues that Wolfinger and Rosenstone (1980) presented from 1972 for which we have data in 2008. On the two economic issues (the government guaranteeing jobs and providing health insurance), nonvoters have more liberal views than voters in both elections, and the gap between them has increased for both issues. In 2008, there is a 10.2 percentage-point difference between nonvoters and voters believing that it is the government's responsibility to guarantee jobs, and a 12.5 percentage-point difference between voters and nonvoters believing that people should "get by on their own." In 1972 these gaps were only 7.8 percentage points and 4.6 percentage points, respectively.

While overall opinion changed on abortion from 1972 to 2008, representativeness on this issue did not change very much. The proportion of individuals taking extreme positions on abortion has increased, and in these extreme positions voters are least representative of nonvoters. For example, from 1972 to 2008, underrepresentation of extreme pro-life positions increased: the gap between nonvoters and voters taking this position was 3.6 percentage points in 1972, compared to a 9.5 percentage-point difference in 2008.

Finally, the issue on which there was the greatest improvement in the representativeness of voters is that of women's roles. Between 1972 and 2008, all segments of the electorate seem to have converged on the response in favor of women's equality. Although there were substantial differences between voters and nonvoters on whether "women's place is in the home" and whether "women are equal," in 1972, in 2008 these differences had all but disappeared. The largest representational bias on this issue remained a liberal one, with almost 87 percent of voters believing that women are equal, compared to only 80 percent of nonvoters.

Thus, in comparing the differences between voters and non-voters, we see both expected and interesting changes between 1972 and 2008. Opinion on the role of women in society has become more widely supportive of equality (at least in the voicing of public policy views), and in contrast to liberal fears that social issues now serve to mobilize conservatives, it is *liberal* views on abortion that are overrepresented among the voters.[5] For our purposes, however, the more interesting differences between 1972 and 2008 relate to the role of government in providing jobs or health insurance because these issues relate most directly to the possibly distinctive preferences of voters and nonvoters on redistributive issues. We observe here a greater underrepresentation of nonvoters' more liberal positions on these issues in 2008 as compared to 1972. Whether this difference is merely a function of the two particular time points we selected for observation or instead reflects a more fundamental difference between voters and nonvoters is addressed in the next section.

6.3 Who Votes Matters: Policy Differences between Voters and Nonvoters

In this part of the analysis we seek to document more broadly the contours of voters' policy representativeness over time. We want to overcome the potential hazards of comparing the 1972 and 2008 elections as endpoints and instead comment on changes in voter representativeness across the entire time period. This also allows us to assess whether such representativeness shifts slowly—as one might expect were policy views largely structured by the longer-term, enduring demographic predictors of turnout—or whether it reflects more short-term, election-specific factors. To the extent to which we observe the latter we would likely draw some inferences regarding the importance of election specific factors such as elite mobilization and candidate positioning.

According to Meltzer and Richard (1981), periods of increasing inequality should be associated with increased demand for government redistribution. Because we believe that increasing economic inequality was likely accompanied by an increasing divergence in the economic needs and priorities of poorer and wealthier individuals, and that this divergence would be reflected in increasingly distinctive policy preferences across social class (Schlozman, Burns & Verba 1999), we expected to find voters to be less representative—especially on redistributive issues— in 2008 than they were in 1972.

Our evidence on this point is drawn from the biennial American National Election Studies (NES) surveys between 1972 and 2008, which

---

5. We are of course not claiming that the issue of abortion is causing this overrepresentation of liberal views. The result could simply be caused by wealthy citizens having more liberal views on abortion *and* voting more frequently than poor voters.

Table 6.2. Issue Preferences of Nonvoters and Voters, 1972 and 2008 (NES).

	1972			2008		
	% of Nonvoters	% of Voters	Difference[a]	% of Nonvoters	% of Voters	Difference[a]
Govt Jobs Scale						
Govt Should Guarantee Jobs	37.1	29.3	−7.8	38.6	28.4	−10.2
Middle of the Road[b]	19.4	24.6	5.2	23.3	20.7	−2.6
People on Their Own	43.5	46.1	2.6	38.1	50.9	12.8
Number of Respondents	490	1,482		207	719	
Govt Health Insurance Scale						
Govt Health Insurance	48.3	43.7	−4.6	59.1	46.6	−12.5
Middle of the Road[b]	15.8	14.2	−1.6	16.0	14.9	−1.1
Private Insurance	35.8	42.1	6.3	24.9	38.5	13.6
Number of Respondents	240	718		460	1,523	
Abortion Legal[c]						
Always	21.3	26.2	4.9	33.4	42.0	8.6
For Personal Reasons (1972)/ For Other Reasons if Need	15.9	18.4	2.5	14.6	18.9	4.3

Table 6.2. (Continued.)

Established (2008)						
Only if Woman's Life or Health in Danger (1972)/ Only if Rape, Incest, or Women's Life or Health in Danger (2008)	49.8	45.8	−4.0	29.9	26.5	−3.4
Only if Rape, Incest, or Women's Life or Health in Danger (2008)	13.2	9.6	−3.6	22.1	12.6	−9.5
Never	593	1,621		247	784	
Women's Roles Scale						
Women's Equality	43.7	51.0	7.3	80.3	86.7	6.4
Middle of the Road	16.8	21.2	4.4	11.1	7.4	−3.7
Woman's Place Is Home	39.5	27.8	−11.7	8.7	5.9	−2.8
Number of Respondents	572	1,588		234	776	

Notes: Entries in the first two columns for each year are column percentages. Entries in the "Difference" column are the difference between the group's share of voters and nonvoters. Computed by the authors using data from the American National Election Studies Time Series Cumulative File, 1972 and 2008; see appendix 6.1 for question-wording details.

[a] Positive numbers indicate overrepresentation among voters, while negative numbers indicate underrepresentation among the voters.

[b] The NES asked different questions on abortion in 1972 and 2008, both with four response categories. In both years, the question included "Always" and "Never" as response categories. In 1972, the additional two categories were: "Only if the mother's life and health of the mother was in danger" and "If, due to personal reasons, the woman would have difficulty caring for the child." In 2008, the additional two response categories were "Only in the case of rape, incest or when the woman's life is in danger" and "For reasons other than rape, incest or danger to the woman's life, but only after the need for the abortion has been clearly established." See appendix 6.1 for additional question-wording details.

include a series of policy preference questions asked of voters and nonvoters.[6] We consider citizens' preferences and attitudes as reflected in their political views, their preferences on redistributive issues, and their preferences on values-based issues. Figure 6.1 documents the policy differences between voters and nonvoters in presidential election years between 1972 and 2008, focusing on three redistributive policy questions: support for government spending on health; support for providing services; and support for government guaranteeing jobs (see appendix 6.1 for precise question wording).

We describe these questions as redistributive because they indicate the degree to which respondents support governmental services or policies that redistribute resources to the poor. For each question, respondents

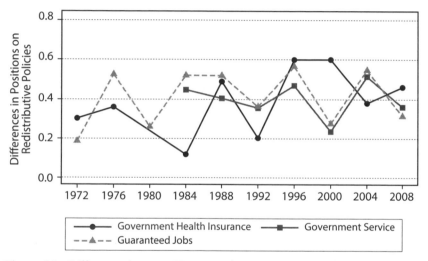

Figure 6.1. Differences between Voters' and Nonvoters' Attitudes on Redistributive Policies, 1972–2008.
Note: Plotted values are the weighted mean difference between voters' and nonvoters' attitudes on each issue in the specified year. Values greater than 0 indicate that voters (as a group) are more conservative than nonvoters (as a group) on the specific policy question; values less than 0 indicate that voters are more liberal than nonvoters. All mean differences are significant at $p < .05$, except 1972 for guaranteed jobs, 1984 for government health insurance, and 2000 for government service. Computed by the authors using data from the American National Election Studies Time Series Cumulative File, 1972–2008; see appendix 6.1 for question-wording details.

6. The NES is restricted to citizens.

are asked to place themselves on a 7-point scale, with the high point indicating the most conservative policy position (opposing redistribution) and the low point indicating the most liberal policy position (supporting redistribution). In figure 6.1 we plot the difference between the mean score of voters and the mean score of nonvoters on each issue. Positive values thus indicate that voters are more conservative than nonvoters, while negative values indicate that voters are more liberal than nonvoters.

As shown in figure 6.1, we find consistent differences between voters and nonvoters on each of these issues. In each year since 1972, voters are more conservative than are nonvoters in their beliefs regarding how much the government should do to provide jobs, health insurance, and services. More specifically, except for the difference between voters and nonvoters on government health insurance and job guarantees in 1972 and on government health insurance in 1984, the difference between voters and nonvoters is statistically significant in each election. Substantively, the mean differences on all three issues are typically greater than .4 on a 7-point scale. This suggests that voters are about one-half a scale position more conservative than are nonvoters. As we expected, then, there are notable, consistent and substantial differences between voters and nonvoters on redistributive issues—and the conventional wisdom should be updated accordingly.

Next we consider the representativeness of voters on two different sets of issues that we refer to as values-based issues and political attitudes. We present these results in separate graphs. We expect the responses to the first set of questions, including party identification, party ideology, and candidate preference, to be most sensitive to the particular electoral context (i.e., the nature of the issues, campaign strategy, etc.). We therefore expect these attitudes—and candidate preference, in particular—to be most likely to change election by election.

In contrast, the second set of issues are largely motivated by some sense of "values": the role of women/women's equality, aid to blacks, and defense spending. While we are not arguing that this is a coherent set of opinions that share common demographic or attitudinal sources, we do believe that each of these likely reflects more personal, fundamental symbolic beliefs than the other issues we consider. As such, we expect them to likely exhibit little sensitivity to election-specific contexts.

We turn to the representativeness of voters and nonvoters on political attitudes first. The party identification and political ideology measures are based on the standard NES 7-point party identification and political ideology questions.[7] The vote preference measure is based on

7. See appendix 6.1 for details on question wording.

respondents' thermometer rankings of the two major presidential candidates in each election year. We first compute the difference between voters' evaluations of the Republican and Democratic candidates and then compute the same value for nonvoters. We then take the difference between these two scores and then, for graphing purposes, rescale it to be comparable to values on a 7-point scale.

Figure 6.2 presents the mean differences between voters and nonvoters on party identification, political ideology, and candidate vote preference for 1972 through 2008.[8] The values that are plotted for each attitude or preference (i.e., the vertical axis values) are the mean differences between voters and nonvoters for each attitude or preference. Based

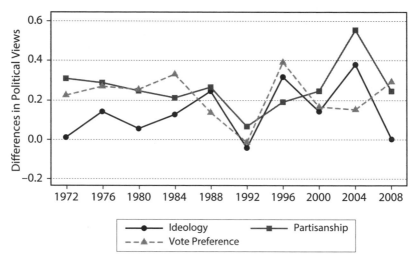

Figure 6.2. Differences between Voters and Nonvoters on Ideology, Partisanship, and Vote Preference.
Note: Plotted values are the weighted mean difference between voters and nonvoters on each opinion item in the specified year. Values greater than 0 indicate that voters (as a group) are more conservative than nonvoters (as a group) on the specific attitude; values less than 0 indicate that voters are more liberal than nonvoters. Mean differences on partisanship (except 1992 and 1996) and vote preference (except 1988, 1992, 2000, and 2004) are significant at p < .05. Mean differences on ideology are significant at p < .05 only in 1988, 1996, and 2004. Computed by the authors using data from the American National Election Studies Time Series Cumulative File, 1972–2008; see appendix 6.1 for question-wording details.

---

8. Mean differences are computed using the NES supplied weights.

on our general knowledge of the interrelationships among partisanship, ideology, and vote choice, we expected these three measures to move largely in sync with each other, and that is mostly what we see. And because vote preference is necessarily tied to candidate characteristics, we see this difference between voters and nonvoters varying the most from election to election, as we would expect.

We note that in many of these elections we observe statistically significant differences between voters and nonvoters on partisanship and vote preference. These differences are statistically significant in six of ten elections for vote preference and eight of ten elections for partisanship. Statistically significant differences between voters and nonvoters on ideology are less common, observed in only two elections, 1988 and 1996, though in seven of the ten elections voters in our sample are ideologically more conservative than nonvoters.[9] Thus we find that voters are more conservative than nonvoters on partisanship, candidate preference, and ideology, although the evidence is more robust for partisanship and candidate preference.

Figure 6.3 presents the mean differences between voters and nonvoters on values-based issues for 1972 through 2008. Our expectations of null findings here are generally supported. The magnitude of the difference between voters and non-voters on aid to blacks and defense spending is generally less than 0.1. Larger differences between voters and nonvoters on women's equality are observed, and are statistically significant in four years (1972, 1980, 1992, and 2000), but even these differences disappear in the two most recent elections. Generally, then, we find little or no systematic differences between voters and nonvoters on these values-based issues.

6.4 A More Detailed Look at Preferences: 2004

To compare the preferences of voters and nonvoters on a broader set of issues we utilize the 2004 NAES. Because the Annenberg policy questions are more timely queries regarding citizens' issue positions than the long-standing questions of political attitudes included on the NES, they provide another perspective on the representativeness of voters in 2004. They also offer the advantage of a substantially larger sample size than the NES.

---

9. Ideology could be interpreted differently by different respondents, and differently across elections. Some respondents might be emphasizing a social dimension in their evaluation of ideology, others might be emphasizing an economic dimension in their evaluation of ideology.

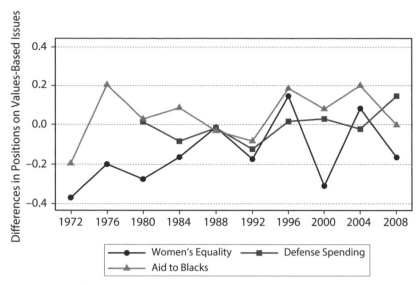

Figure 6.3. Differences between Voters' and Nonvoters' Attitudes on
Values-Based Issues.
Note: Plotted values are the weighted mean difference between voters' and
nonvoters' attitudes on each issue in the specified year. Values greater than 0
indicate that voters (as a group) are more conservative than nonvoters (as a
group) on the specific policy question; values less than 0 indicate that voters are
more liberal than nonvoters. Mean differences on women's equality are
significant at p < .05 in 1972, 1980, 1992, and 2000. Mean differences on aid to
blacks are significant at p < .05 in 1976. Computed by the authors using data
from the American National Election Studies Time Series Cumulative File,
1972–2008; see appendix 6.1 for question-wording details.

Although the particular questions differ from those used in the NES
and reported in earlier tables, we note that these issues, too, can be
viewed more broadly as income-based (both tables 6.3 and 6.4), as
politically-based (table 6.5), and as values-based (table 6.6). In addition,
the NAES also included a series of questions regarding security issues
(table 6.7), and legal issues (table 6.8), which we discuss as well.

The NAES offers five questions that we consider to be redistributive in
nature: whether the respondent favors making union organizing easier,
government health insurance for workers, government health insurance
for children, more federal assistance to schools, or increasing the minimum wage. The differences between voters and nonvoters on these
issues are reported in table 6.3. We also examine voter and nonvoter
attitudes on seven economic policy questions, and these differences are
reported in table 6.4. These issues include making permanent the tax

Table 6.3. Preferences of Nonvoters and Voters on Redistributive Issues (NAES 2004).

Issue	% of Nonvoters	% of Voters	Difference[a]
Government Health Insurance for Workers			
Favor	82.1	68.1	14.0
(N)	(4,959)	(16,795)	
Government Health Insurance for Children			
Favor	88.1	76.6	11.4
(N)	(5,140)	(17,378)	
Making Union Organizing Easier			
Favor	65.9	53.5	12.4
(N)	(2,663)	(9,146)	
More Federal Assistance to Schools[b]			
Favor	78.6	66.9	11.7
(N)	(7,559)	(24,559)	
Increasing the Minimum Wage			
Favor	88.3	80.5	7.8
(N)	(1,105)	(3,851)	

Notes: Cell entries in columns 1 and 2 are the percentage of respondents favoring the policy identified in each row, with the number of cases in parentheses. Unless otherwise noted, the percentage favoring consists of all respondents who said they *somewhat favor, favor,* or *strongly favor* the policy. The complement of each reported percentage is made of all respondents who said they *somewhat oppose, oppose, neither favor nor oppose, strongly oppose, don't know,* or refused to answer. Cell entries in the "Difference" column are the difference between the percentage of nonvoters and voters favoring each issue. Computed by the authors from the National Annenberg Election Study, 2004; see appendix 6.1 for question-wording details.

[a] Higher values indicate that the nonvoters are more liberal than the voters on the issue. Each difference is statistically significant at the 95 percent confidence level.

[b] This "favorable" category includes those who responded that they wanted more federal assistance to schools. The complement of this reported percentage is made of all respondents who said they wanted the same amount, less, or no federal assistance to schools and those who said *don't know* or refused to answer.

cuts enacted during the administration of President George W. Bush, school vouchers, trade agreements, investing Social Security in the stock market, eliminating overseas tax breaks, eliminating the estate tax, and reimporting drugs.[10] Note that the format of the Annenberg questions

10. See appendix 6.1 for a fuller description of the NAES questions and the notes in tables 6.3 and 6.4 for additional details on our coding of responses.

Table 6.4. Preferences of Nonvoters and Voters on Economic Policies (NAES 2004).

Issue	% of Nonvoters	% of Voters	Difference[a]
Making Bush Tax Cuts Permanent			
Favor	53.8	54.3	−0.50
(N)	(4,266)	(14,652)	
School Vouchers			
Favor	53.2	46.4	6.8
(N)	(15,154)	(49,572)	
More Trade Agreements			
Favor	46.1	40.3	5.7
(N)	(15,154)	(49,572)	
Social Security in the Stock Market			
Favor	57.0	54.5	2.5
(N)	(11,413)	(37,642)	
Eliminating Overseas Tax Breaks to Cut Taxes for Companies that Create Jobs			
Favor	71.4	74.0	−2.6
(N)	(4,037)	(13,996)	
Eliminating the Estate Tax			
Favor	58.2	64.4	−6.1
(N)	(4,593)	(15,363)	
Re-importing Drugs			
Favor	72.0	77.1	−5.1
(N)	(5,990)	(20,318)	

Notes: Cell entries in columns 1 and 2 are the percentage of respondents favoring the policy identified in each row, with the number of cases in parentheses. Unless otherwise noted, the percentage favoring consists of all respondents who said they *somewhat favor, favor,* or *strongly favor* the policy. The complement of each reported percentage consists of all respondents who said they *somewhat oppose, oppose, neither favor nor oppose, strongly oppose, don't know,* or refused to answer. Cell entries in the "Difference" column are the difference between the percentage of nonvoters and voters favoring each issue. Computed by the authors using data from the National Annenberg Election Study, 2004; see appendix 6.1 for question-wording details.

[a] Higher values indicate that the nonvoters are more favorable than voters on the issue. Each difference (except on Bush tax cuts) is statistically significant at the 95 percent confidence level.

generally is to ask whether respondents favor or oppose a policy. When respondents were given the option to say whether they strongly favor or strongly oppose, we collapsed the categories into favor or oppose. Thus, in the tables that follow, we present the proportion of voters who say they favor the policy, compared to the proportion of nonvoters who favor the policy.

The largest differences between voters and nonvoters across the entire set of issues we describe are almost all on redistributive issues (as reported in table 6.3). On every redistributive issue except one, the difference in support between voters and nonvoters is over 11 percentage points. The largest difference observed is 14.7 percentage points on support for government health insurance for workers. And on every issue it is the nonvoters who have the more liberal position overall. Only on support for increasing the minimum wage is the difference less than 11 percentage points, and that is mostly because even voters support this.

On most of the economic policy questions (reported in table 6.4) we also see differences between voters and nonvoters, but here it is more difficult to characterize these differences as either more liberal or more conservative. What we can report is that voters are significantly less favorable than nonvoters on school vouchers, creating more trade agreements, and having social security in the stock market. Voters are significantly more favorable than nonvoters on eliminating overseas tax breaks, eliminating the estate tax, and reimporting drugs.

The distribution of responses to the redistributive questions we saw on the previous table compared to the smaller difference between groups we see on the more complicated economic questions on this table do an excellent job of illustrating our point: the voters may be representative of the electorate on some issues, but they are *not* representative of the electorate on issues that go to the core of the role of government in modern democracies.

Respondents' self-reports on party identification and ideology in the 2004 NAES, as shown in table 6.5, broadly follow the contours identified in the 2004 NES, with Republicans being overrepresented among voters compared to their proportion of nonvoters. As shown in table 6.5, Republicans make up 34.5 percent of voters compared to 18.4 percent of nonvoters, and conservatives comprise 38.2 percent of voters and 32.2 percent of nonvoters. Both surveys suggest that conservatives are also overrepresented among voters, but the magnitude of these differences is smaller than those for partisanship.[11]

---

11. Given the difference in question design, we do not make too much of the small differences here.

Table 6.5. Political Attitudes of Nonvoters and Voters (NAES 2004).

Identification	% of Nonvoters	% of Voters	Difference
Party ID[a]			
Democrat	28.4	33.3	4.9
Independent	32.1	25.2	−7.0
Republican	18.4	34.5	16.0
Other	21.1	7.1	−14.0
N	(18,885)	(62,537)	
Ideology[b]			
Liberal	24.0	23.3	−0.7
Moderate	43.8	38.5	−5.3
Conservative	32.2	38.2	6.0
N	(18,885)	(62,537)	

Notes: Entries are computed by authors using data from the National Annenberg Election Study, 2004; see appendix 6.1 for question-wording details.

[a]Respondents who identified as *strong, moderate,* or *weak* Democrats/Republicans are coded as partisans. Respondents who said *don't know* or refused to respond are classified as other.

[b]Respondents who said they were *conservative* or *very conservative* are classified as conservative; respondents who said they were *liberal* or *very liberal* are classified as liberal. Respondents who said they were *moderate, don't know,* or refused to answer are classified as moderate.

Table 6.6 presents nine issues included in the NAES postelection study that measure what we have termed values-based issues, though this categorization is perhaps too broad for this large set of diverse issues. Five of these issues focus on abortion or stem cell research funding and legality, two focus on same-sex marriage issues, and two focus on gun control. The largest difference between voters and nonvoters on these issues is only 6 percentage points and is on the question of gun control, where over 62 percent of nonvoters favor increased gun control, compared to only 56 percent of voters. Every other observed difference is less than 5 percentage points, and the direction of bias is not consistent: sometimes more liberal positions are favored, sometimes more conservative positions are favored by the voters compared to the nonvoters. Thus, on these values issues, we do not see the set of voters as being unrepresentative of the electorate.

The NAES includes data on seven "security" issues ranging from those focusing on the war in Iraq, to military spending, the 9/11 Commission recommendations and the Patriot Act. We can see in table 6.7 that, with one exception, the differences between voters and nonvoters on these

Table 6.6. Preferences of Nonvoters and Voters on Values-Based Issues (NAES 2004).

Issue	% of Nonvoters	% of Voters	Difference
More Gun Control[a]			
Favor	62.5	56.5	−6.0
(N)	(8,323)	(27,393)	
Assault Weapons Ban			
Favor	69.5	74.4	4.8
(N)	(3,279)	(10,662)	
State Law Allowing Same-sex Marriage			
Favor	31.8	32.0	1.7
(N)	(4,915)	(15,811)	
Stem Cell Research Funding			
Favor	63.7	67.6	3.9
(N)	(2,979)	(10,165)	
Banning Late-term Abortions			
Favor	41.5	44.0	2.5
(N)	(6,085)	(20,044)	
Federal Marriage Amendment			
Favor	38.6	41.1	2.5
(N)	(18,885)	(62,537)	
Additional Stem Cell Lines			
Favor	66.7	62.9	−3.8
(N)	(1,376)	(4,646)	
Making Abortion More Difficult			
Favor	37.0	36.7	−0.2
(N)	(2,436)	(8,373)	
Banning All Abortions			
Favor	32.4	28.9	−3.5
(N)	(15,237)	(49,810)	

Notes: Entries are computed by the authors using data from the National Annenberg Election Study, 2004; see appendix 6.1 for question-wording details.

Entries in columns 1 and 2 are the percentage of respondents favoring the policy identified in each row, with the number of cases in parentheses. Unless otherwise noted, the percentage favoring consists of all respondents who said they *somewhat favor*, *favor*, or *strongly favor* the policy. The complement of each reported percentage consists of all respondents who said they *somewhat oppose*, *oppose*, *neither favor nor oppose*, *strongly oppose*, *don't know*, or refused to answer. All differences are statistically significant at greater than 95 percent confidence level except for "Making Abortion More Difficult."

[a] This percentage represents those who responded that they wanted more gun control. The complement of this reported percentage consists of all respondents who said they wanted the same amount, less, or no gun control and those who said don't know or refused to answer.

Table 6.7. Preferences of Nonvoters and Voters on Security Issues (NAES 2004).

Issue	% of Nonvoters	% of Voters	Difference
Keeping Troops in Iraq until Govt. Stable			
Favor	43.0	60.6	−17.6
(N)	(11,271)	(38,041)	
911 Commission Recommendations			
Favor	44.5	48.6	−4.1
(N)	(1,215)	(4,097)	
Spending More on Rebuilding Iraq			
Favor	10.5	8.3	2.2
(N)	(7,559)	(24,559)	
Moving Troops from Europe and Korea			
Favor	55.4	57.7	−2.3
(N)	(2,356)	(8,139)	
Spending More on Homeland Security			
Favor	51.7	49.1	2.5
(N)	(7,559)	(24,559)	
Spending More on Military[a]			
Favor	42.1	45.4	−3.3
(N)	(7,559)	(24,559)	
Patriot Act Is Good for Country[b]			
Favor	54.6	56.6	−2.0
(N)	(6,616)	(21,591)	

Notes: Entries are computed by the authors using data from the National Annenberg Election Study, 2004; see appendix 6.1 for question-wording details.

Entries in columns 1 and 2 are the percentage of respondents favoring the policy identified in each row, with the number of cases in parentheses. Unless otherwise noted, the percentage favoring consists of all respondents who said they *somewhat favor*, *favor*, or *strongly favor* the policy. The complement of each reported percentage is made of all respondents who said they *somewhat oppose*, *oppose*, *neither favor nor oppose*, *strongly oppose*, *don't know*, or refused to answer. All differences are statistically significant at greater than 95 percent confidence level except for "911 Recommendations."

[a] This percentage represents those who responded that they wanted more spending on the military. The complement of this reported percentage consists of all respondents who said they wanted the same amount, less, or no spending on the military and those who said *don't know* or refused to answer.

[b] This percentage represents those who responded that the Patriot Act was good for the country. The complement of this reported percentage consists of all respondents who said they thought the Patriot Act was *neither good nor bad*, *bad*, *don't know*, or refused to answer.

Table 6.8. Preferences of Nonvoters and Voters on Legal Policies (NAES 2004).

Issue	% of Nonvoters	% of Voters	Difference
Limiting Malpractice Awards			
Favor	53.1	64.4	−11.3
(*N*) *p*-value	(1,749)	(6,027)	
Limiting Lawsuits			
Favor	56.4	69.3	−12.8
(*N*) *p*-value	(1,921)	(6,574)	

Notes: Computed by the authors using data from the National Annenberg Election Study, 2004; see appendix 6.1 for question-wording details.

Unless otherwise noted, the percentage favoring consists of all respondents who said they *somewhat favor*, *favor*, or *strongly favor* the policy. The complement of each reported percentage consists of all respondents who said they *somewhat oppose*, *oppose*, *neither favor nor oppose*, *strongly oppose*, *don't know*, or refused to answer. All differences are statistically significant at greater than 95 percent confidence level.

issues are, as in the case of the values-based issues from the NES, quite modest. The most dramatic exception is on support for keeping troops in Iraq or bringing them home, in which case there is more than a 15 percentage-point difference between nonvoters and voters, with voters preferring that the troops stay in Iraq. The difference in support for keeping troops in Iraq is striking; it might be because voters are less likely than nonvoters to have relatives serving there. But it is a fascinating example of the voters *not* being representative of the electorate on a vitally important public policy issue.

Finally, in table 6.8 we report significant and large differences in the legal policy attitudes of voters compared to nonvoters. There is a substantial difference between the two groups on limiting malpractice awards, with voters more strongly supportive of such limitations than nonvoters. An even larger difference appears on the question of limiting lawsuit awards, with nearly 70 percent of voters supporting such limitations, compared to only 56 percent of nonvoters. These figures are consistent with the more conservative positions taken by voters on the redistributive issues we examined earlier.

All told, our findings on the large and consistent differences in the redistributive policy positions of voters versus nonvoters that we observed in the case of a limited number of broad policy issues included in the NES are sustained when examining more timely and detailed policy positions drawn from the NAES data. The magnitude of the differences observed on values-based and policy-oriented questions pales in comparison to what we find for economic issues.

And so we repeat: voters are *not* representative of nonvoters on redistributive issues. This has been true since 1972, in every election and for every redistributive issue we examine.[12]

6.5 Conclusion

Our initial interest in evaluating the representativeness of voters in contemporary American politics was stimulated largely by normative concerns associated with representation in modern democratic societies. The conventional wisdom established by Wolfinger and Rosenstone (1980) is that it does not matter who votes because voters and nonvoters share similar policy preferences. However, they noted that this was based on a comparison of preferences across a wide range of issues, and that in fact voters and nonvoters did differ on particular issues. In our analysis of preferences of voters and nonvoters across ten elections, we, too, find that on some issues voters are more liberal than nonvoters; that on some issues voters are more conservative than nonvoters; and that on some issues, voters' and nonvoters' preferences are about the same. Yet the pattern Wolfinger and Rosentsonte described for 1972 obscures the distinct difference between the preferences of voters and non-voters on issues related to redistributive policies. We consistently find on issues of economic redistribution—those issues most related to income and economic inequality—voters have more conservative policy preferences than nonvoters.

Revising the conventional wisdom according to our evidence is thus important in both normative and practical empirical respects. Both elected officials and citizens alike tend to think of elections as mandates of sorts, though it is extremely difficult to know what policies they are mandates for. Elections merely record which candidate is preferred by a majority of the voters to the other candidate. Elections do *not* record the reasons for the choices of those voters. The outcomes of elections do not tell us what specific preferences motivate voters to choose one candidate over the other. What our work has shown is that the electoral victory of any one candidate cannot be presumed to be reflective of the broader electorate in terms of preferences on redistributive policies.

---

12. We also examined voter/nonvoter preferences based on the NES validated vote measure for the limited number of years for which it is available. Our general findings hold when comparing validated voters and validated nonvoters: there are few differences on values-based issues for voters versus nonvoters; there are differences in partisanship and vote preference, but not ideology, for voters versus nonvoters; and for most observations, there are significant differences between voters and nonvoters on redistributive issues, though the magnitude of these differences is smaller than when we use the self-reported vote.

We have offered in this chapter a more extended analysis of the extent to which voters represent nonvoters. We take issue with the claim that voters are indeed representative of nonvoters. Our evidence deviates from that offered by Wolfinger and Rosenstone (1980) in one very important respect: in every election year from 1972 through 2008, voters and nonvoters differ substantively on most issues relating to the role of government in redistributive policies. In addition to these differences being evident in every election since 1972, we also note that the nature of the electoral bias is clear as well: voters are substantially more conservative than nonvoters on redistributive issues.

Appendix 6.1: Survey Question Wording

A6.1.1 The American National Election Studies

Representative introductions to the 7-point scale responses are included below:

- Government Health Insurance: There is much concern about the rapid rise in medical and hospital costs. Some feel there should be a government insurance plan which would cover all medical and hospital expenses. Suppose these people are at one end of a scale, at point 1. Others feel that medical expenses should be paid by individuals, and through private insurance like Blue Cross or some other company paid plans. Suppose these people are at the other end, at point 7. And of course, some people have opinions somewhere in between at points 2, 3, 4, 5 or 6. Where would you place yourself on this scale, or haven't you thought much about this?
- Government Guaranteeing Jobs: Some people feel that the government in Washington should see to it that every person has a job and a good standard of living. Suppose these people are at one end of a scale, at point 1. Others think the government should just let each person get ahead on his/her own. Suppose these people are at the other end, at point 7. And, of course, some other people have opinions somewhere in between, at points 2, 3, 4, 5 or 6. Where would you place yourself on this scale, or haven't you thought much about this?
- Government Services: Some people think the government should provide fewer services, even in areas such as health and education, in order to reduce spending. Suppose these people are at one end of a scale, at point 1. Other people feel that it is important for

the government to provide many more services even if it means an increase in spending. Suppose these people are at the other end, at point 7. And of course, some other people have opinions somewhere in between, at points 2, 3, 4, 5, or 6. Where would you place yourself on this scale, or haven't you thought much about this?

- Women's Roles: Recently there has been a lot of talk about women's rights. Some people feel that women should have an equal role with men in running business, industry, and government. Suppose these people are at one end of a scale, at point 1. Others feel that a woman's place is in the home. Suppose these people are at the other end, at point 7. And of course, some people have opinions somewhere in between, at points 2, 3, 4, 5, or 6. Where would you place yourself on this scale, or haven't you thought much about this?

- Aid to blacks: Some people feel that the government in Washington should make every effort to improve the social and economic position of blacks. Suppose these people are at one end of a scale, at point 1. Others feel that the government should not make any special effort to help blacks because they should help themselves. Suppose these people are at the other end, at point 7. And, of course, some other people have opinions somewhere in between, at points 2, 3, 4, 5 or 6). Where would you place yourself on this scale, or haven't you thought much about it?

- Defense Spending: Some people believe that we should spend much less money for defense. Others feel that defense spending should be greatly increased. And, of course, some other people have opinions somewhere in between at points 2, 3, 4, 5, or 6. Where would you place yourself on this scale, or haven't you thought much about this?

Representative question wording used to measure political views between 1972 and 2008:

- Party Identification: Generally speaking, do you usually think of yourself as a Republican, a Democrat, an independent, or what? (IF REPUBLICAN OR DEMOCRAT) Would you call yourself a strong (REP/DEM) or a not very strong (REP/DEM)? (IF INDEPENDENT, OTHER [1966 AND LATER: OR NO PREFERENCE]:) Do you think of yourself as closer to the Republican or Democratic Party?

- Ideology: We hear a lot of talk these days about liberals and conservatives. When it comes to politics, do you usually think of yourself as extremely liberal, liberal, slightly liberal, moderate or middle of the road, slightly conservative, extremely conservative, or haven't you thought much about this?

- Candidate/Vote Preference (1978 and later): I'd like to get your feelings toward some of our political leaders and other people who are in the news these days. I'll read the name of a person and I'd like you to rate that person using something we call the feeling thermometer. Ratings between 50 and 100 mean that you feel favorably and warm toward the person; ratings between 0 and 50 degrees mean that you don't feel favorably toward the person and that you don't care too much for that person. You would rate the person at the 50 degree mark if you don't feel particularly warm or cold toward the person. If we come to a person whose name you don't recognize, you don't need to rate that person. Just tell me and we'll move on to the next one.

- Abortion (1972 and 1976): There has been some discussion about abortion during recent years. Which one of the opinions on this page best agrees with your view?

  1. Abortion should never be permitted.
  2. Abortion should be permitted only if the life and health of the woman is in danger.
  3. Abortion should be permitted if, due to personal reasons, the woman would have difficulty in caring for the child.
  4. Abortion should never be forbidden, since one should not require a woman to have a child she doesn't want.

- Abortion (1980 and later): There has been some discussion about abortion during recent years. Which one of the opinions on this page best agrees with your view?

  1. By law, abortion should never be permitted.
  2. The law should permit abortion only in case of rape, incest, or when the woman's life is in danger.
  3. The law should permit abortion for reasons other than rape, incest, or danger to the woman's life, but only after the need for the abortion has been clearly established.
  4. By law, a woman should always be able to obtain an abortion as a matter of personal choice.

A6.1.2 The National Annenberg Election Study

Question wording for the policy preference questions is provided below. Possible response categories are included in tables 6.3 and 6.4.

- Making Union Organizing Easier: Do you favor or oppose making it easier for labor unions to organize?

- Government Health Insurance for Children: Do you favor or oppose the federal government helping to pay for health insurance for all children?
- Social Security in the Stock Market: Do you favor or oppose allowing workers to invest some of their Social Security contributions in the stock market?
- School Vouchers: Do you favor or oppose the federal government giving tax credits or vouchers to parents to help send their children to private schools?
- Favoring Federal Assistance for Schools: Providing financial assistance to public elementary and secondary schools—should the federal government spend more on it, the same as now, less, or no money at all?
- Favoring Military Spending: Military defense—should the federal government spend more on it, the same as now, less, or no money at all?
- Reinstateing the Draft: Do you think the United States should put the military draft back into operation?
- Spending to Rebuild Iraq: Rebuilding Iraq—should the federal government spend more on it, the same as now, less, or no money at all?
- Troops in Iraq: Do you think the United States should keep troops in Iraq until a stable government is established there, or do you think the United States should bring its troops home as soon as possible?
- Implementing 9/11 Commission Recommendations: As you may know, the 9/11 Commission has recently released its final report on what the government knew about potential terrorist attacks before 9/11, and made recommendations on what the government should do to prevent future attacks. Based on what you know about the report, do you think the government should adopt all of the commission's recommendations, most of them, just some of them, or none of them?
- Gun Control: Restricting the kinds of guns people can buy—should the federal government do more about it, do the same as now, do less about it, or do nothing at all?
- Assault Weapons Ban: The current federal law banning assault weapons is about to expire. Do you think the U.S. Congress should pass this law again, or not?
- Banning All Abortions: The federal government banning all abortions—do you favor or oppose the federal government doing this?

- Making Abortion More Difficult: Laws making it more difficult for a woman to get an abortion—do you favor or oppose this?
- Party Identification: Generally speaking, do you think of yourself as a Democratic, a Republican, an independent, or something else?
- Ideology: Generally speaking, would you describe your political views as very conservative, conservative, moderate, liberal, or very liberal?

Seven

··

Conclusion

As we finished writing this book in January 2013 many aspects of the 2012 presidential election had yet to be carefully examined, including who voted, whether who voted mattered for who won, and, critically, how the winner would govern. Claims that who voted could drive the outcome were fairly common in October 2012, but concern with the validity of those claims had essentially disappeared by election day. Instead, the political banter shifted to what would now transpire, given that President Barack Obama had won reelection.

It is this disjuncture between observations of who votes, and what policies will be produced postelection, that we have sought to address in this volume. In the 2012 presidential election, the media devoted large amounts of space to reporting on Bayesian averages of horse-race polls in order to predict the winner of the election. This focus may have crowded out coverage of the implications of the election for policy outcomes. Little attention was being paid as to why these voters were behaving as they were. If one believes that it is important for government to be responsive to the preferences of all citizens, then our emphasis on the differences in preferences of voters and nonvoters on *policies* rather than on *candidates* should be incorporated in careful analyses of public opinion. And these analyses should include the opinions of both voters and nonvoters.

We began writing this book thinking that who votes matters in terms of the issues that officials address, the policies they enact, and how a democratic government responds to the preferences of its citizens. We also believed that each of these consequences has substantial normative significance.

Our analysis of turnout in U.S. presidential elections since 1972 has proceeded against a backdrop of seismic changes in economic inequality, and with a particular interest in the income bias of voters. The importance of the substantial and sustained income bias that we have documented is underscored by our findings on the consistent differences in the policy preferences of voters and nonvoters. Voters are significantly more conservative than nonvoters on redistributive issues, and they have been in every election since 1972. If we had to point to our most important empirical finding of the many that we report, this is it. Voters may be more liberal than nonvoters on social issues, but on redistributive issues they are not. These redistributive issues define a fundamental relationship between citizens and the state in a modern industrialized democracy and are central to ongoing conflicts about the scope of government. It is on these issues that voters offer a biased view of the preferences of the electorate.

And it is not just that voters have different preferences than nonvoters on redistributive issues. In addition, the parties are failing to convince lower-income voters that they are offering distinctive choices on these issues. Whether perception or reality, this perceived lack of choices undermines the extent to which elections function as a linkage mechanism between citizen preferences and government policies.

7.1 The Politics of Candidate Choices and Policy Choices

Key to our effort to advance the study of turnout to a more explicitly political perspective is to consider the role of the policy positions that candidates offer in motivating voters. The predominant emphasis in the study of voter turnout for the past decade or more has been about voter mobilization and political competitiveness. When voters choose a president, they may indeed be influenced by various aspects of the candidacy, party, and campaign. But what we have emphasized is that presidential elections are choices about the policies that will govern the nation.

These policies can become an important benefit for citizens who must decide whether voting is worth the effort. We have shown that when individuals believe candidates offer distinctive choices they are more likely to vote. But not all eligible citizens perceive candidates as offering distinctive positions. In chapter 5 we observed that individuals in the highest income quintile are consistently most likely to perceive ideological differences between the major party presidential candidates, while individuals in the lowest quintile are least likely to see these differences. Moreover, the magnitude of these differences in perception increased dramatically in 2004 and 2008, with high-income individuals becoming increasingly likely to see differences between the two candidates.

Our initial reaction to this finding was to suspect that these changes may have had something to do with differences between wealthy and poor individuals in how they perceive the candidates' issue positions. This thought was at least partly true: since 1980, and especially in 2004 and 2008, individuals in the highest income quintile increasingly placed the Democratic candidate on the liberal end of the 7-point scale and also increasingly placed the Republican candidate on the conservative end of the scale. In other words, these individuals reported seeing the major candidates become more extreme, consistent with descriptions of polarization in contemporary American politics.[1]

At the same time, individuals in the poorest quintile increasingly placed both candidates closer to the middle of the 7-point scale. This moderate scale placement is quite stable from 1980 onward for the Democratic candidate, and only slightly less stable for the Republican candidate. In short, the poor do not seem to see as much of a difference in the policy positions of the two presidential candidates.

These observations are relevant to our argument about the political consequences of economic inequality for voter turnout. While some theories of political inequality might predict a decrease in income bias in turnout since 1972 because increasing economic inequality mobilizes the poor to vote, our empirical evidence of stability in income bias contradicts this expectation. The argument we presented in chapter 1 was that *if* candidates do not offer relevant choices during a period of increasing economic inequality then the poor will not be mobilized, and therefore income bias in turnout will not decrease. We also argued that *if* candidates do offer relevant choices during a period of increasing economic inequality, then the poor could be mobilized, and income bias in turnout would decrease. Our evidence suggests that, indeed, poor people are substantially less likely to perceive policy differences between the parties on redistributive issues, notably failing to see that one party offers a distinctive *left* choice relative to the other. Given that we observe no change in income bias in turnout, this result is consistent with our first argument.

Why don't poor people perceive a larger ideological difference between the parties? We speculate on a number of relevant points that might be fruitful to consider. Numerous studies of public opinion in the United States suggest the importance of education, especially, but also income, to the level of information citizens acquire and how this information influences the development and influence of policy and

---

1. See Han & Brady (2007) or Poole & Rosenthal (1997) for a description of polarization in the legislature.

partisan attitudes on other political orientations and behaviors such as vote choice (Delli Carpini & Keeter 1996). More specifically, Bartels (2008) finds that individuals with higher levels of income have higher levels of political knowledge. While the sources of these differences might be diverse—variations in political interest and media exposure are obvious suspects—the implications for our findings are clear. Since poor citizens have less information about politics generally, their perceptions of presidential candidate policy positions are likely based on less information and therefore might be less accurate or more uncertain than the perceptions of those with higher levels of information.[2]

We also argue that these information differences are not simply a function of individual taste and choice but also reflect the political environment. We know that individuals' engagement in politics is influenced by elite mobilization and political issues (Holbrook & McClurg 2005; Rosenstone & Hansen 1993), as well as institutional characteristics of elections and parties, as illustrated in comparative studies of voter turnout (Blais 2006; Franklin 2004). One could also argue that variations in information across income groups may directly result from the political campaign strategies adopted by both major parties, both of which focus most mobilization efforts on individuals who have voted previously.

Highton and Wolfinger (2001) report, for example, that in 1992 and 1996, nonvoters were far less likely to be contacted by phone or in person by a political party. Other research also suggests that both parties are more likely to contact more highly educated, wealthier individuals than they are to contact less-educated and poorer individuals (Goldstein & Ridout 2002; Panagopoulos & Wielhouwer 2008; Parry et al. 2008).[3] While much of this party contact may be focused on fund raising, the contacts are also likely to include appeals that contain policy information. The problem here is that most of these efforts are targeted toward registered voters or habitual voters, and thus low-income individuals are least likely to be reached in this way. This seems to us to be a key feature of contemporary election campaigns that may result in low income individuals having less information than wealthy individuals.

7.2 Turnout and Institutions

Our analyses span a period of major changes in electoral laws in the United States, many of which were passed with the intention

---

2. We note that this does not mean that the perceptions of the wealthy are without uncertainty or error.
3. See Abrajano (2010) for an analysis of this specific to Hispanics.

of increasing turnout of underrepresented demographic groups. Our evidence indicates that both election day registration and absentee voting have positive effects on turnout. It appears that early voting's potentially positive effects are dependent on the length of the early voting period. When registration is closed farther in advance of election day it lowers turnout—a causal relationship that we have established with more confidence than earlier cross-sectional studies could do. Taken together, this evidence shows that electoral reforms over the past several decades have modestly increased voter turnout in presidential elections. Our findings on whether these reforms have succeeded in increasing the turnout of groups such as the poor or less educated are not as crisp. Our results suggest that election day registration may have its largest effect on those in the second and third income quintiles, and that members of the very lowest income group may be those least likely to take advantage of it.

For decades the United States has been identified as a unique case in the study of voter turnout worldwide, primarily based on the low level of U.S. turnout compared to that of other advanced industrial democracies (Jackman 1987; Lijphart 1997; Powell 1986). Most of these discussions attribute lower turnout in the United States to various aspects of election rules. Many other countries have either compulsory registration, or systems that put the primary burden of registration on the state, rather than one that places the primary burden for registration on the individual citizen, as is the case in the United States.

Claims of the burdens of the American electoral system have often been used as rationales for policy makers to adopt registration and balloting procedures that make it easier for individuals to overcome the cost of voting. As we discussed in chapter 4, some of the claims of reformers have been met, with electoral reforms such as absentee voting and election day registration leading to modest increases in voter turnout. But the effects of these reforms seem unlikely to overcome the turnout disparity between the United States and other Western democracies. What is less often discussed as an explanation for low turnout in the United States are the choices offered (or the lack thereof) by the candidates.

We caution, however, that these findings on the effects of electoral reforms and candidate choices are contingent on the politics of the period that we studied. To the extent that future campaigns and candidates seek to mobilize supporters more through these alternative voting methods, these reforms might offer greater potential for increasing turnout and reducing disparities in voter turnout across demographic groups. And to the extent that candidates offer distinctive policy choices that envision different levels of redistribution or distinctive roles of government, the poor and rich alike might view casting a ballot as worth the effort.

We believe that it is important to note that other institutional changes have occurred over the period of our analysis—changes that are likely relevant to understanding the broad contours of voter turnout in the United States. For example, increasing proportions of individuals now live in one-party-dominant congressional districts, and presidential campaigns have increasingly honed their campaign strategies to targeting only states where their efforts could be pivotal to yielding an important set of electoral votes—battleground states. To the extent that citizens in many districts or states are not exposed to competitive parties seeking their votes, they will be less likely to be contacted to vote and less likely to be exposed to information about their choices.

Organized labor is another important institutional feature of American politics today that has undergone tremendous change (Hirsch & Macpherson 2003). Even highly competitive election campaigns offering truly distinctive policy options to citizens must somehow overcome the conflicting demands on citizens' time and attention to convey useful and relevant electoral information. For most of the twentieth century, labor unions provided an important linkage between the Democratic Party and its constituents, helping to translate and make real why Democratic candidates were offering relevant policies. That the proportion of unionized workers has declined so dramatically over the past forty years, and the political power of labor waned, suggests that an important means of translating politics to poorer and less educated individuals has weakened greatly in electoral politics today.

7.3 On Turnout and Political Inequality

The distinctiveness of the United States in comparative studies of turnout is largely based on its substantially lower level of turnout compared to other contemporary democracies. But it has also been distinctive with regard to the especially strong relationship between income and turnout (Beramendi & Anderson 2008). Not all countries have the strong level of income bias in turnout that the United States does. One potential explanation is the nature of the party system and the policy choices offered in other countries.

Our findings on the substantial income bias of voters in the United States are not new. Schlozman, Verba, and Brady's (2012) study of political engagement in the United States underscores the fact that income bias in political participation in the United States today is as evident as it was several decades ago—despite the legal reforms, despite the expanded role of government in citizens' lives, and despite the broader reach of modern political campaigns.

As we have shown that voters and nonvoters have different preferences on redistributive issues, our findings punctuate the importance of this income bias as it relates to turnout. Turnout has always been unequal in the United States: the wealthy vote more than the poor. But this does not mean that a high level of income bias is an unchangable characteristic of U.S. elections. If candidates took positions perceived by poor voters to offer more distinct choices, then income bias could decrease.

The potential power of the ballot is that each eligible person has one to cast—despite different levels of education and income or different levels of other social resources that are distributed unevenly in our society. The bulk of recent scholarship that has focused on elected officials being differentially responsive to different groups of constituents has focused on comparing responsiveness to the wealthy to responsiveness to the poor. And this literature largely confirms that elected officials are more responsive to the wealthy than to the poor (Bartels 2008; Gilens 2012). But literature looking specifically at responsiveness to voters versus responsiveness to nonvoters also suggests that there are indeed policy consequences of who votes, that elected officials are more responsive to voters than to nonvoters (Griffin 2005; Martin 2003).

Given this evidence that elected officials do respond more to voters than nonvoters, it is important to repudiate the conventional wisdom that who votes does not matter. Voters are less supportive of government redistribution than are nonvoters. To the extent that elected officials respond to voters, we expect that public policies regarding redistribution and inequality will be less generous than they would in the case of universal turnout. As Wolfinger and Rosenstone explained in their concluding comments, "Citizens who are underrepresented at the polls . . . are less able to command the attention of elected officials and affect their decisions on public policy" (1980, 111).

Who votes now? And does it matter? Our answer to the first question was a lengthy one. Our answer to the second is more direct: Yes!

References ....

Abrajano, Marisa A. 2010. *Campaigning to the New American Electorate: Advertising to Latino Voters*. Palo Alto, CA: Stanford University Press.

Abrajano, Marisa A., & R. Michael Alvarez. 2010. *New Faces, New Voices: The Hispanic Electorate in America*. Princeton, NJ: Princeton University Press.

Abramson, Paul R., John H. Aldrich, & David W. Rohde. 2003. *Change and Continuity in the 2018 and 2010 Elections*. Washington, DC: CQ Press.

Adams, James, Jay Dow, & Samuel Merrill. 2006. "The Political Consequences of Alienation-Based and Indifference-Based Voter Abstention: Applications to Presidential Elections." *Political Behavior* 28(1): 65–86.

Adams, James, and Samuel Merrill. 2003. "Voter Turnout and Candidate Strategies in American Elections." *Journal of Politics* 65(1): 161–89.

Aldrich, John H. 1993. "Rational Choice and Turnout." *American Journal of Political Science* 37: 246–78.

American National Election Studies. 2010. *Time Series Cumulative Data File*. Data set, accessed at http://www.electionstudies.org. Ann Arbor MI: American National Election Studies.

American Political Science Association. Task Force on Inequality and American Democracy. 2004. "American Democracy in an Age of Rising Inequality." *Perspectives on Politics* 2(4): 651–66.

Annenberg Public Policy Center. 2004. *2004 National Annenberg Election Survey*. Data set, accessed at http://www.annenbergpublicpolicycenter.org/ResearchDataSets.aspx. Philadelphia: Annenberg Public Policy Center.

Arvizu, John R., & F. Chris Garcia. 1996. "Latino Voting Participation: Explaining and Differentiating Latino Voting Turnout." *Hispanic Journal of Behavioral Sciences* 18: 104–28.

Ashenfelter, Orley, & Stanley Kelley. 1975. "Determinants of Participation in Presidential Elections." *Journal of Law and Economics* 18: 721.

Atkeson, Lonna Rae. 2003. "Not All Cues Are Created Equal: The Conditional Impact of Female Candidates on Political Engagement." *Journal of Politics* 65(4): 1040–61. Available at http://www.jstor.org/stable/3449920.

Barreto, Matt A. 2005. "Latino Immigrants at the Polls: Foreign-Born Voter Turnout in the 2002 Election." *Political Research Quarterly* 58(1): 79–86. Available at http://prq.sagepub.com/content/58/1/79.abstract.

Barreto, Matt. A., Matthew J. Streb, Mara Marks, & Fernando Guerra. 2006. "Do Absentee Voters Differ from Polling Place Voters? New Evidence from California." *Public Opinion Quarterly* 70(2): 224–34.

Bartels, Larry. 2008. *Unequal Democracy: The Political Economy of the New Gilded Age*. Princeton, NJ: Princeton University Press.

Beck, Paul Allen, & M. Kent Jennings. 1979. "Political Periods and Political Participation." *American Political Science Review* 73: 737–50.

Bennett, Stephen Earl, & David Resnick. 1990. "The Implications of Nonvoting for Democracy in the United States." *American Journal of Political Science* 34: 771–802.

Beramendi, Pablo, & Christopher J. Anderson, eds. 2008. *Democracy, Inequality and Representation: A Comparative Perspective*. New York: Russell Sage Foundation.

Berent, Matthew K., Jon A. Krosnick, & Arthur Lupia. 2011. "The Quality of Government Records and 'Over-estimation' of Registration and Turnout in Surveys: Lessons from the 2008 ANES Panel Study's Registration and Turnout Validation Exercises". Working Paper nes012554. Ann Arbor, MI: American National Election Studies.

Bergan, Daniel E., Alan S. Gerber, Donald P. Green, & Costas Panagopoulos. 2005. "Grassroots Mobilization and Voter Turnout in 2004." *Public Opinion Quarterly* 69(5): 760–77.

Bernstein, Robert A., Anita Chadha, & Robert Montjoy. 2003. "Cross-State Bias in Voting and Registration Overreporting in the Current Population Surveys." *State Politics & Policy Quarterly* 3(4): 367–86. Available at http://spa.sagepub.com/content/3/4/367.abstract.

Blais, André 2006. "What Affects Voter Turnout?" *Annual Review of Political Science* 9: 111–25.

Brians, Craig Leonard, & Bernard Grofman. 1999. "When Registration Barriers Fall, Who Votes? An Empirical Test of a Rational Choice Model." *Public Choice* 99(1–2): 161–76.

———. 2001. "Election Day Registration's Effect on U.S. Voter Turnout." *Social Science Quarterly* 82(1): 170–83.

Brown, Robert D., & Justin Wedeking. 2006. "People Who Have Their Tickets but Do Not Use Them—"Motor Voter," Registration, and Turnout Revisited." *American Politics Research* 34(4): 479–504.

Bullock, Charles S., & M. V. Hood. 2006. "A Mile-Wide Gap: The Evolution of Hispanic Political Emergence in the Deep South." *Social Science Quarterly* 87(5): 1117–35. Available at http://dx.doi.org/10.1111/j.1540-6237.2006.00419.x.

Burden, Barry C. 2000. "Voter Turnout and the National Election Studies." *Political Analysis* 8(4): 389–98.

Burnham, Walter Dean. 1980. "The Appearance and Disappearance of the American Voter". In *Electoral Participation: A Comparative Analysis*, ed. Richard Rose. Beverly Hills, CA: Sage, 35–73.

———. 1987. "The Turnout Problem". In *Elections American Style*, ed. A. James Reichley. Washington, DC: Brookings Institution Press, 113–14.

————. 1988. "The Class Gap." *New Republic* 999: 30–33.

Campbell, Angus, Philip E. Converse, Warren E. Miller, & Donald E. Stokes. 1960. *The American Voter*. New York: Wiley.

Cassel, Carol. A. 2002. "Hispanic Turnout: Estimates from Validated Voting Data." *Political Research Quarterly* 55(2): 391–408.

Cemenska, Nathan, Jan E. Leighley, Jonathan Nagler, & Daniel P. Tokaji. 2010. *Report on the 1972–2008 Early and Absentee Voting Dataset*. Washington, DC: Pew Charitable Trusts. Accessed at http://www.pewtrusts.org/uploadedFiles/wwwpewcenteronthestatesorg/Initiatives/MVW/Non-Precinct_Laws_1972-2008.pdf.

Cho, Wendy K. Tam. 1999. "Naturalization, Socialization, Participation: Immigration and (Non-)Voting." *Journal of Politics* 61: 1140–55.

Citrin, Jack, Eric Schickler, & John Sides. 2003. "What if Everyone Voted? Simulating the Impact of Increased Turnout in Senate Elections." *American Journal of Political Science* 47(1): 75–90.

Congressional Budget Office. 2011. *Trends in the Distribution of Household Income Between 1979 and 2007*. Technical report. Washington, DC: U.S. Congress.

Conway, Margaret M., David W. Ahren, & Gertrude A. Steuernagel. 2004. *Women and Political Participation: Cultural Change in the Political Arena*. 2nd ed. Washington, DC: CQ Press.

Cox, Gary W., & Michael C. Munger. 1989. "Closeness, Expenditures, and Turnout in the 1982 United States House Elections." *American Political Science Review* 83(1): 217–31.

Crocker, Royce. 1996. *Voter Registration and Turnout: 1948–1994*. CRS Report for Congress 96-932. Washington, DC: Congressional Research Service.

Danziger, Sheldon, & Peter Gottschalk. 1995. *America Unequal*. New York: Russell Sage Foundation and Harvard University Press.

Darmofal, David. 2005. "Socioeconomic Bias, Turnout Decline, and the Puzzle of Participation." Unpublished manuscript.

Delli Carpini, Michael X., & Scott Keeter. 1996. *What Americans Know about Politics and Why It Matters*. New Haven, CT: Yale University Press.

DeNavas-Walt, Carmen, Bernadette D. Proctor, & Jessica C. Smith. 2009. *Income, Poverty, and Health Insurance Coverage in the United States: 2008*. Current Population Reports, P60-236. Washington, DC: U.S. Census Bureau.

Dennis, Jack, & Diana Owen. 2001. "Popular Satisfaction with the Party System and Representative Democracy in the United States." *International Political Science Review* 22(4): 399–415.

DeSipio, Louis, Natalie Masuoka, & Christopher Stout. 2006. The Changing Non-Voter: What Differentiates Non-Voters and Voters in Asian American and Latino Communities? Technical Report 06-11. Irvine, CA: Center for the Study of Democracy. Available at http://repositories.cdlib.org/csd/06-11.

Downs, Anthony. 1957. *An Economic Theory of Democracy*. New York: HarperCollins.

Ellis, Christopher R., Joseph Daniel Ura, & Jenna Ashley-Robinson. 2006. "The Dynamic Consequences of Nonvoting in American National Elections." *Political Research Quarterly* 59(2): 227–33.

Endersby, James W., Steven E. Galatas, & Chapman B. Rackaway. 2002. "Closeness Counts in Canada: Voter Participation in the 1993 and 1997 Federal Elections." *Journal of Politics* 64(2): 610–31.

Engelen, Bart. 2006. "Solving the Paradox—The Expressive Rationality of the Decision to Vote." *Rationality and Society* 18(4): 419–41.

Erikson, Robert S. 1981. "Why Do People Vote? Because They Are Registered." *American Politics Research* 9(3): 259–76.

Erikson, Robert, & Kent Tedin. 2011. *American Public Opinion*. Vol. 8. New York: Pearson.

Farley, Reynolds. 1996. *The New American Reality: Who We Are, How We Got Here, Where We Are Going*. New York: Russell Sage Foundation.

Fenster, Mark J. 1994. "The Impact of Allowing Day of Registration Voting on Turnout in U.S. Elections from 1960 to 1992." *American Politics Quarterly* 22(1): 74–87.

Ferejohn, John A. & Morris P. Fiorina. 1974. "Paradox of Not Voting—Decision Theoretic Analysis." *American Political Science Review* 68(2): 525–536.

———. 1975. "Closeness Counts Only in Horseshoes and Dancing." *American Political Science Review* 69(3): 920–25.

Fiorina, Morris P. 1976. "Voting Decision—Instrumental and Expressive Aspects." *Journal of Politics* 38(2): 390–413.

Fitzgerald, Mary. 2005. "Greater Convenience but Not Greater Turnout—The Impact of Alternative Voting Methods on Electoral Participation in the United States." *American Politics Research* 33(6): 842–67.

Francia, Peter L., & Paul S. Herrnson. 2004. "The Synergistic Effect of Campaign Effort and Electon Reform on Voter Turnout in State Legislative Elections." *State Politics and Policy Quarterly* 4(1): 74–93.

Franklin, Daniel P., & Eric E. Grier. 1997. "Effects of Moter Voter Legislation: Voter Turnout, Registration, and Partisan Advantage in the 1992 Presidential Election." *American Politics Quarterly* 25: 104–17.

Franklin, Mark N. 2004. *Voter Turnout and the Dynamics of Electoral Competition in Established Democracies since 1945*. Cambridge: Cambridge University Press.

Freeman, Richard. 2004. "What, Me Vote?" In *Social Inequality*, ed. Kathryn M. Neckerman. New York: Russell Sage Foundation, 703–28.

Gay, Claudine. 2001. "The Effect of Black Congressional Representation on Political Participation." *American Political Science Review* 95(3): 589–602.

Giammo, Joseph D., & Brian J. Brox. 2010. "Reducing the Costs of Participation: Are States Getting a Return on Early Voting?" *Political Research Quarterly* 63(2): 295–303.

Gibson, Campbell, and Kay Jung. 2002. *Historical Census Statistics on Population Totals by Race, 1790 to 1990, and by Hispanic Origin, 1970 to 1990, for the United States: Regions, Divisions, and States*. Working

Paper Series no. 56. Washington DC: U. S. Census Bureau, Population Division.

Gibson, Martha. 1991. "Public Goods, Alienation, and Political Protest: The Sanctuary Movement as a Test of the Public Goods Model of Collective Rebellious Behavior." *Political Psychology* 12(4): 623–51.

Gilens, Martin. 2012. *Affluence and Influence: Economic Inequality and Political Power in America*. Princeton, NJ: Princeton University Press and Russell Sage Foundation.

Goldstein, Kenneth M., & Travis N. Ridout. 2002. "The Politics of Participation: Mobilization and Turnout over Time." *Political Behavior* 24(1): 3–29.

Gottschalk, Peter, & Sheldon H. Danziger. 2005. "Inequality of Wage Rates, Earnings, and Family Income in the United States, 1975–2002." *Review of Income and Wealth* 51: 231–54.

Granberg, Donald, & Soren Holmberg. 1991. "Self-Reported Turnout and Voter Validation." *American Journal of Political Science* 35: 448–59.

Green, Donald P., & Alan S. Gerber. 2008. *Get Out the Vote: How to Increase Voter Turnout*. second ed. New York: Brookings Institution Press.

Gronke, Paul, Eva Galanes-Rosenbaum & Peter A. Miller. 2007. "Early Voting and Turnout." *Political Science and Politics* 40(4): 639–45.

Hacker, Jacob S. 2006. *The Great Risk Shift: The New Economic Insecurity and the Decline of the American Dream*. New York: Oxford University Press.

Han, Hahrie, & David W. Brady. 2007. "A Delayed Return to Historical Norms: Congressional Party Polarization after the Second World War." *British Journal of Political Science* 37(3): 505–31.

Hanmer, Michael J. 2007. "An Alternative Approach to Estimating Who Is Most Likely to Respond to Changes in Registration Laws." *Political Behavior* 29(1): 1–30.

Hanmer, Michael J. 2009. *Discount Voting: Voter Registration Reforms and Their Effects*. New York: Cambridge University Press.

Henderson, John, & Sara Chatfield. 2011. "Who Matches? Propensity Scores and Bias in the Causal Effects of Education on Participation." *Journal of Politics* 73(3): 646–58.

Herron, Michael C. 1999. "Postestimation Uncertainty in Limited Dependent Variable Models." *Political Analysis* 8(1): 83–98.

Highton, Benjamin. 1997. "Easy Registration and Voter Turnout." *Journal of Politics* 59(2): 565–75.

Highton, Benjamin, & Arthur L. Burris. 2002. "New Perspectives on Latino Voter Turnout in the United States." *American Politics Research* 30(3): 285–306.

Highton, Benjamin, & Raymond E. Wolfinger. 2001. "The Political Implications of Higher Turnout." *British Journal of Political Science* 31: 179–92.

Hill, David. 2003. "A Two-Step Approach to Assessing Composition Effects of the National Voter Registration Act." *Electoral Studies* 22(4): 703–20.

Hill, Kim Quaile, & Jan E. Leighley. 1992. "The Policy Consequences of Class Bias in American State Electorates." *American Journal of Political Science* 36(2): 351–65.

Hill, Kim Quaile, & Patricia A. Hurley. 1984. "Nonvoters in Voters' Clothing: The Impact of Voting Behavior Misreporting on Voting Behavior Research." *Social Science Quarterly* 65: 199–206.

Hillygus, D. Sunshine. 2005. "The Missing Link: Exploring the Relationship between Higher Education and Political Engagement." *Political Behavior* 27(1): 25–47.

Hinich, Melvin J. 1981. "Voting as an Act of Contribution." *Public Choice* 36: 135–40.

Hirsch, Barry T., & David A. Macpherson. 2003. "Union Membership and Coverage Database from the Current Population Survey." *Industrial and Labor Relations Review* 56(2): 349–54.

Holbrook, Thomas. M., & Scott D. McClurg. 2005. "The Mobilization of Core Supporters: Campaigns, Turnout, and Electoral Composition in United States Presidential Elections." *American Journal of Political Science* 49(4): 689–703.

Jackman, Robert W. 1987. "Political Institutions and Voter Turnout in the Industrial Democracies." *American Political Science Review* 81: 405–23.

———. 1993. "Rationality and Political Participation." *American Journal of Political Science* 37: 279–90.

Jennings, M. Kent. 1979. "Another Look at the Life Cycle and Political Participation." *American Journal of Political Science* 23(4): 755–71.

Jennings, M. Kent, & Gregory B. Markus. 1988. "Political Involvement in the Later Years: A Longitudinal Survey." *American Journal of Political Science* 32(2): 302–16.

Jones, Arthur F., Jr., & Daniel H. Weinberg. 2000. *The Changing Shape of the Nation's Income Distribution, 1947–1998: Consumer Income.* Washington, DC: U.S. Census Bureau.

Kam, Cindy D., & Carl L. Palmer. 2008. "Reconsidering the Effects of Education on Political Participation." *Journal of Politics* 70(3): 612–31.

———. 2011. "Rejoinder: Reinvestigating the Causal Relationship between Higher Education and Political Participation." *Journal of Politics* 73(3): 659–63.

Kam, Cindy D., Elizabeth J. Zechmeister, & Jennifer R. Wilking. 2008. "From the Gap to the Chasm—Gender and Participation among Non-Hispanic Whites and Mexican Americans." *Political Research Quarterly* 61(2): 205–18.

Karp, Jeffrey A., & Susan A. Banducci. 2000. "Going Postal: How All-Mail Elections Influence Turnout." *Political Behavior* 22(3): 223–39.

———. Banducci. 2001. "Absentee Voting, Mobilization, and Participation." *American Politics Research* 29(2): 183–95.

Katz, Jonathan N., & Gabriel Katz. 2010. "Correcting for Survey Misreports Using Auxiliary Information with an Application to Estimating Turnout." *American Journal of Political Science* 54(3): 815–35. Available at http://dx.doi.org/10.1111/j.1540-5907.2010.00462.x.

Key, V. O. 1966. *The Responsible Electorate: Rationality in Presidential Voting 1936–1960.* New York: Random House.

Kingston, Paul W., & Steven E. Finkel. 1987. "Is There a Marriage Gap in Politics." *Journal of Marriage and the Family* 49(1): 57–64.

Knack, Steven. 1995. "Does Motor Voter Work? Evidence from State-Level Data." *Journal of Politics* 57(3): 796–811.

———. 2001. "Election-Day Registration: The Second Wave." *American Politics Research* 29(1): 65–78.

Knack, Steven, & James White. 2000. "Election-Day Registration and Turnout Inequality." *Political Behavior* 22(1): 29–44.

Lazarsfeld, Paul, Bernard Berelson, & Hazel Gaudet. 1948. *The People's Choice.* New York: Columbia University Press.

Leighley, Jan E. & Jonathan Nagler. 1992a. "Individual and Systemic Influences on Turnout—Who Votes, 1984." *Journal of Politics* 54: 718–40.

Leighley, Jan E., & Jonathan Nagler. 1992b. "Socioeconomic Class Bias in Turnout, 1964–1988—The Voters Remain the Same." *American Political Science Review* 86: 725–36.

Leighley, Jan E. & Jonathan Nagler. 2007. "Unions, Voter Turnout, and Class Bias in the US Electorate, 1964–2004." *Journal of Politics* 69(2): 430–441.

Leighley, Jan E., & Arnold Vedlitz. 1999. "Race, Ethnicity and Political Participation: Competing Models and Contrasting Explanations." *Journal of Politics* 61: 1092–1114.

Lijphart, Arend. 1997. "Unequal Participation: Democracy's Unresolved Dilemma." *American Political Science Review* 91(1): 1–14.

Lloyd, Randall. D. 2001. "Voter Registration Reconsidered—Putting First Things First Is Not Enough." *American Politics Research* 29(6): 649–64.

Lyons, William, & John M. Scheb II. 1999. "Early Voting and the Timing of the Vote: Unanticipated Consequences of Electoral Reform." *State and Local Government Review* 31(2): 147–52.

Martin, Paul S. 2003. "Voting's Rewards: Voter Turnout, Attentive Publics, and Congressional Allocation of Federal Money." *American Journal of Political Science* 47(1): 110–27.

Martinez, Michael D., & Jeff Gill. 2005. "The Effects of Turnout on Partisan Outcomes in U.S. Presidential Elections 1960–2000." *Journal of Politics* 67(4): 1248–74.

Mayer, Alex. 2011. "Does Education Increase Participation?" *Journal of Politics* 73(3): 633–45.

McCarty, Nolan, Keith T. Poole, & Howard Rosenthal. 2008. *Polarized America: The Dance of Ideology and Unequal Riches.* Cambridge, MA: MIT Press.

McDonald, Michael P. 2003. "On the Overreport Bias of the National Election Study Turnout Rate." *Political Analysis* 11(2): 180–86.

McDonald, Michael P., & Samuel L. Popkin. 2001. "The Myth of the Vanishing Voter." *American Political Science Review* 95(4): 963–74.

McDonald, Michael P./United States Election Project. 2011. "Turnout 1980–2010." Available at http://elections.gmu.edu/voter_turnout.htm.

Meltzer, Allan H., & Scott F. Richard. 1981. "A Rational Theory of the Size of Government." *Journal of Political Economy* 89(5): 914–27.

Miller, Nicholas R. 1986. Public Choice and the Theory of Voting: A Survey. In *Annual Review of Political Science*, ed. Samuel Long. Vol. 1. Santa Barbara, CA: Praeger, 1–36.

Miller, Warren E. 1980. "Disinterest, Disaffection, and Participation in Presidential Politics." *Political Behavior* 2(1): 7–32.

Nagler, Jonathan. 1991. "The Effect of Registration Laws and Education on United States Voter Turnout." *American Political Science Review* 85: 1393–1405.

———. 1994. "Scobit: An Alternative Estimator to Logit and Probit." *American Journal of Political Science* 38(1): 230–55.

Neeley, Grant W., & Lillard E. Richardson. 2001. "Who Is Early Voting? An Individual Level Examination." *Social Science Journal* 38(3): 381–92.

Nie, Norman H., Jane Junn, & Kenneth Stehlik-Barry. 1996. *Education and Democratic Citizenship in America*. Chicago: University of Chicago Press.

Nownes, Anthony J. 1992. "Primaries, General Elections, and Voter Turnout: A Multinomial Logit Model of the Decision to Vote." *American Politics Quarterly* 20: 205–26.

Oliver, J. Eric. 1996. "The Effects of Eligibility Restrictions and Party Activity on Absentee Voting and Overall Turnout." *American Journal of Political Science* 40: 498–513.

Pacheco, Julianna S., & Eric Plutzer. 2007. "Stay in School, Don't Become a Parent—Teen Life Transitions and Cumulative Disadvantages for Voter Turnout." *American Politics Research* 35(1): 32–56.

Page, Benjamin I., & Lawrence R. Jacobs. 2009. *Class War? What Americans Really Think about Economic Inequality*. Chicago: University of Chicago Press.

Palfrey, Thomas R., & Howard Rosenthal. 1985. "Voter Participation and Strategic Uncertainty." *American Political Science Review* 79: 62–78.

Panagopoulos, Costas, & Peter W. Wielhouwer. 2008. "Polls and Elections: The Ground War 2000–2004: Strategic Targeting in Grassroots Campaigns." *Presidential Studies Quarterly* 38(2): 347–62.

Parry, Janine A., Jay Barth, Martha Kropf, & E. Terrence Jones. 2008. "Mobilizing the Seldom Voter: Campaign Contact and Effects in High-Profile Elections." *Political Behavior* 30(1): 97–113.

Philpot, Tasha S., Daron R. Shaw, & Ernest B. McGowan. 2009. "Winning the Race: Black Voter Turnout in the Presidential Election." *Public Opinion Quarterly* 73(5): 995–1022.

Piketty, Thomas, & Emmanuel Saez. 2003. "Income Inequality in the United States, 1913–1998." *Quarterly Journal of Political Science* 118(1): 1–39.

———. 2006. The Evolution of Top Incomes: A Historica and International Perspective. Working Paper 11955. Cambridge, MA: National Bureau of Economic Research.

Plane, Dennis L., & Joseph Gershtenson. 2004. "Candidates' Ideological Locations, Abstention, and Turnout in U.S. Midterm Senate Elections." *Political Behavior* 26(1): 69–93.

Plutzer, Eric. 2002. "Becoming a Habitual Voter: Inertia, Resources, and Growth in Young Adulthood." *American Political Science Review* 96(1): 41–56.

Poole, Keith T., & Howard Rosenthal. 1997. *Congress: A Political-Economic History of Roll Call Voting*. New York: Oxford University Press.

Powell, G. Bingham. 1986. "American Voter Turnout in Comparative Perspective." *American Political Science Review* 1986: 17–43.

Ramakrishnan, S. Karthick. 2005. *Democracy in Immigrant America: Changing Demographics and Political Participation.* Stanford, CA: Stanford University Press.

Reiter, Howard L. 1979. "Why Is Turnout Down?" *Public Opinion Quarterly* 43: 297–311.

Rigby, Elizabeth, & Melanie J. Springer. 2011. "Does Electoral Reform Increase (or Decrease) Political Equality?" *Political Research Quarterly* 64(2): 420–434.

Riker, William, & Peter Ordeshook. 1968. "A Theory of the Calculus of Voting." *American Political Science Review* 62: 25–42.

Rocha, Rene R., Caroline J. Tolbert, Daniel C. Bowen, & Christopher J. Clark. 2010. "Race and Turnout: Does Descriptive Representation in State Legislatures Increase Minority Voting?" *Political Research Quarterly* 63(4): 890–907.

Rosenstone, Steven J. 1982. "Economic Adversity and Voter Turnout." *American Journal of Political Science* 26: 25–46.

Rosenstone, Steven J., & John Mark Hansen. 1993. *Mobilization, Participation, and Democracy in America.* New York: Macmillan.

Schildkraut, Deborah J. 2005. "The Rise and Fall of Political Engagement among Latinos: The Role of Identity and Perceptions of Discrimination." *Political Behavior* 27(3): 285–312.

Schlozman, Kay Lehman, Nancy Burns, & Sidney Verba. 1999. " "What Happened at Work Today?" A Multistage Model of Gender, Employment, and Political Participation." *Journal of Politics* 61(1): 29–53.

Schlozman, Kay Lehman, Sidney Verba, & Henry E. Brady. 2012. *The Unheavenly Chorus: Unequal Political Voice and the Broken Promise of American Democracy.* Princeton, NJ: Princeton University Press.

Schuessler, Alexander A. 2000. "Expressive Voting." *Rationality and Society* 12(1): 87–119.

Shaffer, Stephen D. 1982. "Policy Differences between Voters and Non-Voters in American Elections." *Western Political Quarterly* 35(4): 496–510.

Shields, Todd G., and Robert K. Goidel. 1997. "Participation Rates, Socioeconomic Class Biases, and Congressional Elections: A Crossvalidation." *American Journal of Political Science* 41(2): 683–91.

Sides, John, Eric Schickler, & Jack Citrin. 2008. "If Everyone Had Voted, Would Bubba and Dubya Have Won?" *Presidential Studies Quarterly* 38(3): 521–39.

Silver, Brian E., Barbara A. Anderson, & Paul R. Abramson. 1986. "Who Overreports Voting?" *American Political Science Review* 80: 613–24.

Soroka, Stuart N., & Christopher Wlezien. 2010. *Degrees of Democracy: Politics, Public Opinion, and Policy.* Cambridge: Cambridge University Press.

Springer, Melanie J. Forthcoming. *How the States Shaped the Nation: American Electoral Institutions and Voter Turnout, 1920–2000.* Chicago: University of Chicago Press.

Stein, Robert M. 1998. "Early Voting." *Public Opinion Quarterly* 62(1): 57–69.

Stein, Robert M., & Patricia A. Garcia-Monet. 1997. "Voting Early but Not Often." *Social Science Quarterly* 78(3): 657–71.

Stoker, Laura, & M. Kent Jennings. 1995. "Life-Cycle Transitions and Political Participation: The Case of Marriage." *The American Political Science Review* 89(2): 421–33.

Strate, John M., Charles J. Parrish, Charles D. Elder, & Coit Ford. 1989. "Life Span Civic Development and Voting Participation." *American Political Science Review* 83(2): 443–64.

Studlar, Donley T., & Susan Welch. 1986. "The Policy Opinions of British Nonvoters." *European Journal of Political Research* 14(1–2): 139–48.

Tate, Katherine. 1991. "Black Political Participation in the 1984 and 1988 Presidential Elections." *American Political Science Review* 85: 1159–76.

———. 1993. *From Protest to Politics: The New Black Voters in American Elections.* Cambridge MA: Harvard University Press.

Teixeira, Ruy. 2010. *Demographic Change and the Future of Parties.* Washington, DC: Center for American Progress.

Teixeira, Ruy A. 1987. *Why Americans Don't Vote: Turnout Decline in the United States, 1960-1984.* Westport, CT: Greenwood Press.

———. 1992. *The Disappearing American Voter.* Washington, DC: American Enterprise Institute.

Tenn, Steven. 2005. "An Alternative Measure of Relative Education to Explain Voter Turnout." *Journal of Politics* 67(1): 271–82.

———. 2007. "The Effect of Education on Voter Turnout." *Political Analysis* 999: 1000.

Theiss-Morse, Elizabeth. 1993. "Conceptualizations of Good Citizenship and Political Participation." *Political Behavior* 15(4): 355–80.

Timpone, Richard J. 1998. "Ties That Bind: Measurement, Demographics, and Social Connectedness." *Political Behavior* 20(1): 53–77.

Traugott, Santa. 1989. *Validating Self-Reported Votes: 1964–1988.* Technical Report nes010152. Ann Arbor, MI: American National Election Studies.

Verba, Sidney, Nancy Burns, & Kay Lehman Schlozman. 1997. "Knowing and Caring about Politics: Gender and Political Engagement." *Journal of Politics* 59(4): 1051–72.

Verba, Sidney, & Norman H. Nie. 1972. *Participation in America: Political Democracy and Social Equality.* New York: Harper and Row.

Verba, Sidney, Kay Lehman Schlozman, & Henry Brady. 1995. *Voice and Equality: Civic Voluntarism in American Politics.* Cambridge, MA: Harvard University Press.

Verba, Sidney, Kay Lehman Schlozman, Henry Brady, & Norman H. Nie. 1993. "Race, Ethnicity and Political Resources: Participation in the United States." *British Journal of Political Science* 23(4): 453–97.

Weatherford, M. Stephen. 1991. "Mapping the Ties That Bind: Legitimacy, Representation, and Alienation." *Western Political Quarterly* 44(2): 251–76.

———. 1992. "Measuring Political Legitimacy." *American Political Science Review* 86(1): 149–66.

Wolfinger, Raymond E., & Steven J. Rosenstone. 1980. *Who Votes?* New Haven, CT: Yale University Press.

Wong, Janelle S. 2006. *Democracy's Promise: Immigrants and American Civic Institutions.* Ann Arbor: University of Michigan Press.

Zipp, John F. 1985. "Perceived Representativeness and Voting: An Assessment of the Impact of 'Choices' and 'Echoes.' " *American Political Science Review* 79: 50–61.

Index